THIRD EDITION

UNDERSTANDING
THE
ESSAY

EDWARD O. SHAKESPEARE

PETER H. REINKE

ELLIOT W. FENANDER

Longman

Understanding the Essay, third edition

Longman, 10 Bank Street, White Plains, N.Y. 10606

Associated companies:
Longman Group Ltd., London
Longman Cheshire Pty., Melbourne
Longman Paul Pty., Auckland
Copp Clark Pitman, Toronto

Executive editor: Lyn McLean
Production editor: Marie-Josée A. Schorp
Text design: Betty L. Sokol
Cover design: Joseph DePinho, Pinho Associates
Production supervisor: Richard C. Bretan

Library of Congress Cataloging–in–Publication Data

Understanding the essay/[edited by] Edward O. Shakespeare, Peter H.
 Reinke, Elliot W. Fenander.—3rd ed.
   p. cm.
  Includes index.
  ISBN 0-8013-0758-9
  1. Readers (Secondary) 2. English language—Composition and
exercises. 3. Essays. I. Shakespeare, Edward O. II. Reinke,
Peter H. III. Fenander, Elliot W.
PE1121.U54   1992
808.4—dc20   91-11842
                                                            CIP

3 4 5 6 7 8 9 10-MA-9594

Contents

PART THREE:

A Collection of Essays   64

PART FOUR:

For the Interested Reader   222

Preface

In preparing the third edition of *Understanding the Essay* we have recognized that profound changes are occurring in the American cultural heritage and in the acquisition of literacy. Television and rapid electronic retrieval of information, for all their positive impact on society, have reduced the opportunity for concentrated focus on the printed word.

Since essays are probably the most effective literary form for giving readers a brief but thoughtful glimpse into the varied artistic, philosophical, and technical facets of life, we are more than ever convinced that a book of this sort is essential to the development of mature skills in reading, thinking, and writing.

With this awareness, we have made substantial changes in the selection of essays for this third edition. Old favorites that remain timeless we have retained, but newer works that have lost their timeliness we have sacrificed. The substitutions and additions bring a refreshing variety of new subject matter and different authors. Also in response to the current educational needs of students, we have revised the text and the kinds of questions that follow the essays. And in response to teachers' requests, we have added biographical sketches of the authors of the essays.

Like the first two editions of this book, our text has a general theme: how an essayist reveals the abstract and the general through the use of the specific and the detailed. By focusing attention on this theme, we hope that students will see that an author's abstract ideas about, and attitude toward, a subject are shown through such specific devices as word choice, sentence structure, and selection of concrete illustrative detail. In this new edition we have added another theme, one that is becoming increasingly important: how an author may develop an abstract idea by depending on *readers* to bring *their* specific experiences and *their* sense of culture to bear in such a way that *they* make the specific connections necessary to understanding an essay.

Beyond these themes, the text and questions contain explanations of such literary terms as *allusion, irony, paradox, restraint, satire*, and *tone*. As an aid to the student and the instructor, we have listed and defined these terms in a glossary at the end of the book, together with the numbers of the pages of text in which further explanations appear. The examples in the glossary differ from those in the text, so that students can derive a broader understanding of the terms than they could from just one example.

We have organized the index toward an instructive end, and throughout the book we have suggested composition topics and encouraged students to write essays of their own.

Acknowledgments

In preparing the third edition of *Understanding the Essay* we have been especially favored by the advice of our three consultants, Mary Ann Caws, Louis W. Flaccus, and Richard H. Lederer.

Mary Ann Caws, Distinguished Professor of English, French and Comparative Literature at the Graduate School, City University of New York, somehow made time during her recent appointment as Getty Scholar at the Getty Center for the History of Art and the Humanities, to suggest, in witty detail, important changes in the tone of the text and the selection of essays. One should read her two most recent publications, *The Art of Interference* and *Women of Bloomsbury*, to get an absorbing exposure to the eclectic interests of this former president of the Modern Language Association. Mary Ann Caws is a graduate of Bryn Mawr College, with an M.A. degree from Yale University and a Ph.D. degree from the University of Kansas. We could not begin to recite here either the honors conferred on her or the extent of her accomplishments.

Louis Flaccus, now retired to Tamworth, New Hampshire, after an inspiring career as teacher and administrator at Westtown School, Pennsylvania, and as teacher of English at Scarsdale High School, Scarsdale, New York, mailed pages of corrections and helpful suggestions during the progress of the book. Much of the expanded variety in authors and subject matter is the result if his insistence. Louis Flaccus is a graduate of Haverford College, with an M.A. degree from Middlebury College. He is the author of *Collected Poems: 1983–87* and is a freelance editor and writer for newspapers in the vicinity of Tamworth.

Richard Lederer, acclaimed for *Anguished English, Get Thee to a Punnery, Crazy English,* and *The Play of Words,* displays his verbal humor regularly on Public Radio, in newspaper columns, and at guest appearances. Hundreds of former students, however, know him from St. Paul's School in New Hampshire, where he taught for many years. He was also a longtime member of the English Committee of the National Association of Independent Schools. The experience acquired from his several careers was invaluable in his contribution of ideas to the development of this edition of our book. Richard Lederer is a graduate of Haverford College, with an M.A.T. degree from Harvard University and a Ph.D. degree from the University of New Hampshire.

Special thanks are given here to Daniel Catherwood, former student at the Shipley School, for his research and preliminary biographical sketches of authors, and to Skip Shakespeare for her help with proofreading.

We are also grateful to the staff of Longman Publishing Group: to Lyn McLean, executive editor; Aerin Csigay, editorial assistant; and Marie-Josée Schorp, production editor, for their guidance and care.

E.O.S.
P.H.R.
E.W.F.

Credits

"A Fly in Buttermilk" from *Nobody Knows My Name* by James Baldwin. Reprinted by arrangement with the James Baldwin Estate.
"Waiting for Godot, by Samuel Beckett, at The Golden" from *Curtains* by Kenneth Tynan. Copyright 1961 by Kenneth Tynan.
"Do You Want to Make Something Out of It?" from *Thurber Country* by James Thurber. Copyright 1953 by James Thurber. Copyright 1981 by Helen Thurber and Rosemary A. Thurber. Published by Simon & Schuster.

In memory of E.O.S. IV

PART ONE

Defining the Essay

An Introduction

The essay was first honored as a special literary form in the year 1580 in France. Twelve years earlier the young Frenchman who was to be known as the father of the essay had been a 36-year-old practicing lawyer. But the course of his life was changed when his father died in 1568. Gradually the young man withdrew from public life and assumed the management of the family's country estate. There he became absorbed in reading and in reflective thought, and in 1571, in the tower library of the estate, he began writing down notes on ideas that interested him. During the next nine years he wrote and revised, wrote and revised. Finally, in 1580, he published two volumes of the short literary pieces that he had developed from his notes. The name of this Frenchman was Michel Eyquem de Montaigne, and the title of his publication was *Essais.*

Essais is a good title for Montaigne's works. Translated it means *trials* or *attempts* or *experiments,* and this is exactly what these literary pieces were—attempts or trials or experiments at writing personal reflections on a variety of topics of particular interest to Montaigne. Characteristic were such titles as "Of Names," "Smells," and "Of the Art of Conversing." From Montaigne's title *Essais* comes the English term for this literary form, *essays.*

Though Montaigne is called the father of the essay, he did not *invent* the form. Actually, the essay has been in existence ever since the first people who could read and write effectively decided to jot down some ideas that they thought were worth preserving. Thus we can think of the commentaries of Confucius or the dialogues of Plato or the letters of Saint Paul or the *Moral Works* of Plutarch as essays, as nearly every introduction to the essay will tell us. But Montaigne was the first author to write and publish a collection of pieces identified solely with this form.

As you can see from the meaning of *essai,* and from the wide variety of subject matter treated in essays, this particular literary form is so diverse as to be virtually impossible to define. A broad description will have to suffice.

If you have gone on a motor trip into hill or mountain country, you have had the experience of following the ascending curves of a road until you have reached the top of a ridge, and there, spread before you, from the valley below to the blue ranges in the distance, is a spectacular view. Here you often find other tourists, peering through binoculars or taking snapshots. If you have been impressed by such a view, you have probably wanted to record it, either by photograph or by painting. If you like to write, you may have wished to describe the scene in a notebook or journal that you keep. Literary inspiration can be drawn from such natural scenes as booming surf on a storm-whipped beach, peach-colored blossoms on a prickly pear cactus, scarlet maples on a bright New England day in autumn, the first snowfall of the approaching winter. One need look no further than the editorial pages of many newspapers to find short and attractive reflections on such topics.

Essays are by no means confined to nature, however. In fact, many of the best and most memorable essays are written about the writer's thoughts on life in all its variety, the routine and the common, the strange and the unpredictable, the humorous and the trivial, the tragic and the terrifying. A marvelous example is the following essay, which appeared on the front page of the *New York Times,* December 25, 1968, just after astronauts had for the first time circled the moon. Its author, Archibald MacLeish (1892–1982), a poet, essayist, and playwright, was immediately and profoundly inspired.

About the Author

Archibald MacLeish, a graduate of Yale University, with a law degree from Harvard, served this country as an officer in World War I. Then, as author and statesman, he devoted the rest of his long life to expressing his concern for humanity. He is best known for *Nobodaddy*, a blank verse play that probes moral ideas through the stories of Adam and Eve and Cain and Abel, and *J.B.*, a play that explores the meaning of the trials of Job. Because he was a persuasive speaker and scholar as well as a writer, he was appointed librarian of Congress in 1939 and assistant secretary of state in 1944. In this essay, MacLeish helps us to see the exploration of space as more than a great adventure.

A REFLECTION: RIDERS ON EARTH TOGETHER, BROTHERS IN ETERNAL COLD

Archibald MacLeish

December 25, 1968

1   Men's conception of themselves and of each other has always depended on their notion of the earth. When the earth was the World—all the world there was—and the stars were lights in Dante's heaven and the ground beneath men's feet roofed Hell, they saw themselves as creatures at the center of the universe, the sole, particular concern of God—and from that high place they ruled and killed and conquered as they pleased.

2   And when, centuries later, the earth was no longer the World but a small, wet, spinning planet in the solar system of a minor star off at the edge of an inconsiderable galaxy in the immeasurable distances of space—when Dante's heaven had disappeared and there was no Hell (at least no Hell beneath the feet)—men began to see themselves, not as God-directed actors at the center of a noble drama, but as helpless victims of a senseless farce where all the rest were helpless victims also, and millions could be killed in world-wide wars or in blasted cities or in concentration camps without a thought or reason but the reason—if we call it one—of force.

5

3   Now, in the last few hours, the notion may have changed again. For the first time in all of time men have *seen* the earth; seen it not as continents or oceans from the little distance of a hundred miles or two or three, but seen it from the depths of space; seen it whole and round and beautiful and small as even Dante—that "first imagination of Christendom"—had never dreamed of seeing it; as the Twentieth Century philosophers of absurdity and despair were incapable of guessing that it might be seen. And seeing it so, one question came to the minds of those who looked at it. "Is it inhabited?" they said to each other and laughed—and then they did not laugh. What came to their minds a hundred thousand miles and more into space— "half way to the moon" they put it—what came to their minds was the life on that little, lonely, floating planet; that tiny raft in the enormous, empty night. "Is it inhabited?"

4   The medieval notion of the earth put man at the center of everything. The nuclear notion of the earth put him nowhere—beyond the range of reason even—lost in absurdity and war. This latest notion may have consequences. Formed as it was in the minds of heroic voyagers who were also men, it may remake our image of mankind. No longer that preposterous figure at the center, no longer that degraded and degrading victim off at the margins of reality and blind with blood, man may at last become himself.

5   To see the earth as it truly is, small and blue and beautiful in that eternal silence where it floats, is to see ourselves as riders on the earth together, brothers on that bright loveliness in the eternal cold—brothers who know now they are truly brothers.

Some of the other essays in this book are like listening in on the writer's intimate thoughts; others are like a private lesson. Some may be informal and meandering, others sternly structured. Some may be straightforward presentations; others may be in the form of a short story, a fable, a dialogue, a letter. Although some critics and teachers of literature put essays into categories (formal, informal, didactic, personal, editorial, and so on), we will use a different approach.

Essays are no more than explorations of ideas and feelings. They are not the last word on a subject, as a great and learned book might be; they are merely attempts, trials, experiments, *essays*.

So you can see why there can be no complete definition of the essay. At best we can say that most essays are personal— communications directly from writer to reader. Although some essays are carefully organized in a logical or chronological order, many have a less apparent organization. They seem to move with the psychological streams and tributaries of thought, sometimes wandering off, sometimes coming to their destination by fascinating indirection, sometimes flashing with irony or sarcasm, sometimes carefully skirting the bogs of sentimentality. The essay, at its best, is superb writing, an art so subtle in structure and language that it appears to be artless. Besides making its point, it gives the intelligent reader all sorts of "fringe benefits," the subtle delights of perception and insight that only the best authors seem capable of bringing to light with just the right literary turn of phrase.

Many of the essays in this collection were written within the last 30 years, and many of them are short. This does not mean, however, that the best essays are necessarily modern and short. Actually, the heyday of the essay was the eighteenth century, when the printed word had become an affordable and widespread means of communication. Some of the greatest essays in the English language are associated with names from the 1700s and 1800s, like Addison and Steele, Charles Lamb, Benjamin Franklin, Jonathan Swift, Washington Irving, William Hazlitt, and Thomas De Quincey. Without competition from radio and television, those essays could be savored at a leisurely pace. They are just as enjoyable today, as are the earlier essays of Montaigne and Sir Francis Bacon. All they require are the same care and attention to the techniques of close reading that we explain in the text of this book.

You will see that this book is divided into four sections. Part Two contains some important instructions on the analysis of writing techniques. Here you will see that one of the book's themes shows how an author works with specific illustrative details and with great care for word choice and sentence structure to develop certain abstract ideas and generalizations. Another theme shows you how to draw upon the resources of world culture to understand ideas that the author expects readers to know. For instance, MacLeish's essay on the planet Earth is much more meaningful if you know about Dante and if you know about MacLeish's special use of the word *absurd*. These themes are intended to enhance your enjoyment of good literature, and to help you with your own writing techniques.

Part Three is a collection of essays loosely arranged according to style and subject matter. You may not be expected to read all these essays, but if you become interested, we hope you will read those that are not assigned as well as those that are. If you read on, you will especially enjoy the essays in Part Four.

The glossary and index at the end of the book should help you with the literary terms used throughout the text.

We hope you will find *Understanding the Essay* the beginning of many years of enjoyable reading in other essay collections and in magazines and newspapers. Among magazines, *The New Yorker* is a source of excellent essays on all sorts of subjects, as are *Harper's* and the *Atlantic*. The *New Republic* is a weekly collection of essays on national and world events. The *Smithsonian* has essays on art, history, and science; and *Natural History* and *Scientific American* have essays on the natural sciences. *Time* and *Newsweek* invariably include at least one essay each week, and the Sunday *New York Times Magazine* is full of interesting essays. On the editorial and op-ed pages of the daily and Sunday newspapers, there are many essays, varying in quality from excellent to poor.

We believe that the principles discussed in this book will help you directly in reading other literature and in writing compositions.

PART TWO

How to Read the Essay

The Abstract and the Specific

As we noted in Part One, a theme of this book is to show how an author uses specific details and examples to present an **abstract** idea. An abstract idea is an idea that has grown above and beyond the **concrete** incidents and situations from which it came. For instance, we talk about abstract ideas like *liberty* and *honor* and *beauty* as though they have a life of their own; then when we are asked to define them, we get lost in related abstractions. "Liberty? Well, it's sort of like freedom, isn't it? I mean, it's like being allowed to do whatever you want." That's about as helpful as saying honor has something to do with honesty, and beauty has something to do with prettiness. To make abstract ideas understandable, we have to use concrete incidents and situations to illustrate them.

The following brief essay about the automated Washington subway uses concrete incidents to illustrate abstract ideas. Read the essay carefully.

About the Author

Roger Starr, born in 1918, went to Lawrenceville School and then to Yale University, where he chaired the *Yale Literary Magazine*. After graduation, he served in the army in World War II, in North Burma and then in the Office of Strategic Services (OSS). Following these duties, he worked briefly for CBS, then joined his father's company in moving barges in New York harbor. The experience gained through association with his father led to management in housing and construction and eventually to his appointment as city housing commissioner of New York.

The reputation that Roger Starr won as an articulate and responsible public citizen made him attractive to the editors of the *New York Times,* and in 1976, after his service to the city, he accepted appointment to the editorial page, for which he has been writing ever since. Among his publications is the book *The Rise and Fall of New York City.* "Helping Hands: Metro Magic" illustrates his abiding concern for the city as a place where people must behave humanely toward each other.

HELPING HANDS: METRO MAGIC

Roger Starr

1985

1   The Washington Metro has no human token sellers. Its machines print fare cards that are good for more than one ride. To make the machine work, the passenger feeds in $1 bills, $5 bills, or nickels, dimes, and quarters, then pushes buttons to tell it how large an investment he wants to make. The Metro system, it turns out, also has a secret fail-safe device.

2   A New Yorker, loose in the Metro on a recent Sunday morning, found himself facing an 80-cent ride (distance counts in Washington). Turning his pockets inside-out, he found he had two $20 bills, two $10s, and 79 cents in coin. The paper-money denominations were too big for the machine. The coins fell one cent short.

3   Before entering the station by escalator, the New Yorker noticed that the station was surrounded by Government office buildings, as deathly quiet on Sunday as raided

speak-easies. He approached an information stand and explained his predicament to the uniformed attendant. What
to do? "Well, sir," the attendant replied, "we have a special
machine for that. You give me your four pennies—and it
turns them into a nickel." The exchange accomplished, the
barrier surpassed, the New Yorker wondered why no one in
New York ever thought of that: reinventing the non-
mechanical heart.

The point of this essay is **implied**, or, as the expression goes,
written between the lines, instead of stated. Getting the implied
point by drawing your own inferences is more creative and more
fun than getting it through the author's or someone else's explanation. We shall now spoil the fun of this essay by explaining
the implications of the concrete illustrations and by explaining
the abstract ideas.

First, the plight of a New Yorker trapped by an automated
system that can't respond to his special condition. We are given
a detailed, straightforward description of his predicament. This
is a concrete illustration, and its implication is that a visitor
who doesn't have appropriate cash for the fully automated
Washington Metro can't use the subway. From this illustration,
we see an abstract idea: the chance of total frustration in dealing with machines instead of people.

Now another concrete illustration. An attendant approached
by the visitor offers to solve the problem by putting the man's
four pennies in a "special machine" that will turn them "into a
nickel." The exchange is thereupon made, and the New Yorker
is on his way. But here the author has left out a detail; here he
has made an implication, and the reader must draw an inference. We don't see this magical machine that converts four pennies into a nickel. Either we can take the story literally and
believe that there is such a machine, or we can infer that the
"special machine" is the attendant himself. The last two words
in the essay, "non-mechanical heart," give us the clue (if we
need one), and we realize that a warmhearted attendant with a
sense of humor has added a penny to give the visitor a nickel.
Out of this illustration comes the abstract idea that kindly human beings can serve us in ways impossible for machines. The

point, or *a* point, of the essay is that the city of New York would be a more humane place if attendants there were similarly accustomed to helping strangers. In fact, the author hints early in the essay that such attendants are a necessary part of the system. Note the last sentence of the first paragraph: "The Metro system, it turns out, also has a secret fail-safe device."

This tedious explanation, longer than the essay, is intended to give you some techniques for drawing inferences and for distinguishing between the specific and the abstract.

Another technique, and one that applies to any subtle, careful, polished writing, is to reread the work. The most experienced readers can be astounded by what they missed in first readings.

Rereadings require special preparation: familiarity with all the words and all the cultural and topical references that the author uses. So keep two lists (preferably in notebooks), one for vocabulary and the other for cultural and topical references. Use a good, clothbound, college-level dictionary for definitions. Paperback dictionaries will not do, and neither will the clothbound ones for sale on bargain counters; they have too few entries, and their definitions are inadequate. Look up all unfamiliar words in an essay. Such a vocabulary-building exercise will greatly increase your pleasure in reading.

For cultural and topical references, too, the dictionary is often helpful. You will also need an encyclopedia and a reference book on familiar quotations.

Now take a look at another essay and see what you can draw from it. This essay, by Annie Dillard, is a vignette from "The Fixed," a chapter in *Pilgrim at Tinker Creek*.

About the Author

Annie Dillard, born April 30, 1945, in Pittsburgh, Pennsylvania, received her A.B. and M.A. degrees from Hollins College, Roanoke, Virginia. A student of science, philosophy, and theology, as well as of literature, she brings to her writings the scientist's discipline of accurate observation, the philosopher's probing of universal questions, and the theologian's fascination with divine mystery.

Her first book, *Tickets for a Prayer Wheel,* is a collection of poems, many of which explore in awe the interaction between the human and the divine. In 1974 she published what has become her best-known book, *Pilgrim at Tinker Creek,* a collection of essays that won a Pulitzer Prize in 1975. Other books are *Holy the Firm, Teaching a Stone to Talk, Living by Fiction, Encounters with Chinese Writers, The Writing Life,* and the autobiographical *An American Childhood.*

FROM *THE FIXED*

Annie Dillard

1974

1   Once, when I was ten or eleven years old, my friend Judy brought in a Polyphemus moth cocoon. It was January; there were doily snowflakes taped to the schoolroom panes. The teacher kept the cocoon in her desk all morning and brought it out when we were getting restless before recess. In a book we found what the adult moth would look like; it would be beautiful. With a wingspread of up to six inches, the Polyphemus is one of the few huge American silk moths, much larger than, say, a giant or tiger swallowtail butterfly. The moth's enormous wings are velveted in a rich, warm brown, and edged in bands of blue and pink delicate as a watercolor wash. A startling "eyespot," immense, and deep blue melding to an almost translucent yellow, luxuriates in the center of each hind wing. The effect is one of a masculine splendor foreign to the butterflies, a fragility unfurled to strength. The Polyphemus moth in the picture looked like a mighty wraith, a beating essence of the hardwood forest, alien-skinned and brown,

with spread, blind eyes. This was the giant moth packed in the faded cocoon. We closed the book and turned to the cocoon. It was an oak leaf sewn into a plump oval bundle; Judy had found it loose in a pile of frozen leaves.

2   We passed the cocoon around; it was heavy. As we held it in our hands, the creature within warmed and squirmed. We were delighted, and wrapped it tighter in our fists. The pupa began to jerk violently, in heart-stopping knocks. Who's there? I can still feel those thumps, urgent through a muffling of spun silk and leaf, urgent through the swaddling of many years, against the curve of my palm. We kept passing it around. When it came to me again it was hot as a bun; it jumped half out of my hand. The teacher intervened. She put it, still heaving and banging, in the ubiquitous Mason jar.

3   It was coming. There was no stopping it now, January or not. One end of the cocoon dampened and gradually frayed in a furious battle. The whole cocoon twisted and slapped around in the bottom of the jar. The teacher fades, the classmates fade, I fade: I don't remember anything but that thing's struggle to be a moth or die trying. It emerged at last, a sodden crumple. It was a male; his long antennae were thickly plumed, as wide as his fat abdomen. His body was very thick, over an inch long, and deeply furred. A gray, furlike plush covered his head; a long, tan furlike hair hung from his wide thorax over his brown-furred, segmented abdomen. His multijointed legs, pale and powerful, were shaggy as a bear's. He stood still, but he breathed.

4   He couldn't spread his wings. There was no room. The chemical that coated his wings like varnish, stiffening them permanently, dried, and hardened his wings as they were. He was a monster in a Mason jar. Those huge wings stuck on his back in a torture of random pleats and folds, wrinkled as a dirty tissue, rigid as leather. They made a single nightmare clump still wracked with useless, frantic convulsions.

5   The next thing I remember, it was recess. The school was in Shadyside, a busy residential part of Pittsburgh. Everyone was playing dodgeball in the fenced playground or racing around the concrete schoolyard by the swings.

Next to the playground a long delivery drive sloped down-hill to the sidewalk and street. Someone—it must have been the teacher—had let the moth out. I was standing in the driveway, alone, stock-still, but shivering. Someone had given the Polyphemus moth his freedom, and he was walking away.

6   He heaved himself down the asphalt driveway by infinite degrees, unwavering. His hideous crumpled wings lay glued and rucked on his back, perfectly still now, like a collapsed tent. The bell rang twice; I had to go. The moth was receding down the driveway, dragging on. I went; I ran inside. The Polyphemus moth is still crawling down the driveway, crawling down the driveway hunched, crawling down the driveway on six furred feet, forever.

Study Guide:

Before rereading Annie Dillard's essay, make sure you understand the appropriate meanings of the following words: *fixed* (in the special sense in which Dillard uses it); *Polyphemus* and *Cyclops* (remember the adventure of Odysseus, also known as Ulysses?); *metamorphosis, pupa, cocoon; to meld; to luxuriate; wraith; swaddling; ubiquitous; thorax; segmented; torture* (special meaning); *wracked;* and *rucked.*

Questions:

1. What outstanding feature of the adult moth pictured in the book would have made biologists name this insect a Polyphemus moth?

2. Where and under what temperature condition had the cocoon been found? What was the month?

3. What important environmental change was made when the cocoon was brought into the classroom and passed from hand to hand?

4. If the cocoon had been left undisturbed, outside, when might the adult have emerged?

5. How did the Mason jar affect the wings of the moth?

6. What does Dillard imply about the teacher as an educator? What does the teacher do that you would consider good instruction? What does the teacher do that you would consider insensitive? What

do you think is Dillard's attitude toward the teacher? What are the clues?

7. How does Dillard feel about the trapped moth? What word choices, what images make you understand how she feels?

8. In line with Question 7, what does Dillard mean in paragraph 3 when she says, "The teacher fades, the classmates fade, I fade"?

9. What does Dillard mean by the last sentence of the essay?

10. What is the point, or what are the points, of this essay? Defend your answer.

Annie Dillard has created some powerful mental images through her choice of words and phrases. Some are literal ("a torture of random pleats and folds"); some are figurative ("wrinkled as a dirty tissue, rigid as leather," and "like a collapsed tent"). We will get into a technical discussion of such word choices later, but you should be on the lookout for the skill and care with which a good writer chooses words and phrases.

Irony and Satire

Partly to show you how different essays can be, we follow with an early-eighteenth-century essay, "Christmas Greens." This essay appeared in the *Spectator* in January of 1712. The *Spectator* was a sheet, published daily, on which were printed informal essays and personal advertisements. It was the result of the inspired collaboration of two Englishmen who had known each other since childhood: Joseph Addison and Richard Steele. This daily sheet was one of the main topics of interest among the upper-middle-class patrons of London coffee houses and among the ladies and gentlemen of that time.

Like the first two essays, "Christmas Greens" uses concrete details to illustrate an abstract idea. But here the similarity ends. First, this essay is in the form of a letter, written by a fictitious Jenny Simper and addressed to a Mr. Spectator. Thus it lacks the directly personal quality of Annie Dillard's style, and whatever point it has to make must come indirectly. Second, the topic of the letter seems ridiculously inappropriate. This essay is apparently not to be taken at face value. The clue to such a suspicion lies in the first part of the opening sentence: "I am a young woman and have my fortune to make, for which reason I come constantly to church to hear divine service and make conquests." To a sensitive reader this statement is a *non sequitur:* the second thought does not logically follow the first.

Sensing this discrepancy, the alert reader wonders what the author, Richard Steele, is up to. Then comes the discovery that the author is saying two different things at once—that though the letter is laughably trivial on the surface, it is quite serious underneath. On the surface, which is the letter itself, Steele uses specific detail to express a young woman's silly request. On a deeper level, which grows out of the inappropriateness of Jenny Simper's reasoning, the author implies a serious idea that is opposite to her request.

The literary device of saying one thing and implying its opposite is a form of **irony**. Irony is a term for situations and for written and spoken observations and inventions in which there is a discrepancy (really an opposition) between what is apparent and what is expected. This quality of discrepancy is often called **incongruity,** a putting together of qualities that do not fit. Ideas or parts that are joined in a discrepant manner are said to be *incongruous*. Incongruity, then, seems to be an inherent quality of irony, but only when the discrepancy is so great as to involve opposites.

There are several forms of irony. The easiest to recognize is *verbal irony,* irony that is consciously, knowingly expressed by the speaker or writer. If it is spoken, the tone of voice and facial expression give the clue to the ironic incongruity.

"Just what I've always wanted!" says a young man as he unwraps a hideous necktie sent by his dear old Aunt Martha, and everyone knows by the sneer in his voice and the curl of his lip that this is a tie that will never be worn.

More difficult to recognize is verbal irony in written form. Here the circumstances must be understood before the irony can be recognized. For instance, if a year later the same young man were to write home from college that he had received another masterpiece from Aunt Martha, his family would understand the irony, but outsiders would not. Thus the writer of irony must be sure either that an area of understanding already exists between writer and reader, or that such an area be established.

A special kind of irony, applicable to this essay, is *dramatic irony*. Dramatic irony appears in two related forms: (1) In which a character, or narrator, unconsciously reveals to other characters and to the audience or reader some knowledge contrary to the impression he or she wishes to make. (2) In which the character, or narrator, acts and reacts in ignorance of some vital, external, contrary knowledge held by one or more of the other characters and by the audience or reader.

Like all other kinds of irony, dramatic irony is based on incongruity. The character's knowledge and intentions are at variance with the reader's superior knowledge and more objective awareness of intentions. In "Christmas Greens" Richard Steele uses dramatic irony. He establishes it through an obvious incongruity in the first line of Jenny's letter. Then to make doubly sure that the irony is not missed, he tops off the incongruity with a hilarious closing line. "Christmas Greens" is ironic because of the **juxtaposition** (the placing side by side) of incongruous details and because of the incongruity between the attitude Jenny expresses and the attitude one would normally expect.

Irony reflects the author's attitude toward the subject, and therefore it may be bitter, funny, satiric, or tragic. In "Christmas Greens" the irony is *satiric*. **Satire** is a humorous or witty device for exposing and ridiculing certain manners and institutions of human society. It implies the author's hope for reforms. Since irony and satire are difficult but extremely important techniques to understand, study "Christmas Greens" with special care. Then read *again* this explanation and the essay.

Sir Richard Steele, born in 1672 in Dublin, Ireland, and educated at Oxford University, is celebrated as an English playwright and essayist. Though his first works were successful comedies, he is far better known for his essays on English customs and morals. In 1709 he formed a partnership with Joseph Addison to publish their essays in a periodical they called the *Tatler.* The *Tatler* was succeeded in 1711 by the *Spectator,* which was succeeded in 1713, for just the one year, by the *Guardian.* Though the two men dissolved their partnership in 1713, the names Addison and Steele and *Tatler* and *Spectator* are virtually synonymous with some of the best and wittiest of English essays.

Richard Steele served briefly in Parliament, and in 1715 he was knighted. He was, however, a spendthrift and free-liver, and in 1729 he died in Wales, debt-ridden and out of favor.

CHRISTMAS GREENS

Richard Steele

January 14, 1712

Mr. Spectator,

1   I am a young woman and have my fortune to make, for which reason I come constantly to church to hear divine service and make conquests; but one great hindrance in this my design is that our clerk, who was once a gardener, has this Christmas so overdecked the church with greens that he has quite spoiled my prospect, insomuch that I have scarce seen the young baronet I dress at these three weeks, though we have both been very constant at our devotions, and don't sit above three pews off.

2   The church, as it is now equipped, looks more like a green-house than a place of worship: the middle aisle is a very pretty shady walk, and the pews look like so many arbours on each side of it. The pulpit itself has such clusters of ivy, holly and rosemary about it, that a light fellow in our pew took occasion to say that the congregation heard the word out of a bush, like Moses. Sir Anthony Love's pew

in particular is so well hedged that all my batteries have no effect. I am obliged to shoot at random among the boughs, without taking any manner of aim. Mr. Spectator, unless you'll give orders for removing these greens, I shall grow a very awkward creature at church, and soon have little else to do there but say my prayers. I am in haste,

Dear sir, Your most obedient servant,
JENNY SIMPER

Study Guide:

Good essayists have fun in choosing words that have several layers of appropriate meanings. Steele, for instance, wants us to enjoy double meanings of *prospect* and *devotions,* each meaning appropriate. In our discussion of reading techniques, we urged you to look up words that are unfamiliar. For an extra measure of care with essays written earlier than the twentieth century, look up familiar words too. Most words have not changed much or at all in the last 300 years, so you should have little difficulty with *prospect, devotions, design,* and *baronet.* The appropriate meaning of *light* may not be so obvious, however. Look it up in the single-volume *Oxford English Dictionary,* a dictionary that specializes in the historical progress of meanings. More obscure is *dress at.* You will have to use the multivolume *Oxford English Dictionary* for that. In fact, you will find Steele's use of the expression defined only under sense 7c. The rewards of such a search are the discovery of the humorous meaning of *dress at* and the discovery of a truly amazing dictionary. Incidentally, a new edition of the *O.E.D.,* as it is commonly referred to, has recently been published. It has many more volumes, costs thousands of dollars, and is available mostly in the libraries of colleges and universities.

Questions:

1. What are the appropriate meanings, in context, of *design, baronet, devotions, dress at,* and *light?*

2. When you become more experienced with literature, you will find that in the eighteenth century would-be lovers often described their flirtations in terms of artillery battering the defenses of their hearts' desires. Where is such a description in "Christmas Greens"? Does it tie in with the earlier use of the word *conquests?*

3. As you have seen in studying "The Fixed," it is through the words and details selected that an author evokes a response and communicates abstract ideas to the reader. In "Christmas Greens" Steele has selected the details with ironic intent to reveal their abstract satiric point.

    a. Examine the first sentence of paragraph 1 up to the semicolon. What is incongruous about the juxtaposition of statements here?

    b. Notice the clause "we have both been very constant at our devotions." Is this a pun? Is its effect ironic?

    c. In paragraph 2, can you see that Jenny has a valid reason for complaint? If so, where does the irony lie?

    d. In the final sentence before the close of the essay, what phrase upsets our expectations and indicates the obvious irony of the satire? Explain.

4. What is the satiric point that Steele is making through these ironic details?

5. Jenny mentions the clerk's former occupation. Is this detail just a humorous embellishment, or does it contribute to the point of the satire?

6. An **allusion** is a reference to a person, saying, or incident from literature, history, mythology, or religion. In paragraph 2 "the word out of a bush" is a biblical allusion to Exodus 3:2. Look up this passage in the Bible. What is the humor in this allusion?

7. In "Christmas Greens" Jenny Simper is a character whose letter is seen by an "audience" of readers. Does Jenny seem to be unaware of the incongruous implications of what she says? Explain how both forms of dramatic irony are used in this essay. Explain their effect.

8. In your dictionary, look up the words *jenny* and *simper*. What humorous purpose is served by such a name?

9. For a reply to Jenny Simper, see pages 251–252.

Style: Appropriateness of Words to Details

Style is the *way* in which an author expresses ideas. In "Christmas Greens" Steele uses an elegantly playful satirical style to express his observations of behavior that he considers ironically frivolous for church. The words are chosen with such punning playfulness and the sentences constructed with such easy grace that the admiring reader might say, "This man really wrote with *style*."

Style is infinite in variety. An author with a sense of good style employs, toward a desired literary end, the best qualities of sentence structure, word choice, organization, taste, and discrimination. In this section we begin a study of one of the characteristics that distinguish good style: choosing words best suited to the purpose of the written work.

"Galapagos Archipelago: The Great Tortoises," the essay that follows, is taken from a much longer entry in the journal kept by the young Charles Darwin when he served as naturalist on H.M.S. *Beagle,* a sailing ship that had been chartered for an expedition of surveying and scientific observation.

The voyage lasted from 1831 until 1836. During this time the *Beagle* made numerous stops at the South American and Australian continents and at many islands in the Atlantic and Pacific oceans. The excerpts are from the account of Darwin's visit to the fantastic Galapagos Archipelago, far off the coast of Ecuador.

The Voyage of the "Beagle," as the famous journal is now known, is crammed with concrete details of Darwin's observations. It also contains some remarkable generalizations about nature. (**Generalization** is a kind of abstract thinking that enables us to lump details into categories. For instance, we categorize as consonants the clicking, popping, hissing, buzzing, humming, and gargling sounds with which we shape words. We make the generalization that these details of speech are distinct from the sounds that we call, by another generalization, vowels.) From Darwin's observations and generalizations eventually came his great abstract theory of evolution, known as the theory of natural selection, first set forth in 1859.

We have selected this passage from Darwin's journal because it is an extraordinary record of minute and accurate detail. (Biologists who go to the Galapagos Islands and take *The Voy-*

age of the "Beagle" with them discover that they recognize place after place that Darwin faithfully described.) Unlike the details in the preceding essays, most in this passage are not selected and arranged to illustrate some controlling abstract idea. Instead, they are set down with scrupulous regard for the student who might later wish to use the information in support of his or her own generalizations and abstract ideas. Nonetheless, the details that Darwin amassed are so exotic that the young naturalist could not resist wondering about their significance to the mysteries of the origin and dispersal of plant and animal species on this planet.

As you read this essay, notice that it is predominantly an example of **literal** description, description as close as possible to the actuality. For this reason it serves as an unusual introduction to appropriate word choice as a matter of style; most literary descriptions have a strong mix of the fanciful or *non*literal. Since Darwin's primary purpose in writing the *Beagle* journal was to provide a detailed and accurate account of his observations, we should expect the style to be straightforward and unadorned, leading to clear, factual descriptions. This is exactly what we find. The second and third sentences of the opening paragraph are good examples. Notice that in describing the volcanic cones on Chatham Island, Darwin uses such words as *truncated, scoriae,* and *cemented,* and such quantitative designations of height as "fifty to a hundred feet." These words are symbolically as close as possible to the objects and attributes that they define. They are said to be words of **denotative** meaning because the images that they evoke in the reader's mind are restricted to a close, or literal, representation of the actuality. Definitions that are narrowed down to such close meanings are called **denotations** (see Glossary of Literary Terms).

Scientific observations should be **objective,** removed from the author's emotional involvement, rather than **subjective,** colored by the author's emotional involvement. A purely objective style can be dull reading, however. *The Voyage of the "Beagle"* is generally acknowledged to be a masterpiece of its kind, so you should notice how Darwin shifts from objective observation to subjective reflection. Notice, too, that in even the most objective descriptions his use of vivid and colorful words, particularly the nouns and the exacting adjectives, prevents the specificity of detail from becoming monotonous.

GALAPAGOS ARCHIPELAGO: THE GREAT TORTOISES

Charles Darwin

September 15, 1835

1   The *Beagle* sailed round Chatham Island, and anchored in several bays. One night I slept on shore on a part of the island, where black truncated cones were extraordinarily numerous: from one small eminence I counted sixty of them, all surmounted by craters more or less perfect. The greater number consisted merely of a ring of red scoriae or slags, cemented together: and their height above the plain of lava was not more than from fifty to a hundred feet: none had been very lately active. The entire surface of this part of the island seems to have been permeated, like a sieve, by the subterranean vapours: here and there the lava, whilst soft, has been blown into great bubbles; and in other parts, the tops of caverns similarly formed have fallen in, leaving circular pits with steep sides. From the regular form of the many craters, they gave to the country an artificial appearance, which vividly reminded me of those parts of Staffordshire, where the great iron-foundries are most numerous. The day was glowing hot, and the scrambling over the rough surface and through the intricate thickets, was very fatiguing; but I was well repaid by the strange Cyclopean scene. As I was walking along I met two large tortoises, each of which must have weighed at least two hundred pounds: one was eating a piece of cactus, and as I approached, it stared at me and slowly stalked away; the other gave a deep hiss, and drew in its head. These huge reptiles, surrounded by the black lava, the leafless shrubs, and large cacti, seemed to my fancy like some antediluvian animals. The few dull-coloured birds cared no more for me, than they did for the great tortoises. . . .

2   The natural history of these islands is eminently curious, and well deserves attention. Most of the organic productions are aboriginal creatures, found nowhere else; there is even a difference between the inhabitants of the different islands; yet all show a marked relationship with those

29

of America, though separated from that continent by an open space of ocean, between 500 and 600 miles in width. The archipelago is a little world within itself, or rather a satellite attached to America, whence it has derived a few stray colonists, and has received the general character of its indigenous productions. Considering the small size of these islands, we feel the more astonished at the number of their aboriginal beings, and at their confined range. Seeing every height crowned with its crater, and the boundaries of most of the lava-streams still distinct, we are led to believe that within a period, geologically recent, the unbroken ocean was here spread out. Hence, both in space and time, we seem to be brought somewhat near to the great fact— that mystery of mysteries—the first appearance of new beings on this earth. . . .

3   I will first describe the habits of the tortoise (*Testudo nigra,* formerly called *Indica*), which has been so frequently alluded to. These animals are found, I believe, on all the islands of the Archipelago; certainly on the greater number. They frequent in preference the high damp parts, but they likewise live in the lower and arid districts. . . . Some grow to an immense size: Mr. Lawson, an Englishman, and vice-governor of the colony, told us that he had seen several so large, that it required six or eight men to lift them from the ground; and that some had afforded as much as two hundred pounds of meat. The old males are the largest, the females rarely growing to so great a size: the male can readily be distinguished from the female by the greater length of its tail. The tortoises which live on those islands where there is no water, or in the lower and arid parts of the others, feed chiefly on the succulent cactus. Those which frequent the higher and damp regions, eat the leaves of various trees, a kind of berry (called *guayavita*) which is acid and austere, and likewise a pale green filamentous lichen (*Usnera plicata*), that hangs in tresses from the boughs of the trees.

4   The tortoise is very fond of water, drinking large quantities, and wallowing in the mud. The larger islands alone possess springs, and these are always situated towards the central parts, and at a considerable height. The tortoises,

therefore, which frequent the lower districts, when thirsty, are obliged to travel from a long distance. Hence broad and well-beaten paths branch off in every direction from the wells down to the sea-coast; and the Spaniards by following them up, first discovered the watering-places. When I landed at Chatham Island, I could not imagine what animal travelled so methodically along well-chosen tracks. Near the springs it was a curious spectacle to behold many of these huge creatures, one set eagerly travelling onwards with outstretched necks, and another set returning, after having drunk their fill. When the tortoise arrives at the spring, quite regardless of any spectator, he buries his head in the water above his eyes, and greedily swallows great mouthfuls, at the rate of about ten in a minute. The inhabitants say each animal stays three or four days in the neighbourhood of the water, and then returns to the lower country; but they differed respecting the frequency of these visits. The animal probably regulates them according to the nature of the food on which it has lived. It is, however, certain, that tortoises can subsist even on those islands, where there is no other water than what falls during a few rainy days in the year.

5   I believe it is well ascertained, that the bladder of the frog acts as a reservoir for the moisture necessary to its existence: such seems to be the case with the tortoise. For some time after a visit to the springs, their urinary bladders are distended with fluid, which is said gradually to decrease in volume, and to become less pure. The inhabitants, when walking in the lower district, and overcome with thirst, often take advantage of this circumstance, and drink the contents of the bladder if full: in one I saw killed, the fluid was quite limpid, and had only a very slightly bitter taste. The inhabitants, however, always first drink the water in the pericardium, which is described as being best.

6   The tortoises, when purposely moving towards any point, travel by night and day, and arrive at their journey's end much sooner than would be expected. The inhabitants, from observing marked individuals, consider that they travel a distance of about eight miles in two or three days.

One large tortoise, which I watched, walked at the rate of sixty yards in ten minutes, that is 360 yards in the hour, or four miles a day,—allowing a little time for it to eat on the road. During the breeding season, when the male and female are together, the male utters a hoarse roar or bellowing, which, it is said, can be heard at the distance of more than a hundred yards. The female never uses her voice, and the male only at these times; so that when the people hear this noise, they know that the two are together. They were at this time (October) laying their eggs. The female, where the soil is sandy, deposits them together, and covers them up with sand; but where the ground is rocky she drops them indiscriminately in any hole: Mr. Bynoe found seven placed in a fissure. The egg is white and spherical; one which I measured was seven inches and three-eighths in circumference, and therefore larger than a hen's egg. The young tortoises, as soon as they are hatched, fall a prey in great numbers to the carrion-feeding buzzard. The old ones seem generally to die from accidents, as from falling down precipices: at least, several of the inhabitants told me, that they had never found one dead without some evident cause.

7   The inhabitants believe that these animals are absolutely deaf; certainly they do not overhear a person walking close behind them. I was always amused when overtaking one of these great monsters, as it was quietly pacing along, to see how suddenly, the instant I passed, it would draw in its head and legs, and uttering a deep hiss fall to the ground with a heavy sound, as if struck dead. I frequently got on their backs, and then giving a few raps on the hinder part of their shells, they would rise up and walk away;—but I found it very difficult to keep my balance. The flesh of this animal is largely employed, both fresh and salted; and a beautifully clear oil is prepared from the fat. When a tortoise is caught, the man makes a slit in the skin near its tail, so as to see inside its body, whether the fat under the dorsal plate is thick. If it is not, the animal is liberated; and it is said to recover soon from this strange operation. In order to secure the tortoises, it is not sufficient to turn them like turtle, for they are often able to get on their legs again.

8   There can be little doubt that this tortoise is an aboriginal inhabitant of the Galapagos; for it is found on all, or nearly all, the islands, even on some of the smaller ones where there is no water; had it been an imported species, this would hardly have been the case in a group which has been so little frequented. Moreover, the old Bucaniers* found this tortoise in greater numbers even than at present: Wood and Rogers also, in 1708, say that it is the opinion of the Spaniards, that it is found nowhere else in this quarter of the world. It is now widely distributed; but it may be questioned whether it is in any other place an aboriginal. The bones of a tortoise at Mauritius, associated with those of the extinct Dodo, have generally been considered as belonging to this tortoise: if this had been so, undoubtedly it must have been there indigenous; but M. Bibron informs me that he believes that it was distinct, as the species now living there certainly is.

Study Guide:

Look up the meanings of the following words and add them to your vocabulary list: *truncated, surmounted, scoriae, permeated, antediluvian, aboriginal, to frequent, succulent, austere, filamentous, lichen, tresses, methodically, to subsist, to ascertain, limpid, pericardium, indiscriminately, fissure, carrion, dorsal, indigenous, distinct.*

Questions:

1. The opening paragraph of this excerpt, while it is scrupulously accurate in detail, evokes a mood. How would you characterize this mood? What literal and *non*literal descriptions contribute to it?

2. Which paragraph in the essay is more intimate in its detail, 3 or 4? Why?

3. Which paragraph hints at the most abstract idea of all? Explain your reason for thinking so. There are generalizations in some of the other paragraphs. What are they? What details are used in support of these generalizations?

4. In what paragraphs is there the most nearly pure use of literal descriptive detail? Explain why the wording would be called literal.

---

*Darwin could be referring to French hunters in Latin America or to buccaneers.

5. Choose an illustrative detail that you found particularly informative and well described. Explain what makes it an example of effective style.

Composition Topic:

Write a literal description of some natural scene or phenomenon. Without resorting to nonliteral descriptions and explanations, be as clear, vivid, and interesting as possible.

Style: Selection of Details and Words

When an essayist selects details to serve the development of a subjective abstract idea, the appropriate words for those details are unlikely to be as literal as Darwin's are in his description of Chatham Island. In writing about the importance of self-control, for instance, an author might compare a hot temper to a volcanic eruption, not meaning at all the literal ejection of lava and ash. Such word choice is nonliteral or fanciful. What follows, in a study of the next essay, "Twins," by E. B. White, is a look at this more fanciful word choice.

As you read "Twins," you will see that it is not simply a recording of detailed observations on a natural phenomenon; it is a remarkable organization of warm and ironic incidents from which emerges a delicately ironic abstract idea. The basic organization is chronological, but White has superimposed on this order some carefully selected details—some seemingly unrelated to the main topic—that give this essay its depth. These details are injected to contrast city with nature, the human animal with lower animals. The result gives the first two paragraphs of the essay a finely ironic cutting edge that may make one feel slightly uncomfortable about one's fellow human beings. But the contrasting details are small, sparingly used, and carefully placed, so that by the end of the essay one comes away feeling compassionate rather than condescending.

One, but not the first, of these details is placed near the end of the first paragraph of "Twins." The sentence is: "Here was a scene of rare sylvan splendor, in one of our five favorite boroughs, and we couldn't have asked for more." By enclosing "in one of our five favorite boroughs" in commas, White points out the contrast. The five boroughs are the Bronx, Brooklyn, Manhattan, Queens, and Staten Island, the five boroughs of New York City. Here, then, in the midst of a densely populated monument to civilization, is unspoiled woodland. At this point in the essay, White has not yet sharpened the edge of his irony. In fact, he implies a fondness for both wilderness and city. But he has set up the contrast, and he has earlier prepared the way for a distinction between the simple beauty of a natural event and some less appealing characteristics of human and humanlike creatures. Through the disciplined use of carefully selected details, White has developed an abstract idea about humankind and nature. He does not, however, *state* the idea; instead, he *shows* it to us. The idea is **implicit** rather than **explicit,** *implied* rather than *explained.*

Not all the details in this essay are so complex in form and purpose as those that make this ironic contrast. Many of the details that White has selected to describe a doe and her fawns are without ulterior motive. These details are distinguished by their simplicity. The chronology of their arrangement and the vividness of their wording make the essay interesting even without its ironic overtones. In the first three sentences of the final paragraph, notice the descriptions of the fawn's rising and sniffing, of the doe's licking her fawn's fur "against the grain," of the fawn's tiptoeing "in little stops and goes."

Simple as these pictures are, however, they are not without contrasts of their own. Notice that playing like a melody throughout the essay is the selection of contrasting details to depict alternating moods in the setting: the sun breaking through the overcast sky, "the shifting light and shade." White's multiple use of contrasts is only one example of the sort of artistry that can be observed in good writing.

As you study these specific details, you should also examine the careful word choice. Notice that there are few adverbs and adjectives, and that these few are chosen for their special vividness and appropriateness. These words have overtones of implied meaning (**connotations**) that go beyond denotation. For instance, see how your mental pictures of incidents in the second paragraph are affected by the adverbs italicized in the following phrases and clauses: "stamped *primly*," "allowing it to swing *crazily*," "the sun broke *weakly* through," "his mother stared *sullenly*." Examine the nouns and verbs, too, for they are chosen with equal care.

About the Author

Elwyn Brooks White (1899–1985), much better known as E. B. White, is the author of "Twins." He got his start as a writer when he was an undergraduate at Cornell University. There he became editor-in-chief of the student newspaper, the *Cornell Daily Sun*. After college E. B. White became a staff writer for *The New Yorker,* and he also wrote for *Harper's* magazine. His wife, the late Katherine S. White, was a renowned editor at *The New Yorker*.

E. B. White is considered one of the two or three outstanding American essayists of the twentieth century. Most of his collections of essays are still in print: *One Man's Meat, The Wild Flag, The Second Tree from the Corner, The Points of My Compass,* and *Letters of E. B. White.* He is also remembered for three of the most beloved of children's books: *Charlotte's Web, Stuart Little,* and *The Trumpet of the Swan.* His best-selling book, however, is a revision of a little text by White's teacher of writing at Cornell, Professor William Strunk. *The Elements of Style,* by Strunk and White, is a required handbook of style in business offices as well as in colleges and high schools, and it is delightful reading.

TWINS

E. B. White

June 19, 1948

1   On a warm, miserable morning last week we* went up to the Bronx Zoo to see the moose calf and to break in a new pair of black shoes. We encountered better luck than we had bargained for. The cow moose and her young one were standing near the wall of the deer park below the monkey house, and in order to get a better view we strolled down to the lower end of the park, by the brook. The path there is not much travelled. As we approached the corner where the brook trickles under the wire fence, we noticed a red deer getting to her feet. Beside her, on legs that were just learning their business, was a spotted fawn, as small

---

*The unusual use of "we" in this essay is a stylistic mannerism of "Notes and Comment" in *The New Yorker,* in which this essay first appeared. You may assume that "we" means "I."

and perfect as a trinket seen through a reducing glass. They stood there, mother and child, under a gray beech whose trunk was engraved with dozens of hearts and initials. Stretched on the ground was another fawn, and we realized that the doe had just finished twinning. The second fawn was still wet, still unrisen. Here was a scene of rare sylvan splendor, in one of our five favorite boroughs, and we couldn't have asked for more. Even our new shoes seemed to be working out all right and weren't hurting much.

2   The doe was only a couple of feet from the wire, and we sat down on a rock at the edge of the footpath to see what sort of start young fawns get in the deep fastnesses of Mittel Bronx. The mother, mildly resentful of our presence and dazed from her labor, raised one forefoot and stamped primly. Then she lowered her head, picked up the afterbirth, and began dutifully to eat it, allowing it to swing crazily from her mouth, as though it were a bunch of withered beet greens. From the monkey house came the loud, insane hooting of some captious primate, filling the whole woodland with a wild hooroar. As we watched, the sun broke weakly through, brightened the rich red of the fawns, and kindled their white spots. Occasionally a sightseer would appear and wander aimlessly by, but of all who passed none was aware that anything extraordinary had occurred. "Looka the kangaroos!" a child cried. And he and his mother stared sullenly at the deer and then walked on.

3   In a few moments the second twin gathered all his legs and all his ingenuity and arose, to stand for the first time sniffing the mysteries of a park for captive deer. The doe, in recognition of his achievement, quit her other work and began to dry him, running her tongue against the grain and paying particular attention to the key points. Meanwhile the first fawn tiptoed toward the shallow brook, in little stops and goes, and started across. He paused midstream to make a slight contribution, as a child does in bathing. Then, while his mother watched, he continued across, gained the other side, selected a hiding place, and lay down under a skunk-cabbage leaf next to the fence, in perfect concealment, his legs folded neatly under him.

Without actually going out of sight, he had managed to disappear completely in the shifting light and shade. From somewhere a long way off a twelve-o'clock whistle sounded. We hung around awhile, but he never budged. Before we left, we crossed the brook ourself, just outside the fence, knelt, reached through the wire, and tested the truth of what we had once heard: that you can scratch a new fawn between the ears without starting him. You can indeed.

Study Guide:

Before rereading "Twins," add to your vocabulary list the following words and their meanings in context: *reducing glass, sylvan, splendor, fastness, mittel, primly, captious, primate, sullenly, ingenuity.*

Questions:

1. At several points in paragraph 1, the selection of incident and detail keeps before us a **contrast** between mankind and nature. Where and how?

2. In paragraph 2 the contrasting details are more obvious and more numerous. The last detail in the paragraph is the most intense in its ironically critical implications. What is the satire in this juxtaposition of human comment and natural incident? How does this satire differ in quality and purpose from that of "Christmas Greens"?

3. In the final paragraph there is only an echo of the ironic details, and the closing sentence is in tender contrast to the closing sentence of paragraph 2. What are the reminders, in the final paragraph, of the ironic contrast?

4. What are the principal abstract ideas illuminated by White's selection of contrasting details?

5. Does White serve his purpose better by ending on a gentle note instead of on the harsher note with which he ended paragraph 2? Explain.

6. What is White implying by his word choice (paragraph 2) in describing the zoo's location in "the deep *fastnesses* of *Mittel* Bronx"?

7. Why is the detail about the "insane hooting" of the "primate" a good selection of words and incident? Why is *primate* a better word here than *ape* or *monkey?*

8. Toward the end of paragraph 3, White says, "We hung around

awhile." Is this informal language inappropriate? Can you explain why White used it? Are there other examples of informal language in this essay?

9. Like a good naturalist and a good writer, White avoids cheap **sentimentality**. There are some poignant moments in this essay, which, in the hands of a less able author, could have descended into weepy rapture. But White avoids this pitfall, first because of the inherent irony he holds before the reader, second because of the **restraint** with which he ends the story. As an amusing exercise write an unrestrained, sentimental ending and tack it onto White's final sentence. Does an unrestrained ending ruin the point of the essay?

Style: Imagery and Figures of Speech

We receive our knowledge of the world around us through sense impressions. These impressions are stored in our minds by processes that involve physical and chemical reactions. Upon suitable stimulation of the brain, the stored impressions can be recalled in the form of images. The vivid recreation of sense impressions through the use of words is called **imagery.**

A writer who builds effects from specific details uses language with great care to evoke precise images. In paragraph 3 of "The Great Tortoises," Darwin describes in literal language the food eaten by tortoises found in high, damp regions: "a kind of berry . . . which is acid and austere." These words suggest denotative images of the objects and qualities that they symbolize. "Austere" suggests not only the severe plainness that we associate with the word today, but also the dry harshness denoted in its Latin and Greek derivations. It is therefore a literally appropriate word.

Authors frequently evoke images that are more complex and, perhaps, more abstract in their meanings than can be easily evoked through literal description. An example of such an image is in the middle of paragraph 1 of "Twins." Here is a description of a fawn's uncoordinated attempts to stand and walk: "on legs that were just learning their business." White might have given a literal description of this incident, but the results would have been too wordy and ponderous for the incident. Instead, he chose an imaginative device for conveying a brief, light, and vivid picture; he suggests the particular awkwardness of the fawn by implying that each leg was learning by itself, independent of the other legs or of any central nervous system. In this description, then, two images are evoked: (1) an imaginary image of each leg activated by its own independent nervous system, and (2) a factual image of all four legs activated by one central, but as-yet-uncoordinated, nervous system. The second (factual) image is conveyed through the first (imaginary) image. Imagery employing our ability to conceive imaginary images in order to evoke factual images is called a **figure of speech,** and the language of such imagery is said to be **figurative** rather than literal.

The two principal forms of figure of speech involve **compari-**

son of an imaginary image to an accurate, factual image. The emphasis, however, is on the imaginary image, so that the final image, the factual one, emerges more through implication than through statement. These two principal forms are called **simile** and **metaphor.**

A **simile** is a *stated* comparison of an imaginary image to the factual image that the author is trying to evoke. Although the images are essentially unlike, the comparison is based on an area of resemblance. The author uses such words as *like, as,* or *than* in stating the comparison. A good example is White's description of the first fawn as being "*as* small and perfect *as* a trinket seen through a reducing glass." A trinket does not literally represent the properties of the fawn, but is an imaginative, or fanciful, comparison on the basis of smallness and perfection.

A **metaphor** is an *implied* comparison of an imaginary image to the factual image that the author is trying to evoke. The author using a metaphor does not merely liken one image to the other, but suggests that the one *is* the other. An example from "Twins" is found toward the end of paragraph 2, where White says the sun "kindled" the white spots on the fawn. Here the factual image, never actually stated, is of the brightening appearance of the fawn's white spots under the light of the emerging sun. The imaginary image is of spots being ignited by the sun. The metaphor implies that the spots are indeed being "kindled."

The important quality to remember about figures of speech is that they are a form of imagery employing imaginary images.

Questions:

1. Where is White's description of the fawn's legs' "just learning their business" played upon in paragraph 3 of "Twins"? What does this imaginary image in paragraph 3 do to help you understand what the second fawn has just accomplished?

2. In the simile comparing the fawn to a trinket seen through a reducing glass, is there a suggestion of the ironic contrast between human attitudes and the natural scene? Explain.

3. What kind of figure of speech is illustrated in the description of the afterbirth?

4. Figures of speech must be appropriate to the context in which they are written. What would be wrong if the sentence in paragraph 2 of "Twins" were changed as follows: "As we watched, the sun broke weakly through, brightened the rich red of the fawns, and made the white spots shine like dimes"?

Inappropriate juxtaposition of figures of speech can be truly ridiculous; for instance, "Rumors burst the dam of secrecy and spread like wildfire." Such a gaffe is called a *mixed metaphor*.

Style: Parallel Construction

For meaning, the English sentence is as dependent on word *order* as it is upon word *choice*. A writer who is careless about placement of adverbial phrases, neglectful about following an introductory participial phrase with the logical grammatical subject, unconcerned about keeping related grammatical elements such as subject and verb close together is guilty not only of confusing the reader but of creating ugly sentences. The English sentence, neatly constructed, is as beautiful as it is meaningful.

One characteristic of an attractive and well-ordered writing style is the arrangement of related elements and ideas in similar structural order. This gives equal weight to the elements arranged in similar syntactical order and is called **parallel construction.** The opening sentence of "Twins" contains a good example of parallel construction: " . . . we went up to the Bronx Zoo *to see the moose calf* and *to break in a new pair of black shoes*."

The narrator's two motives for going to the zoo are expressed in parallel form, as infinitive phrases. The reason for calling the construction parallel can be seen clearly if the infinitive phrases are placed one above the other:

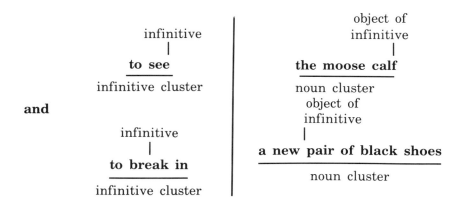

You can understand the value of parallel construction if you substitute the following clause for the second infinitive phrase:

44

"so that we could break in a new pair of black shoes." There is nothing grammatically wrong with such a substitution. But there is an artistic reason for expressing the two activities in parallel form: by giving them equal weight, White sets the tone of the essay and suggests the balancing of the themes he will develop. A style that is devoid of parallel structure is usually clumsy and unnecessarily difficult.

Another characteristic of parallel construction is that it can be used effectively to set off contrasting statements; for instance, "This was no local rebellion; it was a nationwide revolution."

Questions:

1. In each of the three paragraphs of "Twins," find more examples of parallel construction. Be sure to show that the parallel elements are grammatically parallel, that they match each other.

2. Parallel construction need not be confined to elements within a sentence. Sentences expressing related ideas may be expressed in parallel order. Sometimes several paragraphs may be developed in parallel order.

Study MacLeish's essay. What phrases, sentences, and paragraphs are parallel to each other? What purpose does this parallel order serve?

Style: Continuity and Transitions

The reader can never see ahead, with the writer, into the purpose and organization of the writer's work; therefore, the writer is under obligation to give the reader some guidance and a sense of continuity.

As we have pointed out, White is making comments in "Twins" on two kinds of animals, deer and human beings. He must keep us aware of these comments and, at the same time, move the story along. The words "The doe" and "the wire" in the first sentence of the second paragraph of the essay remind us of the doe and the fence in the first paragraph. Then, to remind us that the essay is about the doe and her fawns, White begins the next sentence with "The *mother*." Notice that we are not in doubt as to *what* mother White is referring to. It is "*the* mother," the only mother so far mentioned. Notice also that the identity of mother and doe is further emphasized by the parallel construction of these two sentence beginnings. Thus White makes the **transition** from the first paragraph to the second paragraph.

Transition from the second sentence to the third sentence of paragraph 2 is made by the simple device of the adverbial connector "then." But the transition from sentence 3 to sentence 4, and from sentence 4 to sentence 5, is more difficult to accomplish without breaking the continuity. Notice, first of all, that the word order is changed. Sentence 4 begins with an adverbial phrase, which guides us away from the scene of the deer; and sentence 5 begins with an adverbial clause, which brings us back to the scene. If White had begun the fifth sentence with "The sun broke weakly through," the poor reader would have thought that the sun was breaking through to the monkey house, or that the filling of woodland "with a wild hooroar" somehow helps the sun to break "weakly through." At least, he or she would have been unnecessarily confused for a moment, and there can be no excuse for writing that causes such confusion, even for a moment.

Questions:

1. The second sentence of paragraph 3 of "Twins" might have begun as follows: "In recognition of his achievement, the doe quit her other work." Such a shift would bring the subject closer to its verb. But

what does the shift do to continuity of thought? Is a better transition made by beginning the sentence with "the doe"? Does such a transition justify the separation of subject and verb in this sentence?

2. Transitions are clearly made in paragraph 3 of "Twins." Point out and discuss all the transitional devices in the paragraph.

3. In your next composition underline the transitional devices you have used.

Style: Humor

The following essay, "Early Years in Florida, Missouri," is by Samuel Langhorne Clemens, who derived his pen name, Mark Twain, from the second mark on the fathom line used by Mississippi steamboat crews. Twain's *Life on the Mississippi* tells of his experiences as a pilot on that river before he went on to become one of America's greatest writers. "Early Years in Florida, Missouri" is taken from *Mark Twain's Autobiography,* a book of loosely connected reminiscences and pungent comments.

The style seems casual, but a careful examination reveals a master storyteller and humorist at work. Study the first three paragraphs of the following excerpt, and you will see that the style has a flat, conversational quality. Ten out of 15 sentences are simple or compound; 12 out of the 15 begin with the subject followed by the verb. If you analyze the independent clauses in these first three paragraphs, you will see that 15 out of 19 begin with the subject followed by the verb. The tone is almost monotonous. It is a perfect example of *deadpan* humor. Deadpan gets its name from the makeup that some clowns wear to make their faces expressionless, or "dead." *Pan* is slang for *face*; hence the name *deadpan*. Deadpan humor is funny without seeming to be.

Deadpan humor is the **tone** we will sense in Twain's essay. Tone is a term for the quality of an unspoken bond the writer establishes with the reader. Since the bond is emotional—expressed, implied, or withheld—it cannot be adequately defined. Yet we know it when we sense it through the writer's style. Formal and objective is the tone of Darwin's "Great Tortoises." "More in sorrow than in anger" might be the tone of Annie Dillard's "Fixed." Public, spirited, humorous, kindhearted are elements of tone in Roger Starr's "Helping Hands." Portentous and conscience-driven might describe MacLeish's tone.

The deadpan tone that Twain has created in his description of primitive life in Florida, Missouri, is the same tone that he takes advantage of as he describes the veneer of sophistication in Hartford, Connecticut, in 1877. The deadpan is a purposely flat delivery. Twain accomplishes this at first by the monotonous parallelism of sentence after sentence written with the same construction. He then sustains the deadpan by yet another means—the almost total lack of openly expressed emotional attitude, a mock objective style.

The **humor** of this essay lies in Twain's choice of examples and descriptive language. For instance, when he describes the cracks in the floor of the Missouri church, he says that anything smaller than a peach would fall through them. The mental picture is a funny one. Imagine cracks that wide in a floor of a church! and then imagine the ridiculous idea of anyone's bringing peaches to church! The picture is a good example of the one element that seems characteristic of all humor (though, as we have seen in discussing irony, it is by no means restricted to humor): **incongruity.** Actually, Twain is describing the scene faithfully. The cracks in the puncheon floor *were* that wide, and people *did* surreptitiously munch on peaches in those long-ago country churches. The humor lies in the incongruity of country church manners of the early nineteenth century as contrasted with the pious dignity of New England church manners near the turn of the century.

Humor must be based on reality. It must not stray too far from truth; otherwise it becomes merely silly. To be universally funny it must be a quirky way of looking at something serious. Seen another way, that something serious could be sad or irritating. Humor exposes the differences between what we are and what we would like others to think we are. It exposes the differences between our expectations and our achievements. It exposes the fine line between pride and insecurity. Most important, humor has the peculiar quality of making us laugh. No one knows quite why it makes us laugh. It may be that we laugh because the emphasis of pure humor is more on exposing human incongruities than on exposing human beings. But whatever the cause, there seems to be a tickling quality of bright surprise in the incongruities that humor seizes upon. Somehow we have learned to laugh at such surprises.

In "Early Years in Florida, Missouri," Twain's deadpan tone lets the incongruities speak for themselves. As you look beyond the first three paragraphs, however, you will find that once the deadpan tone has been set, the style becomes more elaborate, and the essay moves on to several other levels of significance, about which you will be asked after you finish the essay. Notice how the thought progresses, and notice the humorous surprises in the incongruities and the position of the *punch lines,* the phrases or clauses that drive home the point. You should also study the language and sentence structure for more than the deadpan tone. Twain, more than any other American author, is credited with the development of a native style. It is a spare style, lacking in literary flourishes; the language and sentence structure are simple, earthy, and direct.

About the Author

When Samuel Langhorne Clemens (1835-1910) was 12, his father died. A year later the young boy went to work as an apprenticed printer for one of the newspapers published in Hannibal, Missouri, the riverfront town to which the Clemens family had moved in 1839. For the next nine years he served as printer not only in Hannibal but later in St. Louis, New York, Philadelphia, and Cincinnati. Such exacting work inspired his respect for the virtues of the clearly written declarative sentence.

In 1857, hoping to make his fortune, Clemens set his sights on South America, but he got no further than New Orleans. There the Mississippi steamboats and his boyhood dream of becoming a pilot proved too strong a lure to resist. Working his way up from cub pilot to pilot, he plied the Mississippi until 1861. In navigating the river, he was familiar with the cries of the leadsmen measuring the depth of the water with a sounding line that had a knot, or "mark," for each fathom (6 feet). At the cry of "Mark twain!" (the second mark), he knew that the depth was safe.

When the Civil War curtailed river traffic, Clemens went west to join his elder brother in Nevada Territory. In Carson City he adopted the name Mark Twain and began his writing career on the staff of the *Virginia City Territorial Enterprise*. Later, as reporter and columnist in San Francisco, he was influenced by the humorist Bret Harte to try his hand at humor. "The Celebrated Jumping Frog of Calaveras County" was the result, and it established his fame.

The rest of Twain's life was a succession of travels, publications, speaking engagements, and boom-and-bust business ventures. Among his best-known books are *The Innocents Abroad, The Adventures of Tom Sawyer, The Prince and the Pauper, The Adventures of Huckleberry Finn* (often cited as the greatest of American novels), *Life on the Mississippi, A Connecticut Yankee in King Arthur's Court,* and *The Mysterious Stranger.*

Though celebrated as a humorist (today we might call him a stand-up comedian), Mark Twain suffered personal tragedies—the loss of two daughters and the long illness and death of his wife—and he early developed a satirical contempt for human greed and cruelty. Hence his description of himself as a misanthrope, and hence the bitterness of some of his last works.

EARLY YEARS IN FLORIDA, MISSOURI

Mark Twain

1877

1   I was born the 30th of November, 1835, in the almost invisible village of Florida, Monroe County, Missouri. I suppose Florida had less than three hundred inhabitants. It had two streets, each a couple of hundred yards long; the rest of the avenues mere lanes, with rail fences and cornfields on either side. Both the streets and the lanes were paved with the same material—tough black mud in wet times, deep dust in dry.

2   Most of the houses were of logs—all of them, indeed, except three or four; these latter were frame ones. There were none of brick, and none of stone. There was a log church, with a puncheon floor and slab benches. A puncheon floor is made of logs whose upper surfaces have been chipped flat with the adz. The cracks between the logs were not filled; there was no carpet; consequently, if you dropped anything smaller than a peach, it was likely to go through. The church was perched upon short sections of logs, which elevated it two or three feet from the ground. Hogs slept under there, and whenever the dogs got after them during services, the minister had to wait till the disturbance was over. In winter there was always a refreshing breeze up through the puncheon floor; in summer there were fleas enough for all.

3   A slab bench is made of the outside cut of a sawlog, with the bark side down; it is supported on four sticks driven into auger holes at the ends; it has no back and no cushions. The church was twilighted with yellow tallow candles in tin sconces hung against the walls. Week days, the church was a schoolhouse.

4   There were two stores in the village. My uncle, John A. Quarles, was proprietor of one of them. It was a very small establishment, with a few rolls of "bit" calicoes on a half a dozen shelves; a few barrels of salt mackerel, coffee, and New Orleans sugar behind the counter; stacks of brooms,

shovels, axes, hoes, rakes, and such things here and there; a lot of cheap hats, bonnets, and tinware strung on strings and suspended from the walls; and at the other end of the room was a counter with bags of shot on it, a cheese or two, and a keg of powder; in front of it a row of nail kegs and a few pigs of lead, and behind it a barrel or two of New Orleans molasses and native corn whisky on tap. If a boy bought five or ten cents' worth of anything, he was entitled to half a handful of sugar from the barrel; if a woman bought a few yards of calico she was entitled to a spool of thread in addition to the usual gratis "trimmin's"; if a man bought a trifle, he was at liberty to draw and swallow as big a drink of whisky as he wanted.

5   Everything was cheap: apples, peaches, sweet potatoes, Irish potatoes, and corn, ten cents a bushel; chickens, ten cents apiece; butter, six cents a pound; eggs, three cents a dozen; coffee and sugar, five cents a pound; whisky, ten cents a gallon. I do not know how prices are out there in interior Missouri now, but I know what they are here in Hartford, Connecticut. To wit: apples, three dollars a bushel; peaches, five dollars; Irish potatoes (choice Bermudas), five dollars; chickens, a dollar to a dollar and a half apiece, according to weight; butter, forty-five to sixty cents a pound; eggs, fifty to sixty cents a dozen; coffee, forty-five cents a pound; native whisky, four or five dollars a gallon, I believe, but I can only be certain concerning the sort which I use myself, which is Scotch and costs ten dollars a gallon when you take two gallons—more when you take less.

Study Guide:

The straightforward language requires sure knowledge of every word. Add these words and their meanings to your list: *adz, auger, tallow, sconce, proprietor, calico, pig* (of lead), *gratis.*

Questions:

1. Where are the punch lines? Does every paragraph have at least one punch line?

2. What is the incongruity in each example of humor?

3. What changes in merchandising attitudes are indicated in this essay? What do these changes imply about the levels of sophistication in Florida, Missouri, and Hartford, Connecticut?

4. Show how concrete detail is used in this essay to produce an abstract impression.

5. Point out the parallel constructions. What is their effect?

6. Choose any of the longer paragraphs; then make a count of the nouns, verbs, adjectives, adverbs, participles, and prepositions. What is the ratio? What does this ratio tell you about a deadpan, objective style?

7. Make a similar count for a paragraph from Annie Dillard's essay. How does the different ratio help to account for the different tone of Dillard's writing?

8. Review "Christmas Greens." At least part of its tone might safely be called deadpan. What difference is there between "Early Years in Florida, Missouri" and "Christmas Greens" in the manner of achieving a deadpan tone?

9. Humor is seldom pure. Witty humor sparkles with clever use of words and images. The emphasis is on cleverness, but human beings are sometimes the butt of its jokes. **Satirical** humor is clever and biting. It often criticizes human beings as well as their behavior. **Sarcastic** humor is invariably injurious to human beings and is therefore funny only to people who are not its targets and who feel no sympathy for its targets. On the other hand, humor that evokes sympathy or pity for the victims of incongruous situations has a pathetic quality that divides our response between laughter and tears.

How would you classify the humor in Twain's essay? Explain. What about the humor of "Christmas Greens"?

10. The final statement of Twain's essay is an example of a **paradox**. A paradox is a statement that is apparently self-contradictory, but that, on examination, turns out not to be self-contradictory. Explain the paradox at the end of Twain's essay.

Style: Allusion

Toward the end of Part One of this book, we stated that one of the themes of the book is to show you how to draw upon the resources of world culture to understand ideas that an author expects the reader to know. We cited as an example Archibald MacLeish's reference to Dante. Dante Alighieri (1265–1321), Italian poet of the Middle Ages, composed one of the greatest works in all of Western literature, *The Divine Comedy.* In it his descriptions of hell (the inferno) are so vivid that to this day they influence our conception of an underworld. So too his descriptions of purgatory and paradise have given us a literary vision of the medieval Christian idea of these worlds. The mere use of Dante's name in MacLeish's essay is intended to call up images of early Christian ideas of hell and the fixed and unchanging stars of heaven. Such references are called **allusions**; they allude to events, people, and ideas that are a part of our accumulated knowledge of world culture.

Allusions are literary shortcuts that forcefully evoke images. They work, however, only if readers have a background of knowledge necessary to understand them. Acquiring that knowledge depends upon a well-developed sense of curiosity. Easy access to a dictionary, an encyclopedia, and a book of familiar quotations sharpens that curiosity. Watching public television and network news and specials; reading in magazines, newspapers, history books, novels; going to the theater and to museums of art and science; asking questions, even at the risk of appearing ignorant—these are ways to expand knowledge and stimulate even more curiosity.

Toward the end of the 1980s, educators became concerned that college students had not acquired in their high school years enough knowledge of world culture to make them culturally "literate." One such person, E. D. Hirsch, Jr., a professor of English, published a book about the subject: *Cultural Literacy.* Because so many people wanted to find out if they were culturally literate or illiterate, the book became an instant best-seller.

The next essay, "Poor but Dumb," by Russell Baker, treats the book in a humorous and satirical vein, but it is serious about cultural literacy. The allusions come thick and fast, so you will have to have an encyclopedia and a good dictionary beside you when you read this essay.

POOR BUT DUMB

Russell Baker

July 14, 1987

1   Do you look blank when they say "William Shakespeare"? Wonder what in the world it means when people say "Sweden" and "Einstein"? Have you ever been embarrassed because everybody laughed when you said: "Elysian Fields? Wasn't he that movie comedian who drank like a fish?"

2   If so, you lack cultural literacy and may as well forget those dreams of becoming rich and famous.

3   Cultural literacy, as explained in a book titled—what else?—*Cultural Literacy,* by E. D. Hirsch Jr., is not as hifalutin a condition as it sounds. All it means is that you are not totally ignorant of the knowledge Americans used to acquire in high school.

4   Nowadays schools don't invariably impart such knowledge. Result: cultural illiteracy, which leads to not getting the sweet jobs.

5   Example: During your interview for an expense-account position with Consolidated Mergers Inc., the vice president for hiring says the job requires a personality combining the warrior instincts of Achilles and the cunning of Ulysses,

and you say, "Tell me more about this Achilles and Ulysses, because if they're anything like herpes I don't want the job."

6   The interviewer smiles and says, "Don't call us, we'll call you." Cultural illiteracy has done you in.

7   Professor Hirsch makes the point that you really don't have to know much to be culturally literate and get in on the good life. Often, he notes, you just have to have heard the name.

8   Einstein, for example. Somebody says "Einstein." All you have to know is: "famous math genius, funny looking hair, theory of relativity." That's enough. You don't have to understand Einstein's theory, or mc squared, or know anything about his life.

9   You can be a substantial ignoramus about Einstein and get all the way to the top in America. But let people see that the name leaves you mystified and you'll still be emptying the trash cans at Quik 'n' Dirtyburger when Social Security time rolls around.

10   The knowledge required to stay culturally literate is in constant flux. Some requirements are never going to change in any foreseeable future. Shakespeare, for instance. For nearly 400 years now, people who said "Shakes which spear?" when somebody else said "Shakespeare" have had trouble getting decent jobs.

11   Spiro Agnew, on the other hand, is a short-timer like all Vice Presidents, and would have disappeared long ago had he not been the first one to plead nolo contendere and resign. (Professor Hirsch says you have to know nolo contendere to be culturally literate, so look it up.)

12   New material is constantly pouring into the fund of knowledge required to stay culturally literate. Much of this material may be hopelessly complicated. Take "Dolby sound," for instance.

13   You are probably as uncertain as I am about what "Dolby sound" is. You probably don't even want to know. I know that reaction. I felt that way myself when "semiotics" and "hermeneutics" and "holistic" came along. I passed up all three, gambling that, like Vice Presidents, they wouldn't last long. Who would want to live in a world

where "hermeneutics" could last as long as Shakespeare, Sweden and Elysian Fields?

14   But the beauty part about "Dolby sound" is, you don't have to know much to be culturally literate. Somebody says "Dolby sound." You immediately say, strictly to yourself of course, "Ah yes, the latest wrinkle in sound recording, supposed to be even better than the last greatest wrinkle."

15   It's not much, but it's enough to save you from asking if Dolby Sound is as big as Puget Sound, and can therefore mean the difference between getting to the top of the world and spending the next 40 years at the Quik 'n' Dirtyburger.

16   The culturally literate person who wants to stay in the mainstream fields dozens of such problems every month.

17   "Quartz watch," for example. To stay culturally literate you look at a few quartz watches. Hey, what do you know! They don't tick!

18   After that you will never look confused when somebody says "quartz watch."

19   Instead of panicking ("Good heavens, did they start making watches out of quartz while I was busy trying to learn what Dolby sound was?") you say to yourself, "Silly watch—doesn't tick," and are hired to manage Consolidated's watchstrap division.

20   Cultural illiteracy is deadly for poor children. They tend to end up in the poorer schools where poorer teachers tend to give up before getting around to Einstein, Achilles and Spiro Agnew. Never mind, little children. Keeping the Quik 'n' Dirtyburger clean is honorable labor.

Study Guide:

Before rereading the essay, make sure of the definitions of the following words, and add them to your vocabulary list: *hifalutin* (or *highfaluting*), *to impart, herpes, flux, nolo contendere.*

Questions:

1. Russell Baker likes to play verbal tricks. In doing so, he compliments his readers, trusting that they will be alert to the fun. The last

sentence of paragraph 1 contains a double allusion based on "Fields." What is the double allusion?

2. Give one example each of Ulysses' cunning instincts and Achilles' warrior instincts.

3. What does "mc squared" have to do with Einstein?

4. Which of the following words might most appropriately be applied to health care: *hermeneutics, semiotics, holistic*?

5. Under which president did Spiro Agnew serve?

6. Baker makes humorous use of several puns and at least one rhyme in this essay. Identify one of each and explain the incongruities that make them funny.

7. How can you tell that "Consolidated Mergers Inc." and "Quik 'n' Dirtyburger" are made-up names?

8. What evidence is in paragraphs 3, 7, 8, 9, and 13–19 to convince us that Baker is poking satirical fun at the book and its title, *Cultural Literacy*?

9. What in paragraphs 7–9 would lead you to believe that Baker is serious about cultural literacy?

10. What does Baker mean by his final paragraph? Is the last sentence supposed to be funny, or is it bitterly sarcastic?

11. This essay is carefully organized. What ideas are repeated and built upon so that the allusions concealed within them are crucially important to that final paragraph?

Style: The Review

A special kind of essay is the review. Every day in newspapers and magazines a number of books, plays, movies, art exhibitions, concerts, recitals, operas, and recordings are reviewed for readers who may be especially interested in one or more of these media of expression. No one review appeals to a large audience, but any one may be highly interesting to a small audience and vitally important to the people and events being reviewed.

Reviews are limited, however, not only in their appeal, but also in their timeliness. This morning's review of last night's theatrical flop will be stale stuff by tomorrow—particularly if it has the graceless style of an article being rushed into print as the harassed reviewer is scribbling the last line. Few morning newspaper reviewers survive such pressure with literary distinction.

Reviewers for weekly and monthly magazines have an easier time, however, and it is among their reviews that one occasionally finds an essay so well written that it remains interesting. One such reviewer was Kenneth Tynan, British theater critic and producer, whose career was distinguished by brilliant sojourns as writer for the London *Observer* and *The New Yorker* and as literary manager of the British National Theatre.

Reading his reviews, one can enjoy Tynan's amazing skill in saying just enough about a play and its production and performance to make his opinions credible without giving too much away. One can also sense Tynan's love of the theater, his lavish praise for what he finds thrilling, his sharp condemnation of what he finds shabby.

Such opinions can easily be overstated, and in the essay that follows, a review of the first Broadway production of *Waiting for Godot*, Tynan's praise of Bert Lahr's performance has elements of overstatement, or exaggeration. The literary term for overstatement is **hyperbole**.

Tynan would probably not have admitted to hyperbole in this case, so we would call it unintended; but Russell Baker uses hyperbole intentionally and for satirical effect in his discussion of jobs won or lost as a consequence of cultural literacy or illiteracy.

The opposite of hyperbole is **understatement**. To understate is to diminish a condition to less than its actual significance. Understatement used as satire may be considered ironic because the image it suggests is nearly contrary to the significance of the actual condition. Because we meet with less understatement than hyperbole, understatement often seems more ironic than does hyperbole, and—ironically—its effect is often more powerful. A famous example of understatement is Queen Victoria's expression of outrage at a tasteless imitation of her by one of her courtiers. "We are not amused," she said.

As you read this review, see how Tynan discloses the puzzling nature of Samuel Beckett's famous play without giving away the story. If you have read or seen the play, you will know that the last sentence of the review is a brilliant metaphor for the theme. Look, too, for allusions, and see if they enrich the essay.

About the Author

Kenneth Tynan (1927–1980) began writing about the theater when he was still in grammar school, and by the time he had finished his undergraduate studies at Oxford, he had already established a reputation as an extraordinarily perceptive reviewer. His reviews, opinions, and "profiles" (biographical sketches) have been collected and published in several books, among which are *Curtains, Tynan Right and Left,* and *The Sound of Two Hands Clapping.*

WAITING FOR GODOT, BY SAMUEL BECKETT, AT THE GOLDEN

Kenneth Tynan

1956

1   Ten days ago *Waiting for Godot* reached New York, greeted by a baffled but mostly appreciative press and preceded by an advertising campaign in which the management appealed for 70,000 intellectuals to make its venture pay. At the performance I saw, a Sunday matinee, the eggheads were rolling in. And when the curtain fell, the house stood up to cheer a man who had never before appeared in a legitimate play, a mighty and blessed clown whose grateful bewilderment was reflected in the tears that speckled his cheeks, a burlesque comic of crumpled mien and baggy eyes, with a nose stuck like a gherkin into a face as ageless as the Commedia dell' Arte: Bert Lahr, no less, the cowardly lion of *The Wizard of Oz,* who played the dumber of Samuel Beckett's two timeless hoboes, and by his playing bridged, for the first time I can remember, the irrational abyss that yawns between the world of red noses and the world of blue stockings.

2   Without him, the Broadway production of Mr. Beckett's play would be admirable; with him, it is transfigured. It is as if we, the audience, had elected him to represent us on stage; to stand up for our rights; to anticipate our reactions, resentful and confused, to the lonely universe into

which the author plunges us. "I'm going," says Mr. Lahr. "We can't go," snaps his partner. "Why not?" pleads Mr. Lahr. "We're waiting for Godot," comes the reply; whereat Mr. Lahr raises one finger with an "Ah!" of comprehension which betokens its exact opposite, a totality of blankest ignorance. Mr. Lahr's beleaguered simpleton, a draughts-player lost in a universe of chess, is one of the noblest performances I have ever seen.

Study Guide:

For your vocabulary list define the following words as used in context: *venture, legitimate* (special use applied to theater), *mien, gherkin, transfigured, beleaguered, draughts-player* (special British use).

Questions:

1. What was a "burlesque comic"? What was the "Commedia dell' Arte"? What are "blue stockings"? What are some other allusions in the essay?

2. Explain the metaphor about "a draughts-player lost in a universe of chess." There are several other indications, all implied rather than stated, that *Waiting for Godot* is difficult to understand. What are they?

3. Samuel Beckett (1906–1989) had an enormous influence on theater during the second half of the twentieth century. He and others of his thinking gave the word *absurd* new meaning (see its use in MacLeish's essay). Look up information on his life and works.

4. Parallel structure moves the essay along in a graceful progression of thought. Point out several examples of it.

5. Do you agree that Tynan is hyperbolic in his praise of Lahr's performance? If so, do you think hyperbole has its usefulness in a review? Discuss.

Composition Topic:

The next time you go to a movie or play, take notes and then write a review. Is it possible to be objective?

PART THREE

A Collection of Essays

The following essays have been chosen for interesting subject matter and effective style. Notice that in some essays the generalizations and the abstract ideas are clearly stated, but that in other essays they are only implied. In either case you should analyze the essay carefully to see how the author's style has shaped words and details toward the expression of generalizations and abstract ideas. Notice also that the meaning of some essays depends heavily upon allusions while the meaning of others does not.

Bernard Levin

One of England's most popular columnists, Bernard Levin writes regularly for the *London Times* and the *Observer*. He is also a critic of theater, movies, and television and has written in that capacity for the *Sunday Times,* the *Guardian,* and the *Daily Express*. For the *Spectator* he has been a parliamentary and political correspondent, writing under the pen name Taper. He is also an observer of human nature and the behavior of human beings under social and political stress. The 1960s were a time of particular interest to Levin, and he published his account of those tumultuous years in a book entitled *The Pendulum Years.*

  "Benign Intentions" is Bernard Levin's review of the science fiction movie *Close Encounters of the Third Kind.* It is much more than a movie review, however.

BENIGN INTENTIONS

Bernard Levin

The Times 23 May 1978

1   What on earth is happening to me? I, who do not normally enter a cinema from one year to the next, have already been twice in 1978. This time it was *Close Encounters of the Third Kind,* a far better film than *Star Wars,* which I saw a few weeks ago. Better in every sense, starting with the "special effects," which in *Star Wars* consisted largely of interminable repetitions of the same shot—the bobbin-like space fighters whizzing about—but which in *Close Encounters* culminated (after a good deal of similar whizzing) in one of the most magnificent spectacles I have seen on a cinema screen, as the giant spaceship comes in to land. It is much better edited too; though the film deliberately leaves much, including the essential point of it, unexplained until the end, there is no irritating feeling of confusion. But much more important, *Close Encounters* is interesting and exciting at far deeper levels; its enormous success, like that of *Star Wars* (and *Close Encounters* seems to be as popular here as in America, while the other film, curiously, does not), is a portent well worth

examining, but it is also saying something on its own account, much more directly and much more effectively.

2   Of all the arguments against the hypothesis that beings from other worlds may visit our earth, only one has ever seemed to me convincing. It is the proposition that any civilization capable of the technology required to send a vehicle through space would be so unimaginably far in advance of our own that it would not need to send its messengers or observers physically across the light-years; it would be able far more easily to devise means by which we could be inspected in the greatest detail, and if necessary communicated with, from afar. One of the most striking things about *Close Encounters* is that it solves this particular philosophical problem with one single, obvious assumption. I suppose I ought not to give away the most significant surprises in the plot, and I suppose that this particular one comes under that heading, so I shall say no more, except that the moment you see the point you see also the rightness of it. The same is true of an even more startling scene; you will see, towards the end of the film, a group of figures in red combat-suits, arriving at the base at which the spacecraft is awaited. The assumption is that they are troops, ready to engage in battle with the unearthly strangers, but when we see them again—taking part in a religious service, which at first reinforces the belief that they are fighting men, now seeking a blessing on their arms—we notice that some of them are elderly and bespectacled, and indeed some of them women, which seems to rule out the hypothesis.

3   And ruled out it emphatically is, in the very last seconds of the film, when we realize at last who they are and what they are there for—and why the hero, in the last glimpse we get of him, is also dressed in the same uniform, and is being asked by the scientist in charge of the project whether there is any history of mental illness in his family.

4   At that point, there is an almost audible click in the mind, and that metaphor is particularly apt; the illumination that dawns as the meaning of the whole film becomes clear is as bright, abrupt and dazzling as that of a light turned on by a switch in a dark room. For it is not only

understanding that dawns; or rather it is not only understanding in the sense of understanding the facts, of seeing
how all the clues come together to provide an explanation.
If that were all, *Close Encounters* would be nothing but
high-class entertainment, and although it *is* high-class entertainment, and could indeed have gone much further
than it does in the explicitness of its philosophical point
without risking its popular appeal, it is also something
very much more—which is, after all, why I have chosen to
discuss it today.

5   Why is almost nobody involved frightened, except at the
first effects of the space visitors, when homes and motor-
cars begin to behave as though they are in the epicentre of
a massive earthquake? (That, I may say, provides one of
the loveliest and most significant items in the whole film,
when all the mechanical toys in the infant's bedroom "come
alive," while he watches the resultant *Boutique Fantasque**
with saucer-eyed wonder untinged by any fear.) I say almost nobody is frightened, because there is one exception,
when the little boy's mother loses a tug-o-war for him (con-
ducted, with a beautiful touch of imagination, through the
cat flap) with whatever it is that is pulling him from her.
She is terrified on his behalf, but he is eager to go and join
his new friends, and before long his confidence is seen to be
abundantly justified.

6   For the point about *Close Encounters*—and this much I
can surely say without disclosing anything—is that everything that happens is firmly rooted in an entirely benign
intention. Whose intention it is we are left to speculate, but
we are given a number of clues to that, too, not least in the
words the priest is speaking in the shot of the service, but
above all in what creatures we see emerging briefly from
the spacecraft and in what manner they return to its interior, now not alone.

7   Within the framework of benignity, there are further
clues. If we are ever to communicate with beings from
other worlds, we must find a common language, which is
unlikely to be an earthly one, particularly Esperanto. In

**The Fantastic Shop*, title of a ballet.

Close Encounters, it is suggested that a means of mutual understanding might be sought in musical tones and in hand movements based on the alphabet for the deaf, and we see both methods demonstrated. But the five-note theme that forms the basis of the former attempt is introduced, spectacularly, in a scene in India, in which a group of robed devotees are chanting it in the form of versicle and response. Why India? And why in this particular setting? Whatever you think the answer to those questions may be, you would be wise to assume that there is an answer, and that the choice was not simply a coincidence.

8   *Close Encounters of the Third Kind* is a film that lingers on the retina of the mind like the image of a light stared at before the eyes are closed. And the reason is that it offers, in addition to great technical skill and great cinematic excitement, a view, and a view, moreover, of great richness and plausibility. If it is possible that beings from space will one day visit our planet—and you would have to be bone-headed well beyond the point of scientific duty to declare that it is *not* possible—then it is worth wondering what such a visit might mean. Not just consist of; mean. This film offers a clear, consistent and powerful choice among possible meanings, and I believe the huge response the film has had reflects a conviction that the makers' guess is the most likely one. And the feeling that I took from the cinema, which I think few who see the film will fail to experience for themselves, is that the thesis is indeed correct. For the final effect of the film is to send us out with an extraordinarily exalted feeling, of the kind that we get before any work of art that expresses—as all true art does and must—the sense of order and harmony, with its irreducible core of mystery, in the universe. In other words, we emerge with the feeling that not only the film, but the universe, has got the answer right.

Study Guide:

1. Before rereading this essay, add to your permanent vocabulary list the following words and the definitions that fit them in context: *benign* (and *benignity*), *interminable, to culminate, portent, hypothesis,*

*explicitness, epicenter, to speculate, Esperanto, mutual, versicle and re-
sponse, plausibility, consistent, thesis, exalted, irreducible.*

2. Bernard Levin's allusion to *Star Wars* is based, as is any allusion, on the assumption that you are familiar with it. If you have not
seen *Star Wars*, then you should obtain a videotape and watch it. And
whether or not you have seen *Close Encounters*, you should watch it
on videotape after having read this review. The two movies provide a
basis for discussion of the philosophical theme that Levin encourages
you to explore.

Questions:

1. In paragraph 4, what is "that metaphor," and what are the metaphors and similes by which Levin explains it?

2. Professional reviewers usually respect an unwritten rule not to
reveal any more of the plot and theme than is necessary to a persuasive discussion of a work. Here, almost like a juggler, Levin keeps plot
and theme in the air. Explain how he keeps them a mystery while
saying just enough to make his point. In which paragraphs does he
perform this literary stunt?

3. Does Levin like the movie? Does he want you to see it? What is
the tone of the essay? What are the concrete examples and specific
clues that lead you to your answers to these questions?

4. In comparing *Close Encounters* with *Star Wars* (paragraph 1),
Levin thinks the popularity of *Close Encounters*, at least in England,
"is a portent worth examining, but it is also saying something on its
own account, much more directly and much more effectively." What is
that "portent" and what is that "something"? Are they tied in with the
final two sentences of the essay?

5. Are some of the sentences in the essay too long and convoluted?
Discuss.

Composition Topic:

Take a notebook with you to the next movie you see, and jot down
ideas and criticisms as they occur to you. Afterwards, write a review
that makes some thematic point without giving away too much of the
movie's plot and theme. Be sure to include specific and interesting
details about the photography, the acting, and the directing.

Peggy and Pierre Streit

Peggy and Pierre Streit were a writer-photographer team who traveled widely in India, Afghanistan, and other parts of Asia during the 1950s.

When the Streits wrote "A Well in India" for the *New York Times Magazine,* they were writing about a country that was very different from most of the land and its people today. The essay remains relevant, however, to some of the poorest and most rural parts of India, and it remains symbolically relevant to our survival on this planet. Indeed, one should read it in light of Archibald MacLeish's "A Reflection: Riders on Earth Together, Brothers in Eternal Cold."

A WELL IN INDIA

Peggy and Pierre Streit

September 20, 1959

1   The hot dry season in India. . . . A corrosive wind drives rivulets of sand across the land; torpid animals stand at the edge of dried-up water holes. The earth is cracked and in the rivers the sluggish, falling waters have exposed the sludge of the mud flats. Throughout the land the thoughts of men turn to water. And in the village of Rampura these thoughts are focused on the village well.

2   It is a simple concrete affair, built upon the hard earth worn by the feet of five hundred villagers. It is surmounted by a wooden structure over which ropes, tied to buckets, are lowered to the black, placid depths twenty feet below. Fanning out from the well are the huts of the villagers— their walls white from sun, their thatched roofs thick with dust blown in from the fields.

3   At the edge of the well is a semicircle of earthen pots and, crouched at some distance behind them, a woman. She is an untouchable—a sweeper in Indian parlance—a scavenger of the village. She cleans latrines, disposes of dead animals and washes drains. She also delivers village babies, for this—like all her work—is considered unclean by most of village India.

4   Her work—indeed, her very presence—is considered polluting, and since there is no well for untouchables in Rampura, her water jars must be filled by upper-caste villagers.

5   There are dark shadows under her eyes and the flesh has fallen away from her neck, for she, like her fellow outcastes, is at the end of a bitter struggle. And if, in her narrow world, shackled by tradition and hemmed in by poverty, she had been unaware of the power of the water of the well at whose edge she waits—she knows it now.

6   Shanti, 30 years old, has been deserted by her husband, and supports her three children. Like her ancestors almost as far back as history records, she has cleaned the refuse from village huts and lanes. Hers is a life of inherited duties as well as inherited rights. She serves, and her work calls for payment of one chapatty—a thin wafer of unleavened bread—a day from each of the thirty families she cares for.

7   But this is the hiatus between harvests; the oppressive lull before the burst of monsoon rains; the season of flies and dust, heat and disease, querulous voices and frayed tempers—and the season of want. There is little food in Rampura for anyone, and though Shanti's chores have continued as before, she has received only six chapatties a day for her family—starvation wages.

8   Ten days ago she revolted. Driven by desperation, she defied an elemental law of village India. She refused to make her sweeper's rounds—refused to do the work tradition and religion had assigned her. Shocked at her audacity, but united in desperation, the village's six other sweeper families joined in her protest.

9   Word of her action spread quickly across the invisible line that separates the untouchables' huts from the rest of the village. As the day wore on and the men returned from the fields, they gathered at the well—the heart of the village—and their voices rose, shrill with outrage: a *sweeper* defying them all! Shanti, a sweeper *and* a woman, challenging a system that had prevailed unquestioned for centuries! Their indignation spilled over. It was true, perhaps, that the sweepers had not had their due. But that

was no fault of the upper caste. No fault of theirs that sun and earth and water had failed to produce the food by which they could fulfill their obligations. So, to bring the insurgents to heel, they employed their ultimate weapon; the earthen water jars of the village untouchables would remain empty until they returned to work. For the sweepers of Rampura the well had run dry.

10   No water: thirst, in the heat, went unslaked. The embers of the hearth were dead, for there was no water for cooking. The crumbling walls of outcaste huts went untended, for there was no water for repairs. There was no fuel, for the fires of the village were fed with dung mixed with water and dried. The dust and the sweat and the filth of their lives congealed on their skins and there it stayed, while life in the rest of the village—within sight of the sweepers—flowed on.

11   The day began and ended at the well. The men, their dhotis wrapped about their loins, congregated at the water's edge in the hushed postdawn, their small brass water jugs in hand, their voices mingling in quiet conversation as they rinsed their bodies and brushed their teeth. The buffaloes were watered, their soft muzzles lingering in the buckets before they were driven off to the fields. Then came the women, their brass pots atop their heads, to begin the ritual of water drawing: the careful lowering of the bucket in the well, lest it come loose from the rope; the gratifying splash as it touched the water; the maneuvering to make it sink; the squeal of rope against wooden pulley as it ascended. The sun rose higher. Clothes were beaten clean on the rocks surrounding the well as the women gossiped. A traveler from a near-by road quenched his thirst from a villager's urn. Two little boys, hot and bored, dropped pebbles into the water and waited for their hollow splash, far below.

12   As the afternoon wore on and the sun turned orange through the dust, the men came back from the fields. They doused the parched, cracked hides of their water buffaloes and murmured contentedly, themselves, as the water coursed over their own shoulders and arms. And finally, as twilight closed in, came the evening procession of women,

stately, graceful, their bare feet moving smoothly over the earth, their full skirts swinging about their ankles, the heavy brass pots once again balanced on their heads.

13   The day was ended and life was as it always was— almost. Only the fetid odor of accumulated refuse and the assertive buzz of flies attested to strife in the village. For, while tradition and religion decreed that sweepers must clean, it also ordained that the socially blessed must not. Refuse lay where it fell and rotted.

14   The strain of the water boycott was beginning to tell on the untouchables. For two days they had held their own. But on the third their thin reserve of flesh had fallen away. Movements were slower; voices softer; minds dull. More and more the desultory conversation turned to the ordinary; the delicious memory of sliding from the back of a wallowing buffalo into a pond; the feel of bare feet in wet mud; the touch of fresh water on parched lips; the anticipation of monsoon rains.

15   One by one the few tools they owned were sold for food. A week passed, and on the ninth day two sweeper children were down with fever. On the tenth day Shanti crossed the path that separated outcaste from the upper caste and walked through familiar, winding alleyways to one of the huts she served.

16   "Your time is near," she told the young, expectant mother. "Tell your man to leave his sickle home when he goes to the fields. I've had to sell mine." (It is the field sickle that cuts the cord of newborn babies in much of village India.) Shanti, the instigator of the insurrection, had resumed her ancestral duties; the strike was broken. Next morning, as ever, she waited at the well. Silently, the procession of upper-caste women approached. They filled their jars to the brim and without a word they filled hers.

17   She lifted the urns to her head, steadied them, and started back to her quarters—back to a life ruled by the powers that still rule most of the world: not the power of atoms or electricity, nor the power of alliances or power blocs, but the elemental powers of hunger, of disease, of tradition—and of water.

Study Guide:

The meanings of the following words are essential to understanding this essay. Add them to your list: *rivulets, torpid, placid, caste, hiatus, monsoon, querulous, audacity, to prevail, insurgents, unslaked, dung, congealed, dhoti, stately, fetid, assertive, to attest to, desultory, instigator, insurrection, bloc.*

Questions:

1. What is an "untouchable" in India? Look this up in an encyclopedia, and then discuss.

2. What conflicts are left unresolved in this essay? Exactly what are the authors criticizing here about social structure? Do we have the same problems in our society? Explain.

3. A **symbol** is an object, person, or incident that stands for or suggests a meaning or idea beyond itself. For instance, the American flag, often cited as an example, is a symbol of our country and also of such abstract ideas as patriotism, democracy, and freedom.

How are the woman sweeper (Shanti) and "water" used symbolically by the authors? What greater ideas do they represent? Turn back to "Twins" for a moment. What is the symbolic significance of the carvings on the beech tree mentioned in paragraph 1 of "Twins"?

4. A **parable** is a story told for its illustration of some moral. The people and events in it are often symbolic. In what way is this essay like a parable?

5. Are there elements of tragedy in this essay? Discuss this question in terms of organization, character, and conflict.

6. Several images are repeated throughout this essay—for instance, images of dust and flesh. There are others. What are they? How is this imagery related to the abstract theme of the essay?

7. What is the authors' attitude toward the reader? Describe the tone of the essay. Does the ratio of nouns and verbs to adverbs and adjectives tell you anything about the tone and style? Explain.

8. Like "Twins," "A Well in India" makes its point by indirection. The restrained final paragraph is the only suggestion of a direct comment. Is this style more or less effective than a direct approach? Explain.

George Orwell

Eric Arthur Blair was born in 1903 in Bengal (India), where his father was a civil servant of the British Empire. At the age of 8, he was sent to St. Cyprian's, an elite boarding school in England, and later to Eton, growing up "an odious little snob," as he described himself. He then made a decision that shaped the rest of his life. Instead of going to Oxford or Cambridge, like most of his classmates, he went to Burma and joined the Imperial Indian Police.

The colonial system so overwhelmed him with guilt and revulsion that he returned to England in 1927, to write. As a laborer in France and a tramp in England, he deliberately acquired the raw material for his first book, *Down and Out in Paris and London,* which he published in 1933 under the pen name George Orwell, symbol of his new identity.

In his rebellion against imperialism, George Orwell now became a Socialist and took an assignment to write about appalling coal mining conditions in northern England. His uncompromisingly honest observations, published in *The Road to Wigan Pier,* criticized not only the coal mining management but also the Socialist party's response (which he found too soft and intellectual).

In 1936 Orwell went to Spain to report on the Spanish civil war. There he joined the Loyalist forces against the Fascists. In 1937, after being severely wounded, he was discharged from the militia. His life now threatened by Soviet-backed Communists, who had betrayed the Socialist Loyalists, he fled Spain. *Homage to Catalonia,* published in 1938, describes these events and his abhorrence of the Communists.

After returning to England, he devoted himself to battling totalitarianism of the Left and of the Right. During World War II he worked for the BBC until 1944, when he became literary editor of the *Tribune,* a Socialist newspaper. In 1945 he published *Animal Farm,* a satire of Soviet totalitarian communism; and in 1949, near death from tuberculosis, he published his final major work, the chilling *1984.* He died in 1950.

Though popularly known as a novelist, George Orwell is regarded as the greatest British political essayist since Jonathan Swift. "Shooting an Elephant," one of his most famous essays, is an outstanding example of the uncompromising honesty that distinguishes his writing. It was written in the early 1930s, after his rejection of imperialism.

SHOOTING AN ELEPHANT

George Orwell

Circa 1933

1   In Moulmein, in Lower Burma,* I was hated by large numbers of people—the only time in my life that I have been important enough for this to happen to me. I was sub-divisional police officer of the town, and in an aimless, petty kind of way anti-European feeling was very bitter. No one had the guts to raise a riot, but if a European woman went through the bazaars alone somebody would probably spit betel juice over her dress. As a police officer I was an obvious target and was baited whenever it seemed safe to do so. When a nimble Burman tripped me up on the football field and the referee (another Burman) looked the other way, the crowed yelled with hideous laughter. This happened more than once. In the end the sneering yellow faces of young men that met me everywhere, the insults hooted after me when I was at a safe distance, got badly on my nerves. The young Buddhist priests were the worst of all. There were several thousands of them in town and none of them seemed to have anything to do except stand on street corners and jeer at Europeans.

2   All this was perplexing and upsetting. For at that time I had already made up my mind that imperialism was an evil thing and the sooner I chucked up my job and got out of it the better. Theoretically—and secretly, of course—I was all for the Burmese and all against their oppressors, the British. As for the job I was doing, I hated it more bitterly than I can perhaps make clear. In a job like that you see the dirty work of Empire at close quarters. The wretched prisoners huddling in the stinking cages of the lock-ups, the grey, cowed faces of the long-term convicts, the scarred buttocks of the men who had been flogged with bamboos—all these oppressed me with an intolerable sense of guilt. But I could get nothing into perspective. I was

*Burma has been renamed Myanmar (pronounced Mee-*ahn*-ma).

young and ill-educated and I had had to think out my problems in the utter silence that is imposed on every Englishman in the East. I did not even know that the British Empire is dying, still less did I know that it is a great deal better than the younger empires that are going to supplant it. All I knew was that I was stuck between my hatred of the empire I served and my rage against the evil-spirited little beasts who tried to make my job impossible. With one part of my mind I thought of the British Raj as an unbreakable tyranny, as something clamped down, in *saecula saeculorum*,* upon the will of prostrate peoples; with another part I thought that the greatest joy in the world would be to drive a bayonet into a Buddhist priest's guts. Feelings like these are the normal by-products of imperialism; ask any Anglo-Indian official, if you can catch him off duty.

3   One day something happened which in a roundabout way was enlightening. It was a tiny incident in itself, but it gave me a better glimpse than I had had before of the real nature of imperialism—the real motives for which despotic governments act. Early one morning the sub-inspector at a police station the other end of the town rang me up on the 'phone and said that an elephant was ravaging the bazaar. Would I please come and do something about it? I did not know what I could do, but I wanted to see what was happening and I got on to a pony and started out. I took my rifle, an old .44 Winchester and much too small to kill an elephant, but I thought the noise might be useful *in terrorem*. Various Burmans stopped me on the way and told me about the elephant's doings. It was not, of course, a wild elephant, but a tame one which had gone "must." It had been chained up, as tame elephants always are when their attack of "must" is due, but on the previous night it had broken its chain and escaped. Its mahout, the only person who could manage it when it was in that state, had set out in pursuit, but had taken the wrong direction and was now twelve hours' journey away, and in the morning the elephant had suddenly reappeared in the town. The Burmese

*Forever and ever.

population had no weapons and were quite helpless against it. It had already destroyed somebody else's bamboo hut, killed a cow and raided some fruit-stalls and devoured the stock; also it had met the municipal rubbish van and, when the driver jumped out and took to his heels, had turned the van over and inflicted violences upon it.

4   The Burmese sub-inspector and some Indian constables were waiting for me in the quarter where the elephant had been seen. It was a very poor quarter, a labyrinth of squalid bamboo huts, thatched with palm-leaf, winding all over a steep hillside. I remember that it was a cloudy, stuffy morning at the beginning of the rains. We began questioning the people as to where the elephant had gone and, as usual, failed to get any definite information. That is invariably the case in the East; a story always sounds clear enough at a distance, but the nearer you get to the scene of events the vaguer it becomes. Some of the people said that the elephant had gone in one direction, some said that he had gone in another, some professed not even to have heard of any elephant. I had almost made up my mind that the whole story was a pack of lies, when we heard yells a little distance away. There was a loud, scandalized cry of "Go away, child! Go away this instant!" and an old woman with a switch in her hand came round the corner of a hut, violently shooing away a crowd of naked children. Some more women followed, clicking their tongues and exclaiming; evidently there was something that the children ought not to have seen. I rounded the hut and saw a man's dead body sprawling in the mud. He was an Indian, a black Dravidian coolie, almost naked, and he could not have been dead many minutes. The people said that the elephant had come suddenly upon him round the corner of the hut, caught him with its trunk, put its foot on his back and ground him into the earth. This was the rainy season and the ground was soft, and his face had scored a trench a foot deep and a couple of yards long. He was lying on his belly with arms crucified and head sharply twisted to one side. His face was coated with mud, the eyes wide open, the teeth bared and grinning with an expression of unendurable agony. (Never tell me, by the way, that the

dead look peaceful. Most of the corpses I have seen looked devilish.) The friction of the great beast's foot had stripped the skin from his back as neatly as one skins a rabbit. As soon as I saw the dead man I sent an orderly to a friend's house nearby to borrow an elephant rifle. I had already sent back the pony, not wanting it to go mad with fright and throw me if it smelt the elephant.

5   The orderly came back in a few minutes with a rifle and five cartridges, and meanwhile some Burmans had arrived and told us that the elephant was in the paddy fields below, only a few hundred yards away. As I started forward practically the whole population of the quarter flocked out of the houses and followed me. They had seen the rifle and were all shouting excitedly that I was going to shoot the elephant. They had not shown much interest in the elephant when he was merely ravaging their homes, but it was different now that he was going to be shot. It was a bit of fun to them, as it would be to an English crowd; besides they wanted the meat. It made me vaguely uneasy. I had no intention of shooting the elephant—I had merely sent for the rifle to defend myself if necessary—and it is always unnerving to have a crowd following you. I marched down the hill, looking and feeling a fool, with the rifle over my shoulder and an ever-growing army of people jostling at my heels. At the bottom, when you got away from the huts, there was a metalled road and beyond that a miry waste of paddy fields a thousand yards across, not yet ploughed but soggy from the first rains and dotted with coarse grass. The elephant was standing eight yards from the road, his left side towards us. He took not the slightest notice of the crowd's approach. He was tearing up bunches of grass, beating them against his knees to clean them and stuffing them into his mouth.

6   I had halted on the road. As soon as I saw the elephant I knew with perfect certainty that I ought not to shoot him. It is a serious matter to shoot a working elephant—it is comparable to destroying a huge and costly piece of machinery—and obviously one ought not to do it if it can possibly be avoided. And at that distance, peacefully eating, the elephant looked no more dangerous than a cow. I

thought then and I think now that his attack of "must" was already passing off; in which case he would merely wander harmlessly about until the mahout came back and caught him. Moreover, I did not in the least want to shoot him. I decided that I would watch him for a little while to make sure that he did not turn savage again, and then go home.

7   But at that moment I glanced round at the crowd that had followed me. It was an immense crowd, two thousand at the least and growing every minute. It blocked the road for a long distance on either side. I looked at the sea of yellow faces above the garish clothes—faces all happy and excited over this bit of fun, all certain that the elephant was going to be shot. They were watching me as they would watch a conjurer about to perform a trick. They did not like me, but with the magical rifle in my hands I was momentarily worth watching. And suddenly I realized that I should have to shoot the elephant after all. The people expected it of me and I had got to do it; I could feel their two thousand wills pressing me forward, irresistibly. And it was at this moment, as I stood there with the rifle in my hands, that I first grasped the hollowness, the futility of the white man's dominion in the East. Here was I, the white man with his gun, standing in front of the unarmed native crowd—seemingly the leading actor of the piece; but in reality I was only an absurd puppet pushed to and fro by the will of those yellow faces behind. I perceived in this moment that when the white man turns tyrant it is his own freedom that he destroys. He becomes a sort of hollow, posing dummy, the conventionalized figure of a sahib. For it is the condition of his rule that he shall spend his life in trying to impress the "natives," and so in every crisis he has got to do what the "natives" expect of him. He wears a mask, and his face grows to fit it. I had got to shoot the elephant. I had committed myself to doing it when I sent for the rifle. A sahib has got to act like a sahib; he has got to appear resolute, to know his own mind and do definite things. To come all that way, rifle in hand, with two thousand people marching at my heels, and then to trail feebly away, having done nothing—no, that was impossible. The crowd would laugh at me. And my whole life, every white

man's life in the East, was one long struggle not to be laughed at.

8   But I did not want to shoot the elephant. I watched him beating his bunch of grass against his knees, with that preoccupied grandmotherly air that elephants have. It seemed to me that it would be murder to shoot him. At that age I was not squeamish about killing animals, but I had never shot an elephant and never wanted to. (Somehow it always seems worse to kill a *large* animal.) Besides, there was the beast's owner to be considered. Alive, the elephant was worth at least a hundred pounds; dead, he would only be worth the value of his tusks, five pounds, possibly. But I had got to act quickly. I turned to some experienced-looking Burmans who had been there when we arrived, and asked them how the elephant had been behaving. They all said the same thing: he took no notice of you if you left him alone, but he might charge if you went too close to him.

9   It was perfectly clear to me what I ought to do. I ought to walk up to within, say, twenty-five yards of the elephant and test his behavior. If he charged, I could shoot; if he took no notice of me, it would be safe to leave him until the mahout came back. But also I knew that I was going to do no such thing. I was a poor shot with a rifle and the ground was soft mud into which one would sink at every step. If the elephant charged and I missed him, I should have about as much chance as a toad under a steam-roller. But even then I was not thinking particularly of my own skin, only of the watchful yellow faces behind. For at that moment, with the crowd watching me, I was not afraid in the ordinary sense, as I would have been if I had been alone. A white man mustn't be frightened in front of "natives"; and so, in general, he isn't frightened. The sole thought in my mind was that if anything went wrong those two thousand Burmans would see me pursued, caught, trampled on and reduced to a grinning corpse like that Indian up the hill. And if that happened it was quite probable that some of them would laugh. That would never do. There was only one alternative. I shoved the cartridges

into the magazine and lay down on the road to get a better aim.

10   The crowd grew very still, and a deep, low, happy sigh, as of people who see the theatre curtain go up at last, breathed from innumerable throats. They were going to have their bit of fun after all. The rifle was a beautiful German thing with cross-hair sights. I did not then know that in shooting an elephant one would shoot to cut an imaginary bar running from ear-hole to ear-hole. I ought, therefore, as the elephant was sideways on, to have aimed straight at his ear-hole; actually I aimed several inches in front of this, thinking the brain would be further forward.

11   When I pulled the trigger I did not hear the bang or feel the kick—one never does when a shot goes home—but I heard the devilish roar of glee that went up from the crowd. In that instant, in too short a time, one would have thought, even for the bullet to get there, a mysterious, terrible change had come over the elephant. He neither stirred nor fell, but every line of his body had altered. He looked suddenly stricken, shrunken, immensely old, as though the frightful impact of the bullet had paralysed him without knocking him down. At last, after what seemed a long time—it might have been five seconds, I dare say—he sagged flabbily to his knees. His mouth slobbered. An enormous senility seemed to have settled upon him. One could have imagined him thousands of years old. I fired again into the same spot. At the second shot he did not collapse but climbed with desperate slowness to his feet and stood weakly upright with legs sagging and head drooping. I fired a third time. That was the shot that did for him. You could see the agony of it jolt his whole body and knock the last remnant of strength from his legs. But in falling he seemed for a moment to rise, for as his hind legs collapsed beneath him he seemed to tower upward like a huge rock toppling, his trunk reaching skywards like a tree. He trumpeted, for the first and only time. And then down he came, his belly towards me, with a crash that seemed to shake the ground even where I lay.

12   I got up. The Burmans were already racing past me

across the mud. It was obvious that the elephant would never rise again, but he was not dead. He was breathing very rhythmically with long rattling gasps, his great mound of a side painfully rising and falling. His mouth was wide open—I could see far down into caverns of pale pink throat. I waited a long time for him to die, but his breathing did not weaken. Finally I fired my two remaining shots into the spot where I thought his heart must be. The thick blood welled out of him like red velvet, but still he did not die. His body did not even jerk when the shots hit him, the tortured breathing continued without a pause. He was dying, very slowly and in great agony, but in some world remote from me where not even a bullet could damage him further. I felt that I had got to put an end to that dreadful noise. It seemed dreadful to see the great beast lying there, powerless to move and yet powerless to die, and not even to be able to finish him. I sent back for my small rifle and poured shot after shot into his heart and down his throat. They seemed to make no impression. The tortured gasps continued as steadily as the ticking of a clock.

13   In the end I could not stand it any longer and went away. I heard later that it took him half an hour to die. Burmans were bringing dahs and baskets even before I left, and I was told they had stripped his body almost to the bones by the afternoon.

14   Afterwards, of course, there were endless discussions about the shooting of the elephant. The owner was furious, but he was only an Indian and could do nothing. Besides, legally I had done the right thing, for a mad elephant has to be killed, like a mad dog, if its owner fails to control it. Among the Europeans opinion was divided. The older men said I was right, the younger men said it was a damn shame to shoot an elephant for killing a coolie, because an elephant was worth more than any damn Coringhee coolie. And afterwards I was very glad that the coolie had been killed; it put me legally in the right and it gave me a sufficient pretext for shooting the elephant. I often wondered whether any of the others grasped that I had done it solely to avoid looking a fool.

Study Guide:

Make a list of the meanings of these words in the context of the essay: *betel juice, to bait, imperialism, to oppress, intolerable, prostrate, despotic, to ravage, "must," mahout, labyrinth, squalid, coolie, conjurer, conventionalized, sahib, resolute, squeamish, senility, pretext.*

Questions:

1. Imperialism is an abstract idea, but Orwell defines the term concretely from his experience. Where and how does he make the transition from the abstract to the concrete?

2. Which one of the following did Orwell know would be the *least* sensible reason for first taking along the .44 Winchester? (a) to intimidate the elephant with noise, (b) to kill the elephant, (c) to impress the Burmans with his command of the situation.

3. Orwell saw the importance of the elephant rifle in clarifying the white man's relationship with the "natives." What was this relationship, and when did Orwell know that he was going to use the rifle to kill the elephant?

4. In Orwell's essay there is a conflict between appearance and reality. As a Britisher in the East, Orwell must put on an act, but he has conscience pangs about his tenuous position. What are these conscience pangs, and how do they manifest themselves?

5. After he has shot the elephant, what excuses does Orwell make to himself for his act? Has he fallen prey to the idea of keeping up appearances? Explain.

6. The latter part of Orwell's essay could have been written as a sensational, emotion-filled account. What effect does Orwell achieve by writing in a restrained manner? In what specific places does he use restraint?

7. Cite several of Orwell's similes, metaphors, and paradoxes that seem especially successful. Why are they successful?

8. What is ironic about Orwell's attitude toward the Coringhee coolie? How is the tone of the whole essay ironic?

9. This essay was written when British colonialism was a controlling influence on Burmese society. Is this situation mirrored in America's recent relations with Central American nations?

10. Read the first sentence of Orwell's essay again. How does this thought serve as a basis for the organization of the essay?

Composition Topic:

Write an essay on the statement in paragraph 7: "He wears a mask, and his face grows to fit it." How does this idea apply to the world of your own experience? How does it apply to race relations?

Robert Benchley

Robert Charles Benchley (1889–1945) received his B.A. degree from Harvard University in 1912. Subsequently drawn to journalism, he first joined the staff of the *New York Herald Tribune*. Then after World War I he became managing editor of *Vanity Fair,* and in 1921 he became drama editor for *Life* (not to be confused with the picture magazine that later became popular). There he was appointed editor in 1924. In 1929 he moved to *The New Yorker,* and as drama editor and writer of special pieces he established his reputation as a uniquely witty critic and droll observer of the current scene.

Hollywood soon discovered Benchley's comic acting talents, and there he became instantly famous for his chaotically funny *Treasurer's Report,* the first all-talking motion picture. This was followed by other films, among them *How to Sleep,* for which he won an Academy Award. Meanwhile, he continued to write, and his essays were collected and published under such book titles as *From Bed to Worse: Or Comforting Thoughts about the Bison* and *My Ten Years in a Quandary, and How They Grew.*

Part of the humor and charm of Benchley's writing and acting is in his willingness to poke fun at himself. However, "What Are Little Boys Made Of?" pokes satirical fun at a kind of popular "science" writing.

WHAT ARE LITTLE BOYS MADE OF?

Robert Benchley

1932

1   Did you know that you have enough resin in your system to rub up a hundred violin A strings? Or enough linoleum to carpet two medium-sized rooms (without bath)? You were probably not aware of these valuable properties lying dormant in your physical make-up, and yet scientists tell us that they are there.

2   As you all were taught in school, our body is made up of millions and millions of tiny particles called the Solar System. These tiny particles are called "aeons," and it would take one of them fifteen billion years to reach the sun if it ever broke loose and *wanted* to get to the sun.

3   Well, anyway, these millions and millions of tiny particles are composed of hydrogen, oxygen, iodine, phosphorus,
Rhode Island, Connecticut. There is also a blueplate dinner
for those who don't like iodine. The action of all these
elements sets up a ferment (C_2HN_4, or common table pep-
per) which sometimes ends in digestion but more often does
not. If any of these agents is lacking in our make-up, due
to our having dressed in a hurry, we say we are "defi-
cient," or perhaps we "feel awful." Even with everything
working I don't feel so hot.

4   It is only recently that doctors have discovered that we
have many more elements in our systems than was originally thought. Whether we have always had them and just
didn't know it, or whether they were brought there and left
by some people who wanted to get rid of them has not been
decided.

5   They tell us that the average 150-pound body (and a
very pretty way to phrase it, too) contains enough carbon
alone to make 9,000 lead pencils (not one of them ever
sharpened, probably).

6   Another item which the doctors tell us we have in abun-
dance is hydrogen—"enough in excess," they put it, "to fill
about a hundred child's balloons." There's a pretty picture
for you! As if we didn't have troubles enough as it is, we
must go about with the consciousness that we have the
makings of one hundred child's balloons inside us, and that
under the right conditions we might float right off our
chairs and bounce against the ceiling until pulled down by
friends!

7   Thinking of ourselves in terms of balloons, lead pencils,
whitewash (we have enough lime in us to whitewash a
chicken coop, says one expert), and matches (we are fools to
bother with those little paper books of matches, for we are
carrying around enough phosphorus to make 2,200 match
heads), all this rather makes a mockery of dressing up in
evening clothes or brushing our hair. We might just as well
get a good big truck and pile ourselves into it in the raw
whenever we want to go anywhere, with perhaps some good
burlap bags to keep the rain off. There is no sense in
trying to look nice when all that is needed is a sandwich-
board sign reading: "Anything on this counter—15 cents."

8   And that is the ultimate insult that these inventory hounds have offered us: they tell us just how much all this truck of which we are made is worth in dollars and cents. They didn't have to do that. Put all our bones, brains, muscles, nerves, and everything that goes into the composition of our bodies on to scales and, at the current market prices, the whole lot would bring just a little over a dollar. This is on the hoof, mind you. If we wanted to tie each element up in little packages with Japanese paper and ribbon, or if we went to the trouble to weather them up a bit and call them antiques, we might be able to ask a little more.

9   For example, the average body, such as might meet another body comin' through the rye, contains only about one tenth of a drop of tincture of iodine at any one time, and one tenth of a drop would hardly be worth the dropper to pick it up for the retail trade. And yet, if *we* don't have that tenth of a drop something happens to our thyroid gland and we sit around the village grocery store all day saying "Nya-ya!" Or to our pituitary gland and we end up wearing a red coat in a circus, billed as Walter, the Cardiff Behemoth: Twice the Size of an Ordinary Man and Only Half as Bright.

10   I don't see why scientists couldn't have let us alone and not told us about this. There was a day when I could bounce out of bed with the lark (I sometimes let the lark get out first, just to shut the window and turn on the heat, but I wasn't far behind), plunge into a cold tub (with just a dash of warm to take off the chill), eat a hearty breakfast, and be off to work with a light heart.

11   But now I get out of bed very carefully, if at all, thinking of those 9,000 lead pencils which are inside me. Too much water seems to be a risk, with all that iron lying around loose. Exercise is out of the question when you consider 2,200 match heads which might jolt up against each other and start a very pretty blaze before you were halfway to work.

12   Suppose that we *are* as full of knickknacks as the doctors say. Why not let the whole matter drop and just forget about it? Now that they have put the thing into our heads, the only way to get it out is for some expert to issue a

statement saying that everyone has been mistaken and that what we are really made of is a solid mechanism of unrustable cast iron and if anything goes wrong, just have a man come up from the garage and look it over.

Study Guide:

1. Look up the meanings of the following words, in context, and add them to your list: *resin, dormant, aeons* (or *eons*), *mockery, ultimate, inventory, behemoth.*

2. This essay pokes satirical fun at a kind of article that appears from time to time in popular magazines. These articles are always presented as serious science, but their authors' underlying assumption is that the reader is ignorant. Thus they reduce the wonders of biochemistry to a sort of ad-man's hokum. Benchley's approach here is a **parody** of this kind of article. A parody is a takeoff, or humorous imitation, of a certain style.

Questions:

1. Paragraph 2 of this essay, instead of assuming that the reader is ignorant, compliments the reader's intelligence and knowledge. Here Benchley's humor plays on what you *know*, not on what you are ignorant of.

    a. Why is "Solar System" just right and all wrong?

    b. What word does Benchley know you would substitute for *aeons*?

    c. How does *aeons* tie in with *time* ("to reach the sun")?

2. The key to Benchley's satire in this essay is his examination of every analogy as though it were literally true; for instance, the comparison of our carbon content to 9,000 lead pencils. How does Benchley lampoon this analogy? What other analogies does he lampoon?

3. Written during the Depression years, this essay mentions prices that today seem unbelievable. Some words and phrases allude to Depression days. The importance of iodine (or the iodide ion) to the function of the thyroid gland, for instance, was medical news in the 1930s. What was a blueplate dinner or blueplate special? What was the Cardiff Giant?

4. In paragraph 5, is Benchley's parenthetic remark about the

phrase "average 150-pound body" sarcastic? What does he mean by the remark? In paragraph 9, how "average" is the "body" in Benchley's allusion to Robert Burns's poem "Coming through the Rye"?

5. Humorous satirists rarely get too far from reality, but Benchley didn't always keep a tight rein on his flights of whimsy. In paragraphs 2, 3, and 10 he digresses into puns and nonsense that some people find too farfetched to be funny and others find hilarious. What is your reaction? Defend it. Do these flights of whimsy depend on Benchley's turning metaphors and analogies into literal images?

6. Is there any deadpan humor in this essay (as in Twain's "Early Years in Florida, Missouri")? How would you characterize the **tone** of the essay?

Janet Flanner

Born in Indianapolis, Indiana, Janet Flanner (1892–1978) attended the University of Chicago from 1912 to 1913, then had a brief career as a movie critic. In 1921 she went to Europe, where she remained for the rest of her life. She was soon drawn to the Left Bank in Paris and the American literary company of such people as Ernest Hemingway, Archibald MacLeish, and Gertrude Stein. Though she tried her hand at fiction, going so far as to write a novel, she was convinced by others and herself that nonfiction was her métier. The editorial staff of *The New Yorker* liked her work and hired her in 1925 to write of France and the Parisian scene. Adopting the pseudonym Genêt, she sent an essay biweekly under the title "Letter from Paris," and for more than 50 years these essays were a feature of the magazine.

Janet Flanner's acute observations in her "letters" recorded the tragic events leading to World War II, events that she found more terrifying than fiction. Among the collections of her essays published as books are *An American in Paris* and *Men and Monuments*. For the style and substance of her reporting she was decorated with the French Legion of Honor in 1947 and received an honorary degree of Doctor of Literature from Smith College in 1958.

The "Letter from Paris" we include here is Janet Flanner's impression of the outbreak of World War II. Its brevity is intended as a terrifying irony.

WAR IN OUR TIME
(DECLARED ON SEPTEMBER 3)

Janet Flanner

1939

The special nature of this war demanded as a primary condition a victim state. Last September, the sacrifice state was to have been Czechoslovakia. This September, the martyr was Poland. The ultimate result would have been the same no matter what the date or the name of the country. Instead of for the theoretical liberty and salvation of Czechoslovakia in 1938, the Allies have gone to war in 1939 for a Poland already in ruins, and so distant that France and England could not fire a shot in Warsaw's defense. The cannons now occasionally rumbling on the Western Front are too far off for the Poles ever to hear the avenging sound. It is these geographic elements, as well as the time now being taken by diplomats traveling like drummers back and forth between Moscow and Berlin to haggle over last-minute concessions, threats, and dickerings, which make this seem an unnatural war. As a matter of fact, it is really a commonplace war, since it is simply a fight for liberty. It is only because of its potential size that it may, alas, prove to be civilization's ruin.

Study Guide and Questions:

1. The title of this essay is an ironic allusion to a statement made in 1938 by England's prime minister Neville Chamberlain, who, after negotiating with Adolf Hitler to temper the latter's warlike threats, assured the anxious British that there would be "peace in our time." The essay itself is full of allusions to countries and circumstances that were frighteningly meaningful in September 1939. A history of the prelude to World War II, with maps of Europe, will give greater depth to your understanding of "War in Our Time."

Instead of using specific, concrete incidents to illustrate the year-long deterioration of negotiations and the seemingly inevitable outbreak of war, Janet Flanner has given us words and phrases like "victim state," "liberty," "Czechoslovakia," "Poland," "Warsaw," "Western Front," and "geographical elements." Each of these evoked powerful images in September 1939; each of them now should evoke images not only of 1939 but also of 1989. Discuss these allusions so that you can see how they enrich the significance of this essay.

2. In a simile, Janet Flanner uses the word *drummer*. Look it up in a good dictionary and see how the colloquial American sense of the word is nicely developed by the rest of the simile.

3. In the last several lines of the essay, Janet Flanner uses sharp contrast for effect. The literary term for such contrast is **antithesis**. What does Janet Flanner see as antithetical in the appearance and the reality of this war?

4. In the next-to-last sentence Janet Flanner has used **understatement**. She refers to the war as "commonplace" and "*simply* a fight for liberty," as though it lacked great significance. By understating in this manner, she prepares the way for the shocking prediction in the final sentence. Imagine the effect of those last two sentences on a reader in September 1939! And do you see the irony in the juxtaposition of "simply" and "a fight for liberty"?

A. M. Rosenthal

Nine years after Abraham Michael Rosenthal (born in 1922) emigrated with his parents and five older sisters from Canada to the United States in 1926, his father, a Russian-born farmer become house painter, died after a fall from a scaffold. In the next several years four of the boy's sisters died in young womanhood.

With the personal courage he discovered in enduring these family tragedies, Rosenthal was determined to enroll for higher education at City College of New York. There he helped to pay for his tuition by working as college correspondent for the *New York Times,* and in 1944 he became a full-fledged reporter for the paper while continuing his education at night. He earned his B.S. degree in social science in 1948.

From 1946 until 1954, A. M. Rosenthal covered the UN for the *Times* and became a traveling reporter from India, Switzerland, Japan, and Poland. In 1959 the government of Poland, angered by his reports, expelled him, but elsewhere he received many awards, including a Pulitzer Prize in 1960.

In 1963 Rosenthal became an editor of the *New York Times* and after waging some important battles for freedom of the press was appointed executive editor, a post he held until 1986. Since stepping down, he has been writing a column for the op-ed page. This column, "On My Mind," often personal in style and humanitarian in outlook, examines the more troubling social problems of our time.

"No News from Auschwitz" was written in 1958, when Rosenthal was reporting from Poland and had just visited Auschwitz, the Nazi concentration camp. It shows his style and outlook in reaction to one of the most horrifying episodes in human history.

NO NEWS FROM AUSCHWITZ

A. M. Rosenthal

August 31, 1958

1   The most terrible thing of all, somehow, was that at Brzezinka the sun was bright and warm, the rows of graceful poplars were lovely to look upon and on the grass near the gates children played.

2   It all seemed frighteningly wrong, as in a nightmare, that at Brzezinka the sun should ever shine or that there

should be light and greenness and the sound of young laughter. It would be fitting if at Brzezinka the sun never shone and the grass withered because this is a place of unutterable terror.

3   And yet, every day, from all over the world, people come to Brzezinka, quite possibly the most grisly tourist center on earth. They come for a variety of reasons—to see if it could really have been true, to remind themselves not to forget, to pay homage to the dead by the simple act of looking upon their place of suffering.

4   Brzezinka is a couple of miles from the better-known southern Polish town of Oswiecim. Oswiecim has about 12,000 inhabitants, is situated about 171 miles from Warsaw and lies in a damp, marshy area at the eastern end of the pass called the Moravian Gate. Brzezinka and Oswiecim together formed part of that minutely organized factory of torture and death that the Nazis called Konzentrationslager Auschwitz.

5   By now, fourteen years after the last batch of prisoners was herded naked into the gas chambers by dogs and guards, the story of Auschwitz has been told a great many times. Some of the inmates have written of those events of which sane men cannot conceive. Rudolf Franz Ferdinand Hoess, the superintendent of the camp, before he was executed wrote his detailed memoirs of mass exterminations and the experiments on living bodies. Four million people died here, the Poles say.*

6   And so there is no news to report about Auschwitz. There is merely the compulsion to write something about it, a compulsion that grows out of a restless feeling that to have visited Auschwitz and then turned away without having said or written anything would be a most grievous act of discourtesy to those who died here.

7   Brzezinka and Oswiecim are very quiet places now; the screams can no longer be heard. The tourist walks silently, quickly at first to get it over with and then, as his mind peoples the barracks and the chambers and the dungeons

*Editors' note: The figure has now been set at 1.2 million prisoners, more than a million of them Jews.

and flogging posts, he walks draggingly. The guide does not say much either, because there is nothing much for him to say after he has pointed.

8   For every visitor, there is one particular bit of horror that he knows he will never forget. For some it is seeing the rebuilt gas chamber at Oswiecim and being told that this is the "small one." For others it is the fact that at Brzezinka, in the ruins of the gas chambers and the crematoria the Germans blew up when they retreated, there are daisies growing.

9   There are visitors who gaze blankly at the gas chambers and the furnaces because their minds simply cannot encompass them, but stand shivering before the great mounds of human hair behind the plate glass window or the piles of babies' shoes or the brick cells where men sentenced to death by suffocation were walled up.

10   One visitor opened his mouth in a silent scream simply at the sight of boxes—great stretches of three-tiered wooden boxes in the women's barracks. They were about six feet wide, about three feet high, and into them from five to ten prisoners were shoved for the night. The guide walks quickly through the barracks. Nothing more to see here.

11   A brick building where sterilization experiments were carried out on women prisoners. The guide tries the door—it's locked. The visitor is grateful that he does not have to go in, and then flushes with shame.

12   A long corridor where rows of faces stare from the walls. Thousands of pictures, the photographs of prisoners. They are all dead now, the men and women who stood before the cameras, and they all knew they were to die.

13   They all stare blank-faced, but one picture, in the middle of a row, seizes the eye and wrenches the mind. A girl, 22 years old, plumply pretty, blonde. She is smiling gently, as at a sweet, treasured thought. What was the thought that passed through her young mind and is now her memorial on the wall of the dead at Auschwitz?

14   Into the suffocation dungeons the visitor is taken for a moment and feels himself strangling. Another visitor goes in, stumbles out and crosses herself. There is no place to pray at Auschwitz.

15   The visitors look pleadingly at each other and say to the guide, "Enough."

16   There is nothing new to report about Auschwitz. It was a sunny day and the trees were green and at the gates the children played.

Study Guide:

1. The meanings of the following words are essential to your understanding of this essay. Add them to your list: *grisly, homage, compulsion, crematorium, to encompass, sterilization* (as applied to the reproductive system).

2. What A. M. Rosenthal is attempting to say to us here is virtually impossible to put into words. The significance of Auschwitz is so horrifying that some people cannot bring themselves to believe that such crimes ever occurred. It is a psychological reaction called *denial.* But the Holocaust (look up the word in an encyclopedia) did happen, and to try to comprehend it we have to read between the lines of Rosenthal's extraordinarily restrained essay. What is our response to the murder of the girl whose photographed face is "smiling gently, as at a sweet, treasured thought"? How can we conceive of this happening to tens, to hundreds, to thousands, to millions?

Questions:

1. Point out examples of **antithesis** in this essay (see Glossary of Literary Terms). How does Rosenthal use this device in organizing the essay and in developing its theme?

2. Why did Rosenthal choose the title "No News from Auschwitz"? How does it reflect the essay's tone? Is there a contrast between the essay's **tone** and what seems to be the author's attitude toward his subject? Discuss. Would outrage have been a more effective tone?

3. Explain the use of restraint in this essay.

4. Repetition of a phrase, a sentence, a paragraph is called **refrain**. What effect does the use of refrain have on this essay?

Composition Topic:

Consider and discuss the total impact of this essay on you as a human being. Write an essay exploring your response.

Jorge Luis Borges

Jorge Luis Borges* (1899–1986) was born in Buenos Aires, Argentina, where he spent his childhood. As a youth he attended day school at the College of Geneva, Switzerland, and then lived for a few years in Spain. After returning to Buenos Aires in 1921, he completed his higher education, and in the 1930s he was appointed professor of English literature at the University of Buenos Aires. In the 1940s he established a reputation as one of South America's most interesting writers, but after incurring the displeasure of Argentina's dictatorial president, Juan Perón, he was demoted, briefly, to "chicken inspector."

In the United States, translations of Borges's poems and short stories began appearing in literary magazines. Two books published in the 1960s bore such unusual titles as *Dreamtigers* and *Imaginary Zoo*. Jorge Luis Borges was now being acclaimed as the greatest contemporary Latino writer. In recognition of his achievements, Harvard University appointed him Elliot Norton Professor of Poetry for the year 1967–1968.

Borges's prose and poetry describe worlds and a mythology of his own creating. Imagine, for instance, the narrator of a story who wonders if he is being dreamt by another character. Some of this almost surrealistic quality may be attributable to the onset of hereditary blindness. In his most creative years he lived a nearly reclusive life, likening himself to "the Minotaur who chooses to stay in the labyrinth where he has been imprisoned."

The essay "Ragnarök" is a **parable**, a story that teaches a moral or religious lesson. The title, from Norse mythology, refers to the destruction of the world in the final battle between the gods and the forces of evil. Translated from Spanish by James E. Irby, "Ragnarök" is from Borges's book entitled *Labyrinths*.

RAGNARÖK

Jorge Luis Borges

1962

1   In our dreams (writes Coleridge) images represent the sensations we think they cause; we do not feel horror because we are threatened by a sphinx; we dream of a sphinx

*Pronounced Hor-heh Loo-ees Bor-hes.

in order to explain the horror we feel. If this is so, how could a mere chronicle of its forms transmit the stupor, the exaltation, the alarm, the menace and the jubilance which made up the fabric of that dream that night? I shall attempt such a chronicle, however; perhaps the fact that the dream was composed of one single scene may remove or mitigate this essential difficulty.

2   The place was the School of Philosophy and Letters; the time, toward sundown. Everything (as usually happens in dreams) was somewhat different; a slight magnification altered things. We were electing officials: I was talking with Pedro Henríquez Ureña, who in the world of waking reality died many years ago. Suddenly we were stunned by the clamor of a demonstration or disturbance. Human and animal cries came from the Bajo.* A voice shouted "Here they come!" and then "The Gods! The Gods!" Four or five individuals emerged from the mob and occupied the platform of the main lecture hall. We all applauded, tearfully; these were the Gods returning after a centuries-long exile. Made larger by the platform, their heads thrown back and their chests thrust forward, they arrogantly received our homage. One held a branch which no doubt conformed to the simple botany of dreams; another, in a broad gesture, extended his hand which was a claw; one of the faces of Janus looked with distrust at the curved beak of Thoth. Perhaps aroused by our applause, one of them—I no longer know which—erupted in a victorious clatter, unbelievably harsh, with something of a gargle and of a whistle. From that moment, things changed.

3   It all began with the suspicion (perhaps exaggerated) that the Gods did not know how to talk. Centuries of fell and fugitive life had atrophied the human element in them; the moon of Islam and the cross of Rome had been implacable with these outlaws. Very low foreheads, yellow teeth, stringy mulatto or Chinese mustaches and thick bestial lips showed the degeneracy of the Olympian lineage. Their clothing corresponded not to a decorous poverty but rather to the sinister luxury of the gambling houses and brothels

*As used here, the Bajo is probably a disreputable part of the city.

of the Bajo. A carnation bled crimson in a lapel and the bulge of a knife was outlined beneath a close-fitting jacket. Suddenly we sensed that they were playing their last card, that they were cunning, ignorant and cruel like old beasts of prey and that, if we let ourselves be overcome by fear or pity, they would finally destroy us.

4   We took out our heavy revolvers (all of a sudden there were revolvers in the dream) and joyfully killed the Gods.

Study Guide:

1. Be sure to know the meanings, in context, of the following words. See what power they give to this extraordinary parable as you read it again: *chronicle, stupor, exaltation, menace, jubilance, to mitigate, clamor, fell* (adjective), *to atrophy, implacable, mulatto, bestial, degeneracy, lineage, decorous, brothel.*

2. Allusions, too, are vital to the strength of this work. Borges's reference to Coleridge, for instance, gets us immediately into a nightmare landscape of indescribable horror. The other allusions give specific intensity to that sensation. To find out about a *sphinx*, read the myth of Oedipus and the accompanying text in *The Greek Myths,* by Robert Graves. See why *Janus,* in Roman mythology, would have more than one face and *Thoth,* in Egyptian mythology, a curved beak. Recognize the religions alluded to in *moon of Islam* and *cross of Rome.* Name the 12 *Olympians.*

Questions:

1. The narrative is full of bizarrely ironic and antithetical events and images. How many adjectives are used in antithetical juxtaposition? Give examples. In what way does the place of the dream become ironic? What other ironies can you discover?

2. Look at the specific descriptions of the Gods in the last third of paragraph 2. Imagine the weird sounds the Gods make. What do these images suggest to you? Do they play upon your subjective reactions? Discuss.

3. See how different the Gods are in paragraph 3. Why does Borges change the appearance of the Gods? What symbolic meaning might you give to a carnation that bled crimson in a lapel? What do these changes in appearance and in descriptive images suggest to you? Is Borges's shortcut evocation of stereotyped cavemen an insensitive attempt at suggesting degeneracy?

4. Who are "we" that "we" should joyfully kill the Gods? Are "we" as dangerous as the Gods? Is Borges giving us some dreadful warning through this parable? In this essay do you see parallels with the history of humankind? Is MacLeish making a similar statement in his essay about the planet Earth? Discuss.

5. Does this essay fit in with "No News from Auschwitz"? Does it fit in with the next essay, "The Assassination"?

Composition Topic:

Write a composition that teaches a lesson through a dream, and try to capture a dreamlike quality to enhance the mood of the essay.

John Updike

John Updike (born in 1932), one of America's most prolific writers, was born and raised in Shillington, Pennsylvania. After receiving his B.A. degree from Harvard University in 1954, he considered a career as an artist, but his keen sense for detail was more strongly drawn toward written expression. In the early 1950s he began working for *The New Yorker,* and there he established his reputation as an outstanding writer. Encouraged by Katherine S. White, he contributed many short stories and essays and continued to do so through the 1960s and 1970s. Recently his work for the magazine has been distinguished by detailed and penetrating literary criticism.

The artist in Updike is obvious in his crafting of verbal images into beautifully constructed sentences, a characteristic not only of his short prose but also of his witty verse and his many novels. His poetry displays a humorously skeptical view of materialistic culture, and his novels show this same skeptical mind in search of some religious meaning in mundane occurrences. The settings for his fiction are often the towns and suburbs of the Middle Atlantic states and New England. Among his best-known novels are *Rabbit, Run; The Centaur; Roger's Version*; and *Rabbit Is Rich*.

John Updike wrote "The Assassination" in an attempt to capture the catastrophic events that began in the late morning on Friday, the 22nd day of November 1963.

THE ASSASSINATION
John Updike

November 1963

1   It was as if we slept from Friday to Monday and dreamed an oppressive, unsearchably significant dream, which, we discovered on awaking, millions of others had dreamed also. Furniture, family, the streets, and the sky dissolved; only the dream on television was real. The faces of the world's great mingled with the faces of landladies who had happened to house an unhappy ex-Marine; cathedrals alternated with warehouses, temples of government with suburban garages; anonymous men tugged at a casket

in a glaring airport; a murder was committed before our eyes; a Dallas strip-tease artist drawled amiably of her employer's quick temper; the heads of state of the Western world strode down a sunlit street like a grim village rabble; and Jacqueline Kennedy became Persephone, the Queen of Hades and the beautiful bride of grief. All human possibilities, of magnificence and courage, of meanness and confusion, seemed to find an image in this long montage, and a stack of cardboard boxes in Dallas, a tawdry movie house, a tiny rented room where some shaving cream still clung to the underside of a washbasin, a row of parking meters that had witnessed a panicked flight all acquired the opaque and dreadful importance that innocent objects acquire in nightmares.

2   What did it mean? Can we hope for a meaning? "It's the fashion to hate people in the United States." This quotation might be from one of a hundred admonitory sermons delivered after President Kennedy's death. In actuality, it occurs in an interview granted in 1959 to a United Press reporter, Aline Mosby, by a young American defector then living in Moscow, Lee Harvey Oswald. The presumed assassin did not seem to be a violent man. "He was too quiet, too reserved," his ex-landlord told reporters. "He certainly had the intelligence and he looked like he could be efficient at doing almost anything." In his room, the police found a map on which was marked the precise path that three bullets in fact took. The mind that might have unlocked this puzzle of perfectly aimed, perfectly aimless murder has been itself forever sealed by murder. The second assassination augmented the first, expanded our sense of potential violence. In these cruel events, democracy seemed caricatured; a gun voted, and a drab Dallas neighborhood was hoisted into history. None of our country's four slain presidents were victims of any distinct idea of opposition or hope of gain; they were sacrificed, rather, to the blind tides of criminality and insanity that make civilization precarious. Between Friday and Monday, three men died: a president, a policeman, and a prisoner. May their deaths be symbols, clues to our deep unease, and omens we heed.

Study Guide:

1. Before rereading this essay, be sure to know the following words and their meanings, in context, and add them to your vocabulary list: *amiably, montage, tawdry, opaque, admonitory, to augment, to caricature, precarious, omen.*

2. Like "War in Our Time," "The Assassination" relies on the *reader's* supplying the specific concrete details to make the abstract ideas and images meaningful. Allusion is indeed a powerful shortcut, but it takes an exceptionally gifted essayist to compress, with this device, the significance of a profound event into less than 500 words. Read an account of the assassination in an encyclopedia or from microfilms of newspapers. See especially a videotape documentary or the *Life* magazine pictorial coverage of those horribly memorable four days.

Questions:

1. How many of the allusions in paragraph 1 are identifiable in news accounts and photographs? Compare the recorded details with Updike's verbal images. What elements are similar? Which of Updike's images seem most effective in evoking the mood in Dallas that weekend?

2. Does Updike's essay express ideas that cannot be found in the detailed news coverage of the assassination? Explain.

3. What is *montage,* and how does Updike suggest this motion picture technique in describing the images in the first paragraph?

4. How is the Greek myth of Persephone effective in our understanding of the role Jacqueline Kennedy played? What is ironic about the phrase "the beautiful bride of grief"?

5. Updike begins his second paragraph with two rhetorical questions. Is Lee Harvey Oswald's quotation an adequate answer? Explain.

6. Concentrate on the sentence "The mind that might have unlocked this puzzle of perfectly aimed, perfectly aimless murder has been itself forever sealed by murder." In context, which phrase is used more *denotatively,* which more *connotatively:* "perfectly aimed," "perfectly aimless"?

7. What contradictions about the assassination does "perfectly aimed, perfectly aimless" intensify? Do recent investigations into possible motives for the assassination make "perfectly aimless" seem less accurate?

8. The writer appears to sense that civilization is on the brink of insanity. What are his reasons for this contention?

9. Updike says the deaths of that November weekend in 1963 are ominous symbols. What other events of the sixties prove that Updike was right? Have "the blind tides of criminality and insanity" ebbed in the past several years?

Washington Irving

Washington Irving (1783–1859), born to a prosperous family in New York City, was a sickly child and such an introspective, romantic youth that two older brothers, concerned for his future, urged upon him the practical career of lawyer. The young man soon tired of law, however, and decided instead to travel.

During his first trip abroad (1804–1806), Washington Irving kept extensive journals, which renewed a childhood love of writing and served as the bases for many of his later works. Upon returning to the United States he set to work on a book that was to be one of the first great pieces of American comic literature, *A History of New York by Diedrich Knickerbocker,* published in 1809. The death of his fiancée that same year, however, so depressed him that after six years of listless dabbling, he sailed for England and did not return for 17 years.

In 1819–1820, still in England, Irving published a collection entitled *The Sketch Book,* which includes "Rip Van Winkle," "The Legend of Sleepy Hollow," and the essay "The Voyage." Cheered by the reception of these stories and essays, Irving traveled extensively in Europe and continued with his writing. Among his published books were *Bracebridge Hall, Tales of a Traveller,* and *Life and Voyages of Christopher Columbus.* In 1828 his interest in Spain prompted a trip to Granada, and his success there as an interpreter of Spanish culture and history led to his later appointment as ambassador to Spain.

In 1846 Washington Irving retired to Tarrytown, on the Hudson River, where earlier he had purchased 10 acres and designed a charming Dutch cottage. There, at "Sunnyside," he lived with his nieces until his death.

"The Voyage," a romantic reflection on crossing the Atlantic, probably combines observations made on several crossings. Since Irving was in precarious health at the time of his first crossing, he may have been thinking of himself when he described the sick sailor at the end of the essay.

THE VOYAGE

Washington Irving

1820

> Ships, ships, I will descrie you
> Amidst the main,
> I will come and try you,

What you are protecting,
And projecting,
　　What's your end and aim.
One goes abroad for merchandise and trading,
Another stays to keep his country from invading,
A third is coming home with rich and wealthy lading.
Halloo! my fancy, whither wilt thou go?*

OLD POEM

1   To an American visiting Europe, the long voyage he has
to make is an excellent preparative. The temporary absence
of worldly scenes and employments produces a state of
mind peculiarly fitted to receive new and vivid impressions.
The vast space of waters that separates the hemispheres is
like a blank page in existence. There is no gradual transition, by which, as in Europe, the features and population of
one country blend almost imperceptibly with those of another. From the moment you lose sight of the land you have
left, all is vacancy until you step on the opposite shore, and
are launched at once into the bustle and novelties of another world.

2   In travelling by land there is a continuity of scene and
a connected succession of persons and incidents, that carry
on the story of life, and lessen the effect of absence and
separation. We drag, it is true, "a lengthening chain" at
each remove of our pilgrimage; but the chain is unbroken:
we can trace it back link by link; and we feel that the last
still grapples us to home. But a wide sea-voyage severs us
at once. It makes us conscious of being cast loose from the
secure anchorage of settled life, and sent adrift upon a
doubtful world. It interposes a gulf, not merely imaginary,
but real, between us and our homes,—a gulf subject to
tempest, and fear, and uncertainty, rendering distance palpable, and return precarious.

3   Such, at least, was the case with myself. As I saw the
last blue line of my native land fade away like a cloud in
the horizon, it seemed as if I had closed one volume of the
world and its concerns, and had time for meditation, before

---

*Where will *you* go?

I opened another. That land, too, now vanishing from my view, which contained all most dear to me in life; what vicissitudes might occur in it, what changes might take place in me, before I should visit it again! Who can tell, when he sets forth to wander, whither he may be driven by the uncertain currents of existence; or when he may return; or whether it may ever be his lot to revisit the scenes of his childhood?

4   I said that at sea all is vacancy; I should correct the impression. To one given to day-dreaming, and fond of losing himself in reveries, a sea-voyage is full of subjects for meditation; but then they are the wonders of the deep, and of the air, and rather tend to abstract the mind from worldly themes. I delighted to loll over the quarter-railing, or climb to the main-top, of a calm day, and muse for hours together on the tranquil bosom of a summer's sea; to gaze upon the piles of golden clouds just peering above the horizon, fancy them some fairy realms, and people them with a creation of my own;—to watch the gentle undulating billows, rolling their silver volumes, as if to die away on those happy shores.

5   There was a delicious sensation of mingled security and awe with which I looked down, from my giddy height, on the monsters of the deep at their uncouth gambols. Shoals of porpoises tumbling about the bow of the ship; the grampus slowly heaving his huge form above the surface; or the ravenous shark, darting, like a spectre, through the blue waters. My imagination would conjure up all that I had heard or read of the watery world beneath me; of the finny herds that roam its fathomless valleys; of the earth; and of those wild phantasms that swell the tales of fishermen and sailors.

6   Sometimes a distant sail, gliding along the edge of the ocean, would be another theme of idle speculation. How interesting this fragment of a world, hastening to rejoin the great mass of existence! What a glorious monument of human invention; which has in a manner triumphed over wind and wave; has brought the ends of the world into communion; has established an interchange of blessings, pouring into the sterile regions of the north all the luxuries

of the south; has diffused the light of knowledge and the charities of cultivated life; and has thus bound together those scattered portions of the human race, between which nature seemed to have thrown an insurmountable barrier.

7   We one day descried some shapeless object drifting at a distance. At sea, every thing that breaks the monotony of the surrounding expanse attracts attention. It proved to be the mast of a ship that must have been completely wrecked; for there were the remains of handkerchiefs, by which some of the crew had fastened themselves to this spar, to prevent their being washed off by the waves. There was no trace by which the name of the ship could be ascertained. The wreck had evidently drifted about for many months; clusters of shell-fish had fastened about it, and long sea-weeds flaunted at its sides. But where, thought I, is the crew? Their struggle has long been over,—they have gone down amidst the roar of the tempest,—their bones lie whitening among the caverns of the deep. Silence, oblivion, like the waves, have closed over them, and no one can tell the story of their end. What sighs have been wafted after that ship! What prayers offered up at the deserted fireside of home! How often has the mistress, the wife, the mother, pored over the daily news, to catch some casual intelligence of this rover of the deep! How has expectation darkened into anxiety—anxiety into dread—and dread into despair! Alas! Not one memento may ever return for love to cherish. All that may ever be known, is, that she sailed from her port, "and was never heard of more!"

8   The sight of this wreck, as usual, gave rise to many dismal anecdotes. This was particularly the case in the evening, when the weather, which had hitherto been fair, began to look wild and threatening, and gave indications of one of those sudden storms which will sometimes break in upon the serenity of a summer voyage. As we sat round the dull light of a lamp in the cabin, that made the gloom more ghastly, every one had his tale of shipwreck and disaster. I was particularly struck with a short one related by the captain.

9   "As I was once sailing," said he, "in a fine stout ship across the banks of Newfoundland, one of those heavy fogs

which prevail in those parts rendered it impossible for us
to see far ahead even in the daytime; but at night the
weather was so thick that we could not distinguish any
object at twice the length of the ship. I kept lights at the
mast-head, and a constant watch forward to look out for
fishing-smacks, which are accustomed to anchor on the
banks. The wind was blowing a smacking breeze, and we
were going at a great rate through the water. Suddenly the
watch gave the alarm of 'a sail ahead!'—it was scarcely
uttered before we were upon her. She was a small schooner,
at anchor, with her broadside towards us. The crew were all
asleep, and had neglected to hoist a light. We struck her
just amidships. The force, the size, and weight of our vessel
bore her down below the waves; we passed over her, and
were hurried on our course. As the crashing wreck was
sinking beneath us, I had a glimpse of two or three half-
naked wretches rushing from her cabin; they just started
from their beds to be swallowed shrieking by the waves. I
heard their drowning cry mingling with the wind. The
blast that bore it to our ears swept us out of all further
hearing. I shall never forget that cry! It was some time
before we could put the ship about, she was under such
headway. We returned, as nearly as we could guess, to the
place where the smack had anchored. We cruised about for
several hours in the dense fog. We fired signal-guns, and
listened if we might hear the halloo of any survivors: but
all was silent—we never saw or heard any thing of them
more."

10   I confess these stories, for a time, put an end to all my
fine fancies. The storm increased with the night. The sea
was lashed into tremendous confusion. There was a fearful,
sullen sound of rushing waves, and broken surges. Deep
called unto deep. At times the black volume of clouds over-
head seemed rent asunder by flashes of lightning which
quivered along the foaming billows, and made the succeed-
ing darkness doubly terrible. The thunders bellowed over
the wild waste of waters, and were echoed and prolonged
by the mountain waves. As I saw the ship staggering and
plunging among these roaring caverns, it seemed miracu-
lous that she regained her balance, or preserved her buoy-

ancy. Her yards would dip into the water: her bow was almost buried beneath the waves. Sometimes an impending surge appeared ready to overwhelm her, and nothing but a dexterous movement of the helm preserved her from the shock.

11   When I retired to my cabin, the awful scene still followed me. The whistling of the wind through the rigging sounded like funereal wailings. The creaking of the masts, the straining and groaning of bulkheads, as the ship labored in the weltering sea, were frightful. As I heard the waves rushing along the sides of the ship, and roaring in my very ear, it seemed as if Death were raging around this floating prison, seeking for his prey: the mere starting of a nail, the yawning of a seam, might give him entrance.

12   A fine day, however, with a tranquil sea and favoring breeze, soon put all these dismal reflections to flight. It is impossible to resist the gladdening influence of fine weather and fair wind at sea. When the ship is decked out in all her canvas, every sail swelled, and careering gaily over the curling waves, how lofty, how gallant she appears—how she seems to lord it over the deep!

13   I might fill a volume with the reveries of a sea-voyage, for with me it is almost a continual revery,—but it is time to get to shore.

14   It was a fine sunny morning when the thrilling cry of "land!" was given from the masthead. None but those who have experienced it can form an idea of the delicious throng of sensations which rush into an American's bosom, when he first comes in sight of Europe. There is a volume of associations with the very name. It is the land of promise, teeming with every thing of which his childhood has heard, or on which his studious years have pondered.

15   From that time until the moment of arrival, it was all feverish excitement. The ships-of-war that prowled like guardian giants along the coast; the headlands of Ireland, stretching out into the channel; the Welsh mountains, towering into the clouds;—all were objects of intense interest. As we sailed up the Mersey, I reconnoitred the shores with a telescope. My eye dwelt with delight on neat cottages, with their trim shrubberies and green grass-plots. I saw

the mouldering ruin of an abbey overrun with ivy, and the taper spire of a village church rising from the brow of a neighboring hill;—all were characteristic of England.

16   The tide and wind were so favorable that the ship was enabled to come at once to her pier. It was thronged with people: some idle lookers-on; others, eager expectants of friends or relatives. I could distinguish the merchant to whom the ship was consigned. I knew him by his calculating brow and restless air. His hands were thrust into his pockets; he was whistling thoughtfully, and walking to and fro, a small space having been accorded him by the crowd, in deference to his temporary importance. There were repeated cheerings and salutations interchanged between the shore and the ship, as friends happened to recognize each other. I particularly noticed one young woman of humble dress, but interesting demeanor. She was leaning forward from among the crowd; her eye hurried over the ship as it neared the shore, to catch some wished-for countenance. She seemed disappointed and sad; when I heard a faint voice call her name. It was from a poor sailor who had been ill all the voyage, and had excited the sympathy of every one on board. When the weather was fine his messmates had spread a mattress on deck in the shade; but of late his illness had so increased, that he had taken to his hammock, and only breathed a wish that he might see his wife before he died. He had been helped on deck as we came up the river, and was now leaning against the shrouds, with a countenance so wasted, so pale, so ghastly, that it was no wonder even the eye of affection did not recognize him. But at the sound of his voice, her eyes darted on his features: it read, at once, a whole volume of sorrow; she clasped her hands, uttered a faint shriek, and stood wringing them in silent agony.

17   All now was hurry and bustle. The meetings of acquaintances—the greeting of friends—the consultations of men of business. I alone was solitary and idle. I had no friend to meet, no cheering to receive. I stepped upon the land of my forefathers— but felt that I was a stranger in the land.

Study Guide:

Irving's rich vocabulary and variety of sentence structure are typical of the influence English authors had on American writers of that time. See how distinctly different Twain's style is in "Early Years in Florida, Missouri." In rereading "The Voyage" you will find your enjoyment enhanced by your understanding of the following words as they are used in context: *to descry, lading, to grapple, palpable, precarious, vicissitudes, reveries, undulating, gambols, communion, to flaunt, oblivion, intelligence, memento, anecdotes, smack* (as in *fishing-smack*), *wretches, bulkheads, weltering, to consign, deference, demeanor.*

Questions:

1. From his travel journals Irving selected the specific incidents for this essay. Atlantic crossings under sail took as long as six weeks, so he had much to choose from. What do the incidents and his reflections upon them tell you about Irving's personality? Be specific.

2. Which of the following sentences comes closest to setting the **theme** for this essay?

   a. "To an American visiting Europe, the long voyage he has to make is an excellent preparative."

   b. "As I saw the last blue line of my native land fade away like a cloud in the horizon, it seemed as if I had closed one volume of the world and its concerns, and had time for meditation, before I opened another."

   c. "The vast space of waters that separates the hemispheres is like a blank page in existence."

   d. "The temporary absence of worldly scenes and employments produces a state of mind peculiarly fitted to receive new and vivid impressions."

3. Explain the last sentence of the essay. How does it tie in with the first three paragraphs of the essay?

4. Irving begins with several abstract statements and then illustrates them with vivid and concrete examples. Describe his process of going from abstract to concrete in this essay, and explain how the tone and the underlying theme of the essay are set by the first three paragraphs.

5. What purpose does the prefatory poem serve?

6. Notice the vivid use of figurative language in the storm scene (paragraphs 10–11). In describing the sea itself (paragraph 10), does

Irving use any images that one does not usually associate with water? What are the effects of the storm imagery?

7. Look at the verbs and participles in paragraph 7. They are remarkably vivid because they are explicit. In your compositions, how successfully can you avoid dull verbs like *to have, to go, to get, to do, to happen,* and the forms of *to be?*

8. Toward the end of paragraph 7, Irving uses a rhetorical device called gradatio, progressing in half-step gradations from "expectation" to "anxiety" to "dread" to "despair." Is this a form of parallel construction? Are there other examples of parallel construction in this essay?

9. Explain and describe on paper how the metaphor developed in the second sentence of paragraph 2 expresses a truth. A long and detailed metaphor of this kind is called an extended metaphor.

10. Could Irving—were he alive—write an essay of this reflective tone about a transatlantic crossing by jetliner? Explain.

E. M. Forster

Left fatherless in early childhood, Edward Morgan Forster (1879–1970), one of England's most respected writers of the twentieth century, was raised by his mother and an aunt, under whose tutelage he developed a love for music, literature, and astronomy. His later, formal, education was a study in contrasts: snobbishness and anti-intellectualism, which he despised, at Tonbridge School in Kent; intellectual freedom and social liberty, which he loved, at King's College, Cambridge.

After receiving degrees in classics and history from Cambridge University, the financially independent Forster traveled extensively in Europe and established his reputation as a novelist who explored subtle misunderstandings in human relationships. *Where Angles Fear to Tread, A Room with a View*, and *Howard's End* are early examples. During World War I he served with the Red Cross in Egypt, and in 1921 he went to India, where he served as personal secretary to the maharajah of Dewas. His experiences in India were the inspiration for his greatest and most famous novel, *A Passage to India*, published in 1924.

In the decades that followed, Forster wrote biographies and plays, and he published several volumes of his collected essays. He was awarded honorary degrees from many universities during his long life, and in 1953 Queen Elizabeth II named him a Companion of Honour.

"The United States" is an essay that shows what Forster discovered about the American scene when he visited in 1947. In reading it, one should realize that England was suffering economic privation after World War II and that the United States was becoming what would eventually be called a superpower.

THE UNITED STATES

E. M. Forster

1947

1   America is rather like life. You can usually find in it what you look for. If you look for skyscrapers or cowboys or cocktail parties or gangsters or business connections or political problems or women's clubs, they will certainly be there. You can be very hot there or very cold. You can explore the America of your choice by plane or train, by

hitch-hike or on foot. It will probably be interesting, and it is sure to be large.

2   I went there for the first time at the age of sixty-eight. By sixty-eight one is so to speak a pilgrim grandfather who knows very clearly what to look for when he disembarks. I had no doubt as to what I wanted to discover in America. It was to provide me with scenery and individuals. The scenery was to be of two sorts—gigantic and homely.* The individuals were not to be representative—I never could get on with representative individuals—but people who existed on their own account and with whom it might therefore be possible to be friends. That is the America I looked for and was to find. My visit was a complete success from my own point of view.

3   After a respectful glance at New York, I went a hundred miles north into the Berkshires. It was April. The trees were leafless—thousands and thousands of birch trees, their trunks whiter than the birch trees here,† milk white, ghost white in the sharp sunshine, covering the sides of the valley and the crests of the hills; and among the birches pushed pine and hemlock—which is like a not very dark green yew. Was I in England? Almost, but not quite. That was again and again to be my sensation, and in the Arizona Desert I was to feel I was almost but not quite in India, and in the Yosemite Valley that it was not quite Switzerland. America is always throwing out these old-world hints, and then withdrawing them in favour of America. To return to the Berkshires: after a few days' quiet the snow descended and silence became absolute. The country became primeval and polar—endless purity, underspreading motionless trees. I can never be grateful enough for those opening days of silence and snow. They imposed proportion. They made me realise that America is not all town: such a generalisation would be truer of England. It is country—controlled no doubt by mechanised gadgets, still it is country. I was glad I had not gaped too long at the New York skyscrapers. Exciting as they are, they mislead.

*Suited to home life; unpretentious. (British usage.)
†England.

They do not epitomise what lies behind them. Presently the snow melted. Where it had lain appeared dark brown earth and occasional pale lilac hepaticas, and the spring began—in double quick time compared to our spring.

4   The Berkshires are homely scenery. Gigantic scenery is more difficult to describe, but I will make an attempt. Suppose yourself walking on a Surrey common near Bagshot. There are a good many fir trees about, the soil is sandy, and the prospect rather dull. Suddenly the common stops, and you are standing without any warning on the brink of a precipice which is one mile deep. One mile into the tortured earth it goes, the other side of the chasm is miles away, and the chasm is filled with unbelievable deposits of rock which resemble sphinxes draped in crimson shawls. That, as far as I can get it into a single sentence, gives you my first impression of the Grand Canyon of the Colorado River, but the Grand Canyon would need many sentences to describe and many books. It is the most astounding natural object I have ever seen. It frightens. There are many colours in it besides crimson—strata of black and of white, and rocks of ochre and pale lilac. And the Colorado River itself is, when one gets down to it, still more sinister, for it is muddy white and very swift, and it rages like an infuriated maggot between precipices of granite, gnawing at them and cutting the Canyon deeper. It was strange after two days amongst these marvels, and terrors, to return to the surface of the earth, and go bowling away in a 'bus between little fir trees.

5   The second item I sought in America was the human, the individual. My work lay mainly in universities, and there and elsewhere I found the individuals I sought. I had expected generosity and hospitality. I had not expected so much tact, charm and sensitiveness; here was the delightful surprise. Wherever I went I found delicate understanding of our troubles in Britain over food and clothing, and a desire to help that was never patronising. This was not confined to the highly educated classes. I recall a cheap eating-house in Nevada where some strangers came up and asked what they could send. I remember the chambermaid in the hotel at Salt Lake City who when I offered her a tip

replied, "I don't like to take your money, brother, you need it more than I do." That is the sort of remark which comes from the heart and goes to the heart, and in the light of it and the warmth of it I found difficulty in examining the defects of the American character. The defects are, I suspect, lack of discrimination, emotionalism, and a tendency to narrow the idea of freedom into freedom to make money. "What else have we fought the war for?" a business acquaintance enquired. But I cannot feel these defects are basic. My friends reassure me against this, and not only my friends; the faces of strangers lighting up everywhere, compassionate, respectful, anxious to help. The individuals I met were mostly of Anglo-Saxon stock; I also knew some Swedish and some Italian farming people, made some Oriental contacts, and had one or two Mexican friends. I did not have the good fortune to get to know any Negroes. On the whole I saw as much of the human landscape as an elderly traveller may reasonably expect, and I liked it.

6   But now comes a qualification. Although the Americans I encountered were full of charitable feelings toward Great Britain, I cannot say that they showed much interest in us otherwise. I have often been asked since my return home: "What do they think about us over there?" Indeed, it is often the only thing English people want to know. The answer, not very flattering to our pride, is that the Americans scarcely think about us at all. They are curious about our Royal Family, they are grateful and appreciative towards Mr. Churchill, they are—or were—enthusiastic over British films. That is all. They do not discuss our Empire. India, over which they have been so critical in the past, is now scarcely in the news and seems to bore them. Even Palestine was seldom mentioned. An explanation of this indifference is that they concentrate, as we all do, on home affairs, and that when they do think of foreign affairs they think of Russia. China to some extent, but mostly Russia. Russia is always weighing on their minds. They are afraid of war, or that their standard of life may be lowered. I shall never forget a dinner party, supposedly given in my honour, at which one of the guests, a journalist, urged that

atomic bombs should be dropped upon the Soviet Union without notice, and quoted with approval a remark which he inaccurately ascribed to Oliver Cromwell:* "Stone dead hath no fellow." "That's good, isn't it, Tom?" he called to another journalist. "Stone dead hath no fellow." Tom agreed that it was very good, and they shouted: "Stone dead hath no fellow" in unison or antiphonically for the rest of the evening. They were cultivated men, but as soon as the idea of Russia occurred to them, their faces became blood red; they ceased to be human. No one seemed appalled by the display but myself, no one was surprised and our hostess congratulated herself afterwards on the success of her party. This obsession over Russia should be realised by all who would understand America, and it explains in part her lack of interest in us.

7   I did not encounter such hysteria elsewhere, and maybe did not frequent the circles where it is likeliest to occur. Most of the people I was with were not influential or highly placed: many of them were teachers, and some of them were young—students, or they practised music or painting or acting or the ballet, or they were doing small commercial jobs or working on the land. My general impression was of good temper and goodwill and hopefulness. I could darken the picture, no doubt. I do not take the Statue of Liberty in New York harbour as seriously as she takes herself. And I did encounter hints of oppression and of violence, and of snobbery. But the main verdict is favourable, and I do beg anyone who happens to have fallen into the habit of nagging at America to drop it. Nagging is so insidious. It often resides not in what is said but in the tone of the voice. It proceeds not from considered criticism but from envy and from discontent—and, of course, life out there is far more comfortable for the average man than it is here. The food is nicer, if dearer, the clothes are nicer and cheaper, the cold drinks are not lukewarm, and the

---

*Shortly before the outbreak of civil war in England, the Houses of Parliament impeached and sentenced to death the Earl of Strafford, first minister and chief supporter of Charles I. In agreement with the sentence, the Earl of Essex (son of Queen Elizabeth's favorite) said, "Stone dead hath no fellow."

railway carriages are not dirty. But these advantages over ourselves should not embitter us against the people who enjoy them. Nor should we charge it against all Americans that their politicians do what our politicians tell them, and tell us, they ought not to do.

8   I chanced to end my three months' visit in the same district of the Berkshires where it had begun. Now it was high summer. The little spring from which I fetched water every day had already begun to flag. The meadows were full of flowers—ox-eye daisies, black-eyed susans, orchids, and an under-carpet of creeping jenny; the meadows sloped down to a brook where the farm hands bathed. There were swallowtail butterflies and fritillaries, and the bobolink, a very agreeable bird, skipped from post to post carolling, and another bird, the phoebe, repeated "phoebe, phoebe, phoebe," whence its name. At night there were fireflies to remind us that this was the latitude of Madrid. Thunderstorms did not disconcert them, and I would watch their flash vanish in the superior brilliancy of lightning, and reappear. Some of them flew at the level of the grass, others across the curtain of birch trees. They were extraordinarily bright; it was a good year for fireflies and the memory of them sparking in the warm rain and the thunder is the latest of my American impressions, and the loveliest.

Study Guide:

Words not to be missed in rereading the essay: *to epitomize, patronizing, discrimination* (denotative and connotative senses), *antiphonally, insidious,* and *to flag.* In looking up these words and adding them to your list, you will have noticed that some British spellings are different from American spellings.

Questions:

1. Who were "Mr. Churchill" and Oliver Cromwell? On what latitudes are the Berkshires and Madrid?

2. The first sentence of this essay is an abstract idea in the form of **analogy**. How does Forster develop this analogy with concrete images?

3. Why did Forster go to America for the first time at the age of 68? In what ways were Forster's impressions formed by his age? How might his views have been different if he had been 28? How might his views have been different if he had written such an essay today?

4. One of the hallmarks of Forster's style is its use of vivid visual description. Find several examples of such description (often in metaphorical terms, but sometimes quite literal) and comment upon their effectiveness.

5. For what audience was this essay originally intended? How do you know?

6. Forster was selective in the sights he chose to see. What was the basis of this selectivity? Why did he pass by New York City in favor of the Berkshires, the Grand Canyon, and other "country" sights? Why did he consider his visit a "complete success"?

7. What impressions about Forster's personality can you form from reading this essay? For instance, is his viewpoint basically liberal or conservative? Is he subjective or objective? How are his feelings uniquely British? Discuss the changes of tone in the essay.

8. What can we as Americans learn about ourselves from this Englishman's portrait of our country? What are the inherent advantages and disadvantages of one's writing about a foreign country?

9. What is the effect of Forster's "ending where he began," in the Berkshires? What other devices does Forster use to organize this essay?

Composition Topic:

Try to do what Forster did in first describing the Grand Canyon; that is, try to describe something unfamiliar in terms of the familiar. Some examples: traveling by bus, train, or plane (assuming one or another is unfamiliar) in terms of traveling by automobile (assuming it is familiar); using a word processor in terms of using a typewriter (or vice versa); telling time by an analog watch in terms of telling time by a digital watch.

William Least Heat Moon

Born in Kansas City, Missouri, in 1939, William Least Heat Moon is the son of Heat Moon, a Sioux Native American. The name Heat Moon is derived from the Moon of Heat, the seventh month. Since he is the last born child of his parents, he is called Least Heat Moon. His Christian name, William Trogdon, comes from a grandfather eight generations back, described by Least Heat Moon as "an immigrant Lancashireman living in North Carolina, who was killed by the Tories for providing food to rebel patriots."

Least Heat Moon attended the University of Missouri and received A.B., M.A., and Ph.D. degrees from Columbia University. From 1965 until 1978 he taught English at Stephens College, Columbia, Missouri. He is now a lecturer at the University of Missouri School of Journalism.

In 1978 Least Heat Moon set out in a Ford half-ton Econoline truck to discover for himself the terrain, people, and customs in the states forming, roughly, the perimeter of the continental United States. Carrying with him a copy of Walt Whitman's *Leaves of Grass* and notebooks and a microcassette recorder, he traveled alone except for an occasional hitchhiker. His accounts of this journey appeared first in the *Atlantic Monthly*. Under the title *Blue Highways: A Journey into America*, they were published as a book by Little, Brown and Company.

"On the old highway maps of America," writes Least Heat Moon, "the main routes were red and the back roads blue. Now even the colors are changing. But in those brevities just before dawn and a little after dusk—times neither day nor night—the old roads return to the sky some of its color. Then, in truth, they carry a mysterious cast of blue, and it's that time when the pull of the blue highway is strongest, when the open road is a beckoning, a strangeness, a place where a man can lose himself."

"Utah 14," an essay from the chapter "West by Southwest" in *Blue Highways,* introduces us to a Hopi student with whom Least Heat Moon strikes up a conversation.

UTAH 14

William Least Heat Moon

1978

1   Dirty and hard, the morning light could have been old concrete. Twenty-nine degrees inside. I tried to figure a

way to drive down the mountain without leaving the sleeping bag. I was stiff—not from the cold so much as from having slept coiled like a grub. Creaking open and pinching toes and fingers to check for frostbite, I counted to ten (twice) before shouting and leaping for my clothes. Shouting distracts the agony. Underwear, trousers, and shirt so cold they felt wet.

2   I went outside to relieve myself. In the snow, with the hot stream, I spelled out *alive*. Then to work chipping clear the windows. Somewhere off this mountain, people still lay warm in their blankets and not yet ready to get up to a hot breakfast. So what if they spent the day selling imprinted ballpoint pens? Weren't they down off mountains?

3   Down. I had to try it. And down it was, Utah 14 a complication of twists and drops descending the west side more precipitately than the east. A good thing I hadn't attempted it in the dark. After a mile, snow on the pavement became slush, then water, and finally at six thousand feet, dry and sunny blacktop.

4   Cedar City, a tidy Mormon town, lay at the base of the mountains on the edge of the Escalante Desert. Ah, desert! I pulled in for gas, snow still melting off my rig. "See you spent the night in the Breaks," the attendant said. "You people never believe the sign at the bottom."

5   "I believed, but it said something about winter months. May isn't winter."

6   "It is up there. You Easterners just don't know what a mountain is."

7   I didn't say anything, but I knew what a mountain was: a high pile of windy rocks with its own weather.

8   In the cafeteria of Southern Utah State College, I bought a breakfast of scrambled eggs, pancakes, bacon, oatmeal, grapefruit, orange juice, milk, and a cinnamon roll. A celebration of being alive. I was full of victory.

9   Across the table sat an Indian student named Kendrick Fritz, who was studying chemistry and wanted to become a physician. He had grown up in Moenkopi, Arizona, just across the highway from Tuba City. I said, "Are you Navajo or Hopi?"

10   "Hopi. You can tell by my size. Hopis are smaller than Navajos."

11   His voice was gentle, his words considered, and smile timid. He seemed open to questions. "Fritz doesn't sound like a Hopi name."

12   "My father took it when he was in the Army in the Second World War. Hopis usually have Anglo first names and long Hopi last names that are hard for other people to pronounce."

13   I told him of my difficulty in rousing a conversation in Tuba City. He said, "I can't speak for Navajos about prejudice, but I know Hopis who believe we survived Spaniards, missionaries, a thousand years of other Indians, even the BIA.* But tourists?" He smiled. "Smallpox would be better."

14   "Do you—yourself—think most whites are prejudiced against Indians?"

15   "About fifty-fifty. Half show contempt because they saw a drunk squaw at the Circle K. Another half think we're noble savages—they may be worse because if an Indian makes a mistake they hate him for being human. Who wants to be somebody's ideal myth?"

16   "My grandfather used to say the Big Vision made the Indian, but the white man invented him."

17   "Relations are okay here, but I wouldn't call them good, and I'm not one to go around looking for prejudice. I try not to."

18   "Maybe you're more tolerant of Anglo ways than some others."

19   "Could be. I mean, I *am* studying to be a doctor and not a medicine man. But I'm no apple Indian—red outside and white underneath. I lived up in Brigham City, Utah, when I went to the Intermountain School run by the BIA. It was too easy though. Too much time to goof around. So I switched to Box Elder—that's a public school. I learned there. And I lived in Dallas a few months. What I'm saying is that I've lived on Hopi land and I've lived away. I hear Indians talk about being red all the way through criticizing

*Bureau of Indian Affairs.

others for acting like Anglos, and all the time they're sitting in a pickup at a drive-in. But don't tell them to trade the truck for a horse."

20   "The Spanish brought the horse."

21   He nodded. "To me, being Indian means being responsible to my people. Helping with the best tools. Who invented penicillin doesn't matter."

22   "What happens after you finish school?"

23   "I used to want out of Tuba, but since I've been away, I've come to see how our land really is our Sacred Circle—it's our strength. Now, I want to go back and practice general medicine. At the Indian hospital in Tuba where my mother and sister are nurse's aides, there aren't any Indian M.D.'s, and that's no good. I don't respect people who don't help themselves. Hopi land is no place to make big money, but I'm not interested anyway."

24   "You don't use the word *reservation*."

25   "We don't think of it as a reservation since we were never ordered there. We found it through Hopi prophecies. We're unusual because we've always held onto our original land—most of it anyway. One time my grandfather pointed out the old boundaries to me: We were way up on a mesa. I've forgotten what they are except for the San Francisco Peaks. But in the last eighty years, the government's given a lot of our land to Navajos, and now we're in a hard spot—eight thousand Hopis are surrounded and outnumbered twenty-five to one. I don't begrudge the Navajo anything, but I think Hopis should be in on making the decisions. Maybe you know that Congress didn't even admit Indians to citizenship until about nineteen twenty. Incredible—live someplace a thousand years and then find out you're a foreigner."

26   "I know an Osage who says, 'Don't Americanize me and I won't Americanize you.' He means everybody in the country came from someplace else."

27   "Hopi legends are full of migrations."

28   "Will other Hopis be suspicious of you when you go home as a doctor?"

29   "Some might be, but not my family. But for a lot of Hopis, the worst thing to call a man is *kahopi*, 'not Hopi.'

Nowadays, though, we all have to choose either the new ways or the Hopi way, and it's split up whole villages. A lot of us try to find the best in both places. We've always learned from other people. If we hadn't, we'd be extinct like some other tribes."

30   "Medicine's a pretty good survival technique."

31   "Sure, but I also like Jethro Tull and the Moody Blues. That's not survival."

32   "Is the old religion a survival technique?"

33   "If you live it."

34   "Do you?"

35   "Most Hopis follow our religion, at least in some ways, because it reminds us who we are and it's part of the land. I'll tell you, in the rainy season when the desert turns green, it's beautiful there. The land is medicine too."

36   "If you don't mind telling me, what's the religion like?"

37   "Like any religion in one way—different clans believe different things."

38   "There must be something they all share, something common."

39   "That's hard to say."

40   "Could you try?"

41   He thought a moment. "Maybe the idea of harmony. And the way a Hopi prays. A good life, a harmonious life, is a prayer. We don't just pray for ourselves, we pray for all things. We're famous for the Snake Dances, but a lot of people don't realize those ceremonies are prayers for rain and crops, prayers for life. We also pray for rain by sitting and thinking about rain. We sit and picture wet things like streams and clouds. It's sitting in pictures."

42   He picked up his tray to go. "I could give you a taste of the old Hopi Way. But maybe you're too full after that breakfast. You always eat so much?"

43   "The mountain caused that." I got up. "What do you mean by 'taste'?"

44   "I'll show you."

45   We went to his dormitory room. Other than several Kachina dolls he had carved from cottonwood and a picture of a Sioux warrior, it was just another collegiate dorm room— maybe cleaner than most. He pulled a shoebox from under

his bed and opened it carefully. I must have been watching a little wide-eyed because he said, "It isn't live rattle-snakes." From the box he took a long cylinder wrapped in waxed paper and held it as if trying not to touch it. "Will you eat this? It's very special." He was smiling. "If you won't, I can't share the old Hopi Way with you."

46   "Okay, but if it's dried scorpions, I'm going to speak with a forked tongue."

47   "Open your hands." He unwrapped the cylinder and ever so gently laid across my palms an airy tube the color of a thunderhead. It was about ten inches long and an inch in diameter. "There you go," he said.

48   "You first."

49   "I'm not having any right now."

50   So I bit the end off the blue-gray tube. It was many intricately rolled layers of something with less substance than butterfly wings. The bite crumbled to flakes that stuck to my lips. "Now tell me what I'm eating."

51   "Do you like it?"

52   "I think so. Except it disappears like cotton candy just as I get ready to chew. But I think I taste corn and maybe ashes."

53   "Hopis were eating that before horses came to America. It's piki. Hopi bread you might say. Made from blue-corn flour and ashes from greasewood or sagebrush. Baked on an oiled stone by my mother. She sends piki every so often. It takes time and great skill to make. We call it Hopi cornflakes."

54   "Unbelievably thin." I laid a piece on a page of his chemistry book. The words showed through.

55   "We consider corn our mother. The blue variety is what you might call our compass—wherever it grows, we can go. Blue corn directed our migrations. Navajos cultivate a yellow species that's soft and easy to grind, but ours is hard. You plant it much deeper than other corns, and it survives where they would die. It's a genetic variant the Hopi developed."

56   "Why is it blue? That must be symbolic."

57   "We like the color blue. Corn's our most important ritual ingredient."

58   "The piki's good, but it's making me thirsty. Where's a water fountain?"

59   When I came back from the fountain, Fritz said, "I'll tell you what I think the heart of our religion is—it's the Four Worlds."

60   Over the next hour, he talked about the Hopi Way, and showed pictures and passages from *Book of the Hopi*. The key seemed to be emergence. Carved in a rock near the village of Shipolovi is the ancient symbol for it:

With variations, the symbol appears among other Indians of the Americas. Its lines represent the course a person follows on his "road of life" as he passes through birth, death, rebirth. Human existence is essentially a series of journeys, and the emergence symbol is a kind of map of the wandering soul, an image of a process; but it is also, like most Hopi symbols and ceremonies, a reminder of cosmic patterns that all human beings move in.

61   The Hopi believes mankind has evolved through four worlds: the first a shadowy realm of contentment; the second a place so comfortable the people forgot where they had come from and began worshipping material goods. The third world was a pleasant land too, but the people, bewildered by their past and fearful for their future, thought only of their own earthly plans. At last, the Spider Grandmother, who oversees the emergences, told them: "You have forgotten what you should have remembered, and now you have to leave this place. Things will be harder." In the fourth and present world, life is difficult for mankind, and he struggles to remember his source because materialism

and selfishness block a greater vision. The newly born infant comes into the fourth world with the door of his mind open (evident in the cranial soft spot), but as he ages, the door closes and he must work at remaining receptive to the great forces. A human being's grandest task is to keep from breaking with things outside himself.

62   "A Hopi learns that he belongs to two families," Fritz said, "his natural clan and that of all things. As he gets older, he's supposed to move closer to the greater family. In the Hopi Way, each person tries to recognize his part in the whole."

63   "At breakfast you said you hunted rabbits and pigeons and robins, but I don't see how you can shoot a bird if you believe in the union of life."

64   "A Hopi hunter asks the animal to forgive him for killing it. Only life can feed life. The robin knows that."

65   "How does robin taste, by the way?"

66   "Tastes good."

67   "The religion doesn't seem to have much of an ethical code."

68   "It's there. We watch what the Kachinas say and do. But the Spider Grandmother did give two rules. To all men, not just Hopis. If you look at them, they cover everything. She said, 'Don't go around hurting each other,' and she said, 'Try to understand things.'"

69   "I like them. I like them very much."

70   "Our religion keeps reminding us that we aren't just will and thoughts. We're also sand and wind and thunder. Rain. The seasons. All those things. You learn to respect everything because you *are* everything. If you respect yourself, you respect all things. That's why we have so many songs of creation to remind us where we came from. If the fourth world forgets that, we'll disappear in the wilderness like the third world, where people decided they had created themselves."

71   "Pride's the deadliest of the Seven Deadly Sins in old Christian theology."

72   "It's *kahopi* to set yourself above things. It causes divisions."

73   Fritz had to go to class. As we walked across campus, I

said, "I guess it's hard to be a Hopi in Cedar City—
especially if you're studying biochemistry."

74   "It's hard to be a Hopi anywhere."

75   "I mean, difficult to carry your Hopi heritage into a
world as technological as medicine is."

76   "Heritage? My heritage is the Hopi Way, and that's a
way of the spirit. Spirit can go anywhere. In fact, it has to
go places so it can change and emerge like in the migrations. That's the whole idea."

Study Guide:

1. Words to know for the second reading and the permanent vocabulary list are *precipitately, mesa, to begrudge, Kachina doll, cosmic.*

2. Allusions to recognize are to *Spaniards* and *missionaries* and
their historic influence on Native Americans of the Southwest and the
West; to *smallpox,* especially as it affected Native Americans; to *noble
savages* as in the philosophical writings of Jean-Jacques Rousseau; to
Jethro Tull and the *Moody Blues;* to the *cranial soft spot;* to the *seven
deadly sins,* and to *migrations.*

Questions:

1. This essay moves from an awareness of physical discomfort to a
celebration of life and the spirit, from acceptance of materialism to
talk of universal benevolence. How do the imagery and the dialogue
reveal these extremes while at the same time showing that the extremes are necessary to the greater whole? Cite specific examples;
there are many.

2. How does Least Heat Moon use the delicate "piki" as a device to
symbolize the juxtaposition of the old ways and the new?

3. How might the Hopi vision of "four worlds" apply to the ways of
life of people in contemporary American white culture?

4. This essay might be called a **didactic**, or teaching, essay. Is
dialogue an effective device for such an essay?

Composition Topic:

Write a didactic essay of your own, using dialogue as the principal
method of making your point. The person you choose to question (or

interview) should have real knowledge—not simply opinions—on the subject matter in question. In the development of this essay, show something of your own personality as well as that of the person being interviewed.

Red Smith

The name Walter Wellesley Smith would mean nothing to most people, but the nickname Red Smith recalls to sports fans and lovers of good writing the best sports columnist in the United States.

Born in 1905 in Green Bay, Wisconsin, Red Smith went to Notre Dame in 1923, already determined to become a newspaper writer. He was no athlete, but attending college when Knute Rockne was football coach and Grantland Rice was writing about "The Four Horsemen of Notre Dame" gave him a taste for sports that the sports editor of the *St. Louis Star* recognized shortly after hiring the young graduate. In the 1930s Smith was lured east by the *Philadelphia Record.* There he established his reputation as an outstanding sports writer, and in 1945 he was hired by the *New York Herald Tribune,* for which he wrote a syndicated column that won nationwide acclaim.

In 1966 the *Tribune* failed, and a year later Smith's beloved wife died. For several years he seemed at loose ends. Troubled by the Vietnam War, he wrote unevenly for *Women's Wear Daily,* but in 1968 he remarried, and in 1971 he was hired by the *New York Times.* There his charmingly witty style and thoughtful insights won him a Pulitzer Prize, and there, until a few months before his death in 1982, he wrote a 900-word column four times a week: "Sports of the Times/Red Smith."

"Leave Us Defense against Solecisms" is an amusing example of Red Smith's love of language and its use in the crafts of sportswriting and sports announcing.

LEAVE US DEFENSE AGAINST SOLECISMS
Red Smith

January 1960

1   It was resolved on New Year's Day to make no New Year's resolutions whatever, but this doesn't rule out suggestions on how other sinners might grow in grace during 1960. It is therefore proposed that during the next 12 months all sports reporters, including those who write for the papers and especially those who broadcast by radio and television, undertake the revolutionary experiment of delivering their reports in English.

2   To be sure this might startle and confuse some of the

clientele, yet 1960 would be a better and brighter year if we could get through it without being advised that the Syracuse University football team, say, has an attack which is difficult to "defense against."

3   Most of the world's sweeping reforms had small beginnings. If we could start by eliminating the barbaric and indefensible use of "defense" as a verb, there might come a day when descriptions of football games didn't twitch, quiver and crawl with such linguistic garbage as "reddogging," "jitterbugging," "blitzing," "stunting," "look-in pass," and bastard nouns like the "keep," the "take" and the "give."

4   It is, of course, idle to dream of tuning in a baseball game and discovering that instead of pumping and dealing, the pitcher is winding up and throwing.

5   Murder of the mother tongue is a form of matricide committed with premeditation by football coaches and encouraged by writers and broadcasters as accessories after the fact.

6   The coachly clan enjoys pretending that butting heads is a science bordering on the occult. Hoping to bewilder and fend off the administration, faculty and alumni, the brothers shroud their sweaty craft in mystery to create the impression that football is an art so involved and technical, so profound, abstruse and esoteric as to be removed from ordinary knowledge and understanding.

7   It was either an illiterate coach or a sly one who misbegot the infinitive "to defense." Maybe he never learned the difference between a noun and a verb, but more likely the corruption was intentional; probably he chose to talk about "defensing the slot-T" because if he were to speak simply about stopping a play it would sound too easy.

8   Most professions and clans, of course, have their own special language. The medical profession talks one tongue and Madison Ave. another. These private tongues serve as a sort of stockade, giving insiders the cozy sense of belonging, mystifying outsiders and keeping them outside.

9   Being thrown into contact with coaches corrupts the language of reporters. Eager to crash the inner circle and eagerer to prove themselves in the know, they borrow the

coachly barbarisms and employ them in tones of arrogant authority.

10   This establishes them as experts, at frightful cost to readers and listeners. They prattle knowingly of splits and gaps and flankers and cornermen, of options and pitches and drawers and traps, of flare passes and swing passes and buttonhook patterns and—may the Curse of Heffelfinger shrivel their busy tongues—of "loaf-of-bread passes."

11   During the regular season the torture has its limits, for as a rule there is only one televised college game on a Saturday, with one pro game Sunday if the local team is on the road.

12   Then the holiday season comes along, and the senses take a horrid clobbering. Even the man who arises feeling fit on New Year's Day, if such there be, is reduced to gibbering idiocy before the first quarter ends in the Rose Bowl.

13   On the first day of this year, happily, an antidote was administered. Rather, it was on the first night of this year, when the afternoon diet of football had ended and the fights came on from Madison Square Garden.

14   Viewers caught the last round of the semi-final between Shotgun Warner and Lee Williams. They saw Williams daze his man with heavy blows to the head, though apparently Warner had taken a substantial lead on points in the early rounds.

15   "We're awaiting the decision for Lee Williams over Don Warner," Jimmy Powers said cheerily, whereupon the judges split three ways for a draw. A little later the Tom McNeely–George Logan bout was stopped and Johnny Addie took the mike.

16   "Logan," he said, "suffered two badly cuts over the left eyebrow."

17   Fans went off to bed as happy as crickets.

Study Guide:

Before rereading this essay, be sure of the meanings of the following words and phrases: **solecism**, *clientele, matricide, premeditation, acces-*

sories after the fact, occult, abstruse, esoteric, to misbeget, stockade, barbarism, to prattle, antidote.

Questions:

1. What are the two senses of *grace* as it is used in paragraph 1? Where else does Red Smith play with words and their meanings?

2. Which of the following statements comes closest to expressing the point of this essay?

   a. Sportswriters and broadcasters should make a New Year's resolution to express themselves in English.
   b. Sports fans enjoy solecisms.
   c. Sportswriters and broadcasters ought to express themselves plainly and informatively.
   d. Coaches and sports reporters need to protect themselves from academic critics.

3. Why is the title for this essay appropriate? Be specific.

4. What is the major figure of speech used in paragraph 3? How is it representative of Smith's satirical approach? Explain.

5. Explain the extended metaphor in paragraph 5.

6. Especially in sports but also in medicine, law, education, and other professions, words and phrases are used in ways that are mysterious to the outsider. Such "in" use of language is called **jargon**. For what purpose, according to Smith, do coaches use jargon? Is his criticism valid?

7. In paragraph 10 Smith explains the corruption of sportswriters' language. Is he objective in his views? Who was Pudge Heffelfinger?

8. How does "the holiday season" give a subtle structure to the essay?

9. Point out examples of hyperbole in this essay. Are they effective as humorous satire?

10. Is satire a better weapon here than schoolteacherish disapproval of solecisms? Explain.

11. To prove Red Smith's point, go to the sports section of your daily paper and cut out for class study an outstanding example of a solecism. Be prepared, however, to discuss why the sports section often contains the most vivid and colorful writing in the entire paper.

Composition Topic:

As though you are writing a sports column for a newspaper, cover a local contest. In vivid style capture the important plays and the essential quality of the playing. Consider how best to organize your thoughts to make your point or points. Can you defend jargon and solecisms in your writing?

James Baldwin

James Arthur Baldwin (1924–1987) was born in Harlem, where he grew up as a racially segregated African-American. When he was only 14, he began preaching in his father's church, but by the time he was 17, he had decided to be a writer. After his clergyman father's death in 1943, he left his family and moved to Greenwich Village, to write and to earn his way by doing odd jobs.

In 1945 Baldwin won a Eugene F. Saxton Memorial Trust Award after impressing Richard Wright, author of *Native Son,* with the unfinished manuscript of a novel; and in 1948 he was granted a Rosenwald Fellowship, which enabled him to move to Paris and write without the oppression of racial discrimination. The novel, published in 1953, is *Go Tell It on the Mountain,* then and now acclaimed worldwide.

Except for occasional business visits, Baldwin did not return to the United States until 1957. By then he had written another novel, *Giovanni's Room,* and an essay collection, the title of which, *Notes of a Native Son,* pays homage to Richard Wright.

Baldwin's other works include several novels, the stage plays *The Amen Corner* and *Blues for Mr. Charlie,* and many essays. Two collections of essays, *Nobody Knows My Name* and *The Fire Next Time,* helped to awaken America to its racial problems.

In the 1960s and 1970s Baldwin's writings and speeches were a strong voice in the civil rights movement; he lectured in 1963 for CORE (Congress of Racial Equality) and was also active in civil rights movements in Paris and Kenya. Until the last year of his life he was not only a prolific writer but also a teacher of writing in colleges and universities. In 1986 the French government made him a commander of the Legion of Honor.

"A Fly in Buttermilk," from *Nobody Knows My Name,* explores the kind of injustice James Baldwin always fought against.

A FLY IN BUTTERMILK

James Baldwin

1958

1   "You can take the child out of the country," my elders were fond of saying, "but you can't take the country out of the child." They were speaking of their own antecedents, I

139

supposed; it didn't, anyway, seem possible that they could be warning me; I took myself out of the country and went to Paris. It was there I discovered that the old folks knew what they had been talking about: I found myself, willy-nilly, alchemized into an American the moment I touched French soil.

2   Now, back again after nearly nine years, it was ironical to reflect that if I had not lived in France for so long I would never have found it necessary—or possible—to visit the American South. The South had always frightened me. How deeply it had frightened me—though I had never seen it—and how soon, was one of the things my dreams revealed to me while I was there. And this made me think of the privacy and mystery of childhood all over again, in a new way. I wondered where children got their strength—the strength, in this case, to walk through mobs to get to school.

3   "You've got to remember," said an older Negro friend to me, in Washington, "that no matter what you see or how it makes you feel, it can't be compared to twenty-five, thirty years ago—you remember those photographs of Negroes hanging from trees?" I looked at him differently. *I* had seen the photographs—but *he* might have been one of them. "I remember," he said, "when conductors on streetcars wore pistols and had police powers." And he remembered a great deal more. He remembered, for example, hearing Booker T. Washington speak, and the day-to-day progress of the Scottsboro case, and the rise and bloody fall of Bessie Smith. These had been books and headlines and music for me but it now developed that they were also a part of my identity.

4   "You're just one generation away from the South, you know. You'll find," he added, kindly, "that people will be willing to talk to you . . . if they don't feel that you look down on them just because you're from the North."

5   The first Negro I encountered, an educator, didn't give me any opportunity to look down. He forced me to admit, at once, that I had never been to college; that Northern Negroes lived herded together, like pigs in a pen; that the campus on which we met was a tribute to the industry and determination of Southern Negroes. "Negroes in the South

form a *community*." My humiliation was complete with his discovery that I couldn't even drive a car. I couldn't ask him anything. He made me feel so hopeless an example of the general Northern spinelessness that it would have seemed a spiteful counterattack to have asked him to discuss the integration problem which had placed his city in the headlines.

6   At the same time, I felt that there was nothing which bothered him more; but perhaps he did not really know what he thought about it; or thought too many things at once. His campus risked being very different twenty years from now. Its special function would be gone—and so would his position, arrived at with such pain. The new day a-coming was not for him. I don't think this fact made him bitter but I think it frightened him and made him sad; for the future is like heaven—everyone exalts it but no one wants to go there now. And I imagine that he shared the attitude, which I was to encounter so often later, toward the children who were helping to bring this future about; admiration before the general spectacle and skepticism before the individual case.

7   That evening I went to visit G., one of the "integrated" children, a boy of about fifteen. I had already heard something of his first day in school, the peculiar problems his presence caused, and his own extraordinary bearing.

8   He seemed extraordinary at first mainly by his silence. He was tall for his age and, typically, seemed to be constructed mainly of sharp angles, such as elbows and knees. Dark gingerbread sort of coloring, with ordinary hair, and a face disquietingly impassive, save for his very dark, very large eyes. I got the impression, each time that he raised them, not so much that they spoke but that they registered volumes; each time he dropped them it was as though he had retired into the library.

9   We sat in the living room, his mother, younger brother and sister, and I, while G. sat on the sofa, doing his homework. The father was at work and the older sister had not yet come home. The boy had looked up once, as I came in, to say, "Good evening, sir," and then left all the rest to his mother.

10   Mrs. R. was a very strong-willed woman, handsome, quiet-looking, dressed in black. Nothing, she told me, beyond name-calling, had marked G.'s first day of school; but on the second day she received the last of several threatening phone calls. She was told that if she didn't want her son "cut to ribbons" she had better keep him at home. She heeded this warning to the extent of calling the chief of police.

11   "He told me to go on and send him. He said he'd be there when the cutting started. So I sent him." Even more remarkably perhaps, G. went.

12   No one cut him, in fact no one touched him. The students formed a wall between G. and the entrances, saying only enough, apparently, to make their intention clearly understood, watching him, and keeping him outside. (I asked him, "What did you feel when they blocked your way?" G. looked up at me, very briefly, with no expression on his face, and told me, "Nothing, sir.") At last the principal appeared and took him by the hand and they entered the school, while the children shouted behind them, "Nigger-lover!"

13   G. was alone all day at school.

14   "But I thought you already knew some of the kids there," I said. I had been told that he had friends among the white students because of their previous competition in a Soapbox Derby.

15   "Well, none of them are in his classes," his mother told me—a shade too quickly, as though she did not want to dwell on the idea of G.'s daily isolation.

16   "We don't have the same schedule," G. said. It was as though he were coming to his mother's rescue. Then, unwillingly, with a kind of interior shrug, "Some of the guys had lunch with me but then the other kids called them names." He went back to his homework.

17   I began to realize that there were not only a great many things G. would not tell me, there was much that he would never tell his mother.

18   "But nobody bothers you, anyway?"

19   "No," he said. "They just—call names. I don't let it bother me."

20   Nevertheless, the principal frequently escorts him through the halls. One day, when G. was alone, a boy tripped him and knocked him down and G. reported this to the principal. The white boy denied it but a few days later, while G. and the principal were together, he came over and said, "I'm sorry I tripped you; I won't do it again," and they shook hands. But it doesn't seem that this boy has as yet developed into a friend. And it is clear that G. will not allow himself to expect this.

21   I asked Mrs. R. what had prompted her to have her son reassigned to a previously all-white high school. She sighed, paused; then, sharply, "Well, it's not because I'm so anxious to have him around white people." Then she laughed. "I really don't know how I'd feel if I was to carry a white baby around who was calling me Grandma." G. laughed, too, for the first time. "White people say," the mother went on, "that that's all a Negro wants. I don't think they believe that themselves."

22   Then we switched from the mysterious question of what white folks believe to the relatively solid ground of what she, herself, knows and fears.

23   "You see that boy? Well, he's always been a straight-A student. He didn't hardly have to work at it. You see the way he's so quiet now on the sofa, with his books? Well, when he was going to _____ High School, he didn't have no homework or if he did, he could get it done in five minutes. Then, there he was, out in the streets, getting into mischief, and all he did all day in school was just keep clowning to make the other boys laugh. He wasn't learning nothing and didn't nobody care if he *never* learned nothing and I could just see what was going to happen to him if he kept on like that."

24   The boy was very quiet.

25   "What were you learning in _____ High?" I asked him.

26   "Nothing!" he exploded, with a very un-boyish laugh. I asked him to tell me about it.

27   "Well, the teacher comes in," he said, "and she gives you something to read and she goes out. She leaves some other student in charge . . ." ("You can just imagine how much reading gets done," Mrs. R. interposed.) "At the end of the

period," G. continued, "she comes back and tells you something to read for the next day."

28   So, having nothing else to do, G. began amusing his classmates and his mother began to be afraid. G. is just about the age when boys begin dropping out of school. Perhaps they get a girl into trouble; she also drops out; the boy gets work for a time or gets into trouble for a long time. I was told that forty-five girls had left school for the maternity ward the year before. A week or ten days before I arrived in the city eighteen boys from G.'s former high school had been sentenced to the chain gang.

29   "My boy's a good boy," said Mrs. R., "and I wanted to see him have a chance."

30   "Don't the teachers care about the students?" I asked. This brought forth more laughter. How could they care? How much could they do if they *did* care? There were too many children, from shaky homes and worn-out parents, in aging, inadequate plants. They could be considered, most of them, as already doomed. Besides, the teachers' jobs were safe. They were responsible only to the principal, an appointed official, whose judgment, apparently, was never questioned by his (white) superiors or confreres.

31   The principal of G.'s former high school was about seventy-five when he was finally retired and his idea of discipline was to have two boys beat each other—"under his supervision"—with leather belts. This once happened with G., with no other results than that his parents gave the principal a tongue-lashing. It happened with two boys of G.'s acquaintance with the result that, after school, one boy beat the other so badly that he had to be sent to the hospital. The teachers have themselves arrived at a dead end, for in a segregated school system they cannot rise any higher, and the students are aware of this. Both students and teachers soon cease to struggle.

32   "If a boy can wash a blackboard," a teacher was heard to say, "I'll promote him."

33   I asked Mrs. R. how other Negroes felt about her having had G. reassigned.

34   "Well, a lot of them don't like it," she said—though I gathered that they did not say so to her. As school time

approached, more and more people asked her, "Are you going to send him?" "Well," she told them, "the man says the door is open and I feel like, yes, I'm going to go on and send him."

35   Out of a population of some fifty thousand Negroes, there had been only forty-five applications. People had said that they would send their children, had talked about it, had made plans; but, as the time drew near, when the application blanks were actually in their hands, they said, "I don't believe I'll sign this right now. I'll sign it later." Or, "I been thinking about this. I don't believe I'll send him right now."

36   "Why?" I asked. But to this she couldn't, or wouldn't, give me any answer.

37   I asked if there had been any reprisals taken against herself or her husband, if she was worried while G. was at school all day. She said that, no, there had been no reprisals, though some white people, under the pretext of giving her good advice, had expressed disapproval of her action. But she herself doesn't have a job and so doesn't risk losing one. Nor, she told me, had anyone said anything to her husband, who, however, by her own proud suggestion, is extremely closemouthed. And it developed later that he was not working at his regular trade but at something else.

38   As to whether she was worried, "No," she told me; in much the same way that G., when asked about the blockade, had said, "Nothing, sir." In her case it was easier to see what she meant: she hoped for the best and would not allow herself, in the meantime, to lose her head. "I don't feel like nothing's going to happen," she said, soberly. "I *hope* not. But I know if anybody tries to harm me or any one of my children, I'm going to strike back with all my strength. I'm going to strike them in God's name."

39   G., in the meantime, on the sofa with his books, was preparing himself for the next school day. His face was as impassive as ever and I found myself wondering—again— how he managed to face what must surely have been the worst moment of his day—the morning, when he opened his eyes and realized that it was all to be gone through

again. Insults, and incipient violence, teachers, and—
exams.

40   "One among so many," his mother said, "that's kind of
rough."

41   "Do you think you'll make it?" I asked him. "Would you
rather go back to _____ High?"

42   "No," he said, "I'll make it. I ain't going back."

43   "He ain't thinking about going back," said his mother—
proudly and sadly. I began to suspect that the boy managed
to support the extreme tension of his situation by means of
a nearly fanatical concentration on his schoolwork; by holding in the center of his mind the issue on which, when the
deal went down, others would be *forced* to judge him. Pride
and silence were his weapons. Pride comes naturally, and
soon, to a Negro, but even his mother, I felt, was worried
about G.'s silence, though she was too wise to break it. For
what was all this doing to him really?

44   "It's hard enough," the boy said later, still in control but
with flashing eyes, "to keep quiet and keep walking when
they call you nigger. But if anyone ever spits on me, I *know*
I'll have to fight."

45   His mother laughs, laughs to ease them both, then looks
at me and says, "I wonder sometimes what makes white
folks so mean."

46   This is a recurring question among Negroes, even
among the most "liberated"—which epithet is meant, of
course, to describe the writer. The next day, with this question (more elegantly phrased) still beating in my mind, I
visited the principal of G.'s new high school. But he didn't
look "mean" and he wasn't "mean": he was a thin, young
man of about my age, bewildered and in trouble. I asked
him how things were working out, what he thought about
it, what he thought would happen—in the long run, or the
short.

47   "Well, I've got a job to do," he told me, "and I'm going to
do it." He said that there hadn't been any trouble and that
he didn't expect any. "Many students, after all, never see G.
at all." None of the children have harmed him and the
teachers are, apparently, carrying out their rather tall or-

ders, which are to be kind to G. and, at the same time, to treat him like any other student.

48   I asked him to describe to me the incident, on the second day of school, when G.'s entrance had been blocked by the students. He told me that it was nothing at all—"It was a gesture more than anything else." He had simply walked out and spoken to the students and brought G. inside. "I've seen them do the same thing to other kids when they were kidding," he said. I imagine that he would like to be able to place this incident in the same cheerful if rowdy category, despite the shouts (which he does not mention) of "nigger-lover!"

49   Which epithet does not, in any case, describe him at all.

50   "Why," I asked, "is G. the only Negro student here?" According to this city's pupil-assignment plan, a plan designed to allow the least possible integration over the longest possible period of time, G. was the only Negro student who qualified.

51   "And, anyway," he said, "I don't think it's right for colored children to come to white schools just *because* they're white."

52   "Well," I began, "even if you don't like it . . ."

53   "Oh," he said quickly, raising his head and looking at me sideways, "I never said I didn't like it."

54   And then he explained to me, with difficulty, that it was simply contrary to everything he'd ever seen or believed. He'd never dreamed of a mingling of the races; had never lived that way himself and didn't suppose that he ever would; in the same way, he added, perhaps a trifle defensively, that he only associated with a certain stratum of white people. But, "I've never seen a colored person toward whom I had any hatred or ill-will."

55   His eyes searched mine as he said this and I knew that he was wondering if I believed him.

56   I certainly did believe him; he impressed me as being a very gentle and honorable man. But I could not avoid wondering if he had ever really *looked* at a Negro and wondered about the life, the aspirations, the universal humanity hidden behind the dark skin. And I wondered, when he told me that race relations in his city were "excel-

lent" and had not been strained by recent developments, how on earth he managed to hold on to this delusion.

57   I later got back to my interrupted question, which I phrased more tactfully.

58   "Even though it's very difficult for all concerned—this situation—doesn't it occur to you that the reason colored children wish to come to white schools isn't because they want to be with white people but simply because they want a better education?"

59   "Oh, I don't know," he replied, "it seems to me that colored schools are just as good as white schools." I wanted to ask him on what evidence he had arrived at this conclusion and also how they could possibly be "as good" in view of the kind of life they came out of, and perpetuated, and the dim prospects faced by all but the most exceptional or ruthless Negro students. But I only suggested that G. and his family, who certainly should have known, so thoroughly disagreed with him that they had been willing to risk G.'s present well-being and his future psychological and mental health in order to bring about a change in his environment. Nor did I mention the lack of enthusiasm evinced by G.'s mother when musing on the prospect of a fair grandchild. There seemed no point in making this man any more a victim of his heritage than he so gallantly was already.

60   "Still," I said at last, after a rather painful pause, "I should think that the trouble in this situation is that it's very hard for *you* to face a child and treat him unjustly because of something for which he is no more responsible than—than *you* are."

61   The eyes came to life then, or a veil fell, and I found myself staring at a man in anguish. The eyes were full of pain and bewilderment and he nodded his head. This was the impossibility which he faced every day. And I imagined that his tribe would increase, in sudden leaps and bounds was already increasing.

62   For segregation has worked brilliantly in the South, and, in fact, in the nation, to this extent: it has allowed white people, with scarcely any pangs of conscience whatever, to *create,* in every generation, only the Negro they

wished to see. As the walls come down they will be forced to take another, harder look at the shiftless and the menial and will be forced into a wonder concerning them which cannot fail to be agonizing. It is not an easy thing to be forced to reexamine a way of life and to speculate, in a personal way, on the general injustice.

63   "What do you think," I asked him, "will happen? What do you think the future holds?"

64   He gave a strained laugh and said he didn't know. "I don't want to think about it." Then, "I'm a religious man," he said, "and I believe the Creator will always help us find a way to solve our problems. If a man loses that, he's lost everything he had." I agreed, struck by the look in his eyes.

65   "You're from the North?" he asked me, abruptly.

66   "Yes," I said.

67   "Well," he said, "you've got your troubles too."

68   "Ah, yes, we certainly do," I admitted, and shook hands and left him. I did not say what I was thinking, that our troubles were the same trouble and that, unless we were very swift and honest, what is happening in the South today will be happening in the North tomorrow.

Study Guide:

1. In rereading this essay be sure to know the meanings of these words: *antecedents, alchemized, to exalt, skepticism, reprisals, pretext, incipient, epithet, aspiration, delusion, to perpetuate, shiftless, menial, to speculate.*

2. In an encyclopedia look up the history of *integration* in the United States, especially the *Brown v. Board of Education of Topeka* decision of May 17, 1954, by the Supreme Court. Also be sure to understand the allusions to Booker T. Washington and Bessie Smith.

Questions:

1. The metaphorical title of the essay is an allusion to a Southern folk song, "Flies in the buttermilk. Shoo! Shoo! Shoo!" What is its connection to the content of the essay?

2. The last sentence of paragraph 61 contains an allusion to the first line of Leigh Hunt's poem "Abou Ben Adhem": "Abou Ben Adhem (may his tribe increase!)." Read all of that poem and then determine if Baldwin is using the allusion as a positive or negative reference to the principal of G.'s school.

3. What do we learn, from the essay, about the author's background? How does this background affect Baldwin's approach to his subject?

4. Why did Baldwin choose to focus mainly on his specific conversations with four people ("an educator"; the student, "G."; the student's mother, "Mrs. R."; and the white school principal) instead of choosing other options in presenting the abstract problems of integration?

5. How do the boy and his mother explain their decision to integrate an all-white high school? How does the school principal explain it? Why don't the two viewpoints agree? Give as many details as you can in answering all three questions, citing specific evidence from the text.

6. Explain, pointing out specific details, how and why the author presents the dramatic tensions between past and present and South and North in this essay. How are these dramatic tensions important? Note, while considering your answers, how the last four paragraphs of the essay connect with the first six paragraphs.

7. How do you personally react to the author's subjective judgments in paragraphs 62 and 68? Do these judgments tally with the evidence he had derived from the interviews? Has subsequent history validated his judgments or not?

8. Point out several specific literary techniques that Baldwin employs that help raise his essay above the level of mere reportage.

Composition Topic:

Write a paragraph on each of the four persons interviewed, describing the personality, psychology, and racial attitude of each.

Robert Chrisman

Essayist, poet, fiction writer, and teacher, Robert Chrisman, born in 1937, is currently president of the Black World Foundation, Oakland, California, and a lecturer in English and African-American and African studies at the University of Michigan at Ann Arbor. He is a graduate of the University of California, Berkeley, and received his M.A. degree from San Francisco State College.

In addition to his work at the University of Michigan, Chrisman has taught courses in writing and in Afro-American literature at San Francisco State College, the University of California at San Francisco, the University of Hawaii, the University of Vermont, and Williams College. His own literary contributions have been published in the *Saturday Review of Literature, Black World, Scanlan's,* and the *Black Scholar.* Indeed, he was founding editor of the *Black Scholar,* an independent forum for presenting contemporary African-American studies and research. As editor he published informative and provocative essays by such well-known authors and critics as Ralph Metcalfe, Jr., Leroi Jones, and Chuck Stone.

"Black Prisoners, White Law" is from *Contemporary Black Thought,* a collection of the best essays from *The Black Scholar.* It is a carefully reasoned essay that shows the importance of seeing life from points of view different from the generally accepted standard.

BLACK PRISONERS, WHITE LAW

Robert Chrisman

1972

1   The first black prisoners in America were the Africans brought to these shores in chains in 1619. Like our brothers in prison today—and like ourselves—those African ancestors were victims of the political, economic and military rapacity of white America. Slave camps, reservations and concentration camps; bars, chains and leg irons; Alcatraz, Cummings and Sing Sing: these are the real monuments of America, more so than Monticello or the Statue of Liberty. They are monuments of a legal inequity which has its roots in the basic laws of the United States and which still endures.

2   To justify and protect its oppression of blacks, white America developed an ideology of white supremacy which shaped the American state, its politics and all its interlocking cultural institutions—education, church, law. Apartheid, generally attributed to 20th-century South Africa, was developed as an instrument of oppression by this country in the 1600's and has its basis in the laws themselves, in the Constitution itself.

3   The function of law is to establish and regulate the political and economic franchise of the citizens within a given state. The Constitution, ironically hailed as a magnificent guarantee of human equality and freedom, deliberately refused franchise to black Americans and Indians and granted it only to white Americans of means. Indeed, black people were defined as a source of white franchise, in the infamous 3/5 clause. This clause gave the slaveholder a preponderance of political power by apportioning him 3/5 constituency for every slave he possessed, *in addition to his own free white constituency.*

4   The right of slaves to escape bondage was also forbidden: In Article IV, Section 2, "No person held to service or labor in one State, under the laws thereof, escaping into another, shall in consequence of any law or regulation therein, be discharged from such service or labor, but shall be delivered up on claim of the party to whom such service or labor may be due." Escaped slaves were to be returned to the slaveowner—by national decree.

5   Designed by agrarian slaveholders and northern industrialists and merchants, the Constitution defined the relationship between their economic interests and their political franchise. Hence its preoccupation with finance and the divisions of power. The Bill of Rights, appended 4 years later, is an afterthought, as a concession to human rights.

6   Black people were governed by the infamous slave codes, which forbade manumission, voting, education, civil status and personal rights and privileges.

7   The Constitution was an apartheid document that guaranteed the continuance of slavery and racism as permanent institutions and perpetuated them as cultural realities. De-

spite the elimination by law of slavery and discrimination, we are still the victims of that racism sanctioned and encouraged by the Constitution.

8   Black people cannot be protected by American law, for we have no franchise in this country. If anything, we suffer double jeopardy: We have no law of our own and no protection from the law of white America which, by its intention and by the very nature of the cultural values which determined it, is inimical to blackness.

9   In the literal sense of the word, we are out-laws. We are most subject to arrest—and the most frequent victims of crime. Over 40% of the prison inmates in the State of California are black. More blacks than whites are executed in the United States—and this does not include lynchings, "self-defense" or police killings. From 1930–1969, 2066 black people were executed to 1751 whites. Four hundred and five black men were executed for rape, as compared to 48 whites during the same period. In his article, "Black Ecology" (*The Black Scholar,* April 1970), Nathan Hare points out that "blacks are about four times as likely to fall victim to forcible rape and robbery and about twice as likely to face burglary and aggravated assault."

10   Being outside the law, black Americans are either victims or else prisoners of a law which is neither enforced nor designed for us—except with repressive intent. For example, gun control legislation was enacted by the United States only after black people began buying guns and endorsing the principle of self-defense, which is a qualitatively different inspiration than the assassination of individuals such as John F. Kennedy and Malcolm X.

11   Furthermore, black leaders who address themselves to the fundamental question—that black Americans must have full political and economic franchise—are arrested or harassed. To list just a few black leaders who have been or are political prisoners: W. E. B. Du Bois, Marcus Garvey, Malcolm X, the Honorable Elijah Muhammad, Martin Luther King, as well as some of the currently embattled brothers and sisters: Rap Brown, Bobby Seale, Angela Davis, Ahmed Evans, Ericka Huggins, the Soledad brothers and Cleveland Sellers. The demand for black equality in

America exposes its most basic contradiction: that as a democracy it cannot endure or allow the full liberation of its black citizens.

12   All black prisoners, therefore, are political prisoners, for their condition derives from the political inequity of black people in America. A black prisoner's crime may or may not have been a political action against the state, but the state's action against him is always political. This knowledge, intuitively known and sometimes transcribed into political terms, exists within every black prisoner.

13   For we must understand that the black offender is not tried and judged by the black community itself, but by the machinery of the white community, which is least affected by his actions and whose interests are served by the systematic subjugation of all black people. Thus the trial or conviction of a black prisoner, *regardless of his offense, his guilt or his innocence,* cannot be a democratic judgment of him by his peers, but a political action against him by his oppressors.

14   Grand juries, the state and federal judges of the Circuit Courts, Superior Courts and Supreme Courts, are appointed, not elected. This fact alone prejudices a fair trial and precludes black representation, for black people do not have a single official in this country who has the power to appoint a judge or grand jury to the bench. Furthermore, because of the appointive nature of most judgeships, judges have no direct responsibility to the persons they try, through recall or election. Nor do trial juries reflect the racial and economic compositions of the populations which they represent. If a city has a 40% black population it should have the same percentage on its juries, in its legal staff and in its judges.

15   It is of course obvious that mugging, theft, pimping and shooting dope are not themselves political actions, particularly when the victims are most often other black people. To maintain that all black offenders are by their actions politically correct is a dangerous romanticism. Black antisocial behavior must be seen in and of its own terms and

be corrected for the enhancement of the black community. But it must be understood that the majority of black offenses have their roots in the political and economic deprivation of black Americans by the Anglo-American state and that these are the primary causes and conditions of black crime. The individual offender and his black community must achieve this primary understanding and unite for our mutual protection and self-determination.

16   Thus the matter of black prisoners and white law involves the basic question of self-determination for all black people. Black people must determine when a black man has violated the black community, and that black community must take the corrective action. As we drive for new economic and cultural institutions, we must also create new legal institutions that will accurately reflect the judgment, the social fabric, the conditions of the black community. As it stands now, only the white American community determines when a black person has offended the black community, and this is a colonial imposition and a political injustice.

17   Most important, the black community outside of bars must never divorce itself from the black community within bars. Freedom is a false illusion in this society; prison is a reality. Black prisoners must be supported by the black community during their incarceration and after they are released.

18   For the black prisoner is the most vulnerable member of our community—in a naked way he is directly at the mercy of the white power structure. It is also apparent that the black prisoner is one of the most valuable members of our community, as well—the organization, the discipline, the fraternity that black men have developed within prison to survive must be developed by us outside the prison if we are to survive.

19   We must employ all means necessary to protect and support black people within prison walls. We are all prisoners, and our unwavering task must be the achievement of organization, unity and total liberation.

Study Guide:

1. For your second reading of this essay, make a list of the following words and be sure to understand their meanings *as they are used in context* (some of the words have quite different meanings in other contexts): *rapacity, inequity, apartheid, to attribute to, franchise, infamous, preponderance, to apportion, constituency, bondage, agrarian, preoccupation, concession, manumission, to perpetuate, to sanction, double jeopardy, inimical, repressive, to harass, to transcribe, subjugation, enhancement, mutual, illusion, incarceration, vulnerable, fraternity.* Be sure to know not only the meanings but also the spellings of *to prejudice* and *to be prejudiced.*

2. Chrisman expects his readers to understand the allusions to Alcatraz, Cummings, Sing Sing, Monticello, South Africa, W. E. B. Du Bois, Marcus Garvey, Malcolm X, Elijah Muhammad, Martin Luther King, Rap Brown, Bobby Seale, Angela Davis, Ahmed Evans, Ericka Huggins, the Soledad brothers, and Cleveland Sellers.

Questions:

1. What was the significance of a slaveholder's having 3/5 constituency for every slave he possessed?

2. To whom is this essay addressed? Is it objective or subjective? Explain. What is its tone?

3. Which of the following statements is the *opposite* of what Chrisman states?

    a. In the literal sense of the word, blacks are *out-laws.*

    b. All black offenders are by their actions politically correct.

    c. Black prisoners today are victims of the political, economic, and military rapacity of white America.

    d. Black men outside of prison are more likely to survive if they develop the techniques of organization and group discipline that their brothers in prison have learned.

4. Which of the following paragraphs most clearly states the main point of the essay: 16, 17, 18, 19? Explain your answer.

5. Is the hyperbole of paragraph 19 effective? Explain.

6. Persuasive writing like Chrisman's has effected changes in our attitudes and in our laws. Is the second sentence of paragraph 12 ("A black prisoner's crime may or may not have been a political action

against the state, but the state's action against him is always political.") still true? Argue the question.

7. How much are you persuaded by this essay? Discuss, taking note that controversy stimulates thinking.

Lillian Ross

Since 1948 Lillian Ross has been writing for *The New Yorker*, where her short stories, biographical profiles, and detailed reports have been delightful and provocative features. An objective observer, she has done some of her best writing in the "Talk of the Town" section of the magazine.

Among her published books are *Picture, Portrait of Hemingway, Reporting, Adlai Stevenson, Reporting Two,* and *Moments with Chaplin.*

"Halloween Party" is from *Takes: Stories from the Talk of the Town,* published in 1983. As you read it, note what careful use Ross makes of lists of observations. The style seems very objective, but her selection of detail gives us a brilliant example of deadpan humor.

HALLOWEEN PARTY

Lillian Ross

November 17, 1980

A letter has arrived from a woman we know:

1   My thirteen-year-old son gave a Halloween costume party for a bunch of boys and girls. I became his financier as he talked endlessly about his Count Dracula costume. Count Dracula seems to have been the most popular Halloween costume for the past ten years—a black satin Count Dracula cape ($18.95), Count Dracula fangs ($1.25), clown whiteface makeup ($2), and Zauders stage blood ($2). The menu for the party included fried chicken, spaghetti, Cokes, salad, and cupcakes with orange or chocolate icing (cost per guest: $7). The candy, for visiting trick-or-treaters as well as for the guests, was orange and black jelly beans, sugar pumpkins, Candy Corn, Tootsie Rolls, Raisinets, Almond Joys, Nestlé Crunch, Baby Ruths, Milky Ways, Heide Jujyfruits, Peanut Chews, and Cracker Jacks (total: $38.65). My son also had eight cookies, six inches in diameter and decorated with black cats ($1.25 each); eight little plastic pumpkins full of hard candies, each with a trembly plastic spider on top ($2.50 each); eight orange-colored balloons that blew up to resemble cats (eighty-five cents each); eight orange-colored lollipops with jack-o'-lantern faces

(seventy cents each); a large paper tablecloth showing a black witch standing over a black caldron with spiders popping out of the caldron ($2.25); matching napkins ($1.10); matching paper cups ($2); matching paper plates ($1.75); a "HAPPY HALLOWEEN" sign ($1.25); a dancing skeleton ($3.99); something called a Happy Spider ($4); a classic jack-o'-lantern, made of a real pumpkin ($4, plus labor). Total investment in props: $181.59. Total investment of labor in jack-o'-lantern, kitchen cleanup, and laundry: $35. Total investment in emotion and puzzlement: indeterminable.

2   I watch the guests arrive. The first one, A, comes as Darth Vader, of "Star Wars." B comes as Luke Skywalker, of "Star Wars." C comes as The Incredible Hulk. D comes as a tramp. E comes as a ghost. F comes as a ballerina. G comes, in one of her mother's old evening gowns, as Bette Midler. All are in an advanced stage of hysteria. A pulls at C's costume. G immediately starts throwing sugar pumpkins at E. They've given themselves an hour before they move the party out to ring doorbells and see what they get. They tear into the fried chicken, most of them eating three bites and wasting the rest. They sprinkle jelly beans on the chicken and on the spaghetti. They pick at the spaghetti, which is on the menu because my son said everybody likes spaghetti. They eat it one strand at a time, dropping a strand on the floor for each strand they consume. They gulp down the Cokes, another "must"—their appetite for the caffeine insatiable. And what are they talking about, these eighth graders who are eying each other fishily? They are talking about their *careers*. They are talking about getting into Exeter. They are talking about Yale and Yale Law School. They are talking about how to get in here and how to get in there. They are talking about who makes more money, the president of Chase Manhattan or the president of General Motors. Nobody is talking kid talk. Nobody is talking about the present time and what to do with it. Nobody is talking about learning. Nobody sounds *young*. A, a pudgy boy who tries to find out the marks of every other child in his class, wants to be "a successful corporation lawyer." He doesn't say just "corporation lawyer." It's

success that he's bent on. He informs my son that he intends to have more money than his uncle, who is a corporation lawyer in Philadelphia. Next, A tells my son that he wants to go to Exeter. Why? "Because Exeter is a stepping-stone to Harvard," he says. Not Exeter for the wonders of Exeter but Exeter because it will be useful *after* he leaves it.

3   B, with his mouth full of Almond Joy, is asking the others a question: "Do you want to be a little fish in a big pond or a big fish in a little pond?"

4   What has that got to do with getting an education? How about the excitement of learning algebra? How about that wonderful grammar teacher who showed you how to recognize the participle absolute? Why aren't you talking about your French teacher's getting you to speak French with an accent that would wow them in Paris? I want to butt in with my questions, but I keep my mouth shut.

5   Now A is talking. His mother, he is saying, has taken him rock climbing, because rock climbing is an impressive activity to put down as his "interest" on the application to Exeter.

6   "But you *hate* rock climbing!" says D, who is a mischief-maker with the face of an angel under his tramp makeup. "You hate to move your *ass*," D adds.

7   All right, who else is here? C, who is wearing a mask of The Incredible Hulk. C is the jock of the group. He has been in training since the age of two in the craft of giving nothing away. He's wary and tight and already immunized to the teeth against charity for its own sake. He, too, wants to be a corporation lawyer; so do B and D. The girls, though—the ballerina and Bette Midler—both want to be big-corporation presidents. They are both relaxed, being well aware of what women's lib has done for them. E, the ghost, is the only one with a simple costume, made of a sheet. A, talking to B, points out that E doesn't have to bother about a costume, because he's rich, very rich. His grandfather lives in Texas and owns real oil wells—not new ones but very old and very productive oil wells. E wants to be a movie director and has promised to give my son, who at the moment wants to be an actor, a starring

part in his first movie. They are pals. Both of them are regarded with suspicion by the ones who want to be corporation lawyers.

8   What else are they saying? They're still talking about Exeter. Apparently, A is obsessed by Exeter—it is he who keeps bringing the conversation back to it.

9   "They ask you to write a "personal letter' to them," this little busybody says. "They say, 'This letter should represent you as accurately as possible.' But then they tell you in the catalogue what they want, so all you have to do is tell it back to them."

10   C finally talks. "The way *you* always figure out what the teacher wants and give it right back to *him*," he says.

11   D squirts a little Coke at A, and the future lawyers get up and make for the door. They cram their loot bags with the orange and black jelly beans, the Candy Corn, the cookies, the trembly spiders, the balloons, the jack-o'-lantern lollipops, and the rest. They make a big point of thanking me loudly. The girls amble out, smiling knowledgeably at each other. E and my son run to catch up to them. They, too, thank me extravagantly. And they all go off, in their disguises, to do their tricks and get their treats. I am left wondering what it's all about.

Study Guide:

In rereading this essay, you should ignore the opening sentence. It is merely a device to get around *The New Yorker*'s "Talk of the Town" mannerism of using *we* instead of *I* (see "Twins"). Words to be looked up and added to the vocabulary list: *indeterminable, insatiable, extravagantly.*

Questions:

1. Is this essay a satire? If so, what are the clues and what is it satirizing?

2. What is the purpose of the four parallel sentences in paragraph 2, each beginning with the word *Nobody*? What purpose is served by paragraph 4?

3. In several places Lillian Ross slips in some judgmental words that reveal a subjective point of view. What and where are they?

4. In the final paragraph, Lillian Ross makes an extraordinarily effective point by bringing us around to the details that are special to a Halloween party, the details that she listed so carefully in paragraph 1. How do the opening and closing paragraphs encapsule the essential, humorous incongruity in the essay? What is that point that is made through this incongruity?

Composition Topics:

1. Can you write a satire on your school's college counseling procedures?

2. Lists can be very effective in telling us about people and activities. Write a composition in which you reveal something about a person's character or intentions by listing the items that he or she packs for a trip.

Alice Walker

Born a daughter of sharecroppers in Eatonton, Georgia, in 1944, Alice Walker early displayed the determination and artistic sensitivity that have made her an outstanding poet, essayist, and novelist. As the civil rights movement was gathering momentum, she entered Spelman College, in Atlanta, Georgia, where she became a civil rights activist. Then she transferred to Sarah Lawrence, in Bronxville, New York, and remained there to earn her B.A. degree in 1965.

Her restless search for a literary voice to explore relations among African-Americans led swiftly to the publication of *Once: Poems* and in 1970 her first novel, *The Third Life of Grange Copeland.* In these literary explorations of African-American relations, she discovered forces that tend to destroy the individual and the family.

Within the artistic control of her prose and poetry one senses the passion of a writer who would stir the reader to active response to these forces rather than to passive observation. Alice Walker might be called a feminist, but by her own definition she is a "womanist." "A womanist," she writes, "is to feminist as purple to lavender."

Revolutionary Petunias and Other Poems, Meridian, and *The Color Purple* are among her later and most powerfully liberating works. They speak not only to women and minorities but to all of us. In addition to writing, Alice Walker has had appointments as a teacher of writing and of African-American literature in several colleges.

In 1974 Alice Walker published a collection of personal essays, *In Search of Our Mothers' Gardens.* The last essay in it is the one we have chosen, "Beauty: When the Other Dancer Is the Self."

BEAUTY: WHEN THE OTHER DANCER IS THE SELF

Alice Walker

1983

1   It is a bright summer day in 1947. My father, a fat, funny man with beautiful eyes and a subversive wit, is trying to decide which of his eight children he will take with him to the county fair. My mother, of course, will not go. She is knocked out from getting most of us ready: I hold my neck stiff against the pressure of her knuckles as she

hastily completes the braiding and then beribboning of my hair.

2   My father is the driver for the rich old white lady up the road. Her name is Miss Mey. She owns all the land for miles around, as well as the house in which we live. All I remember about her is that she once offered to pay my mother thirty-five cents for cleaning her house, raking up piles of her magnolia leaves, and washing her family's clothes, and that my mother—she of no money, eight children, and a chronic earache—refused it. But I do not think of this in 1947. I am two and a half years old. I want to go everywhere my daddy goes. I am excited at the prospect of riding in a car. Someone has told me fairs are fun. That there is room in the car for only three of us doesn't faze me at all. Whirling happily in my starchy frock, showing off my biscuit-polished patent-leather shoes and lavender socks, tossing my head in a way that makes my ribbons bounce, I stand, hands on hips, before my father. "Take me, Daddy," I say with assurance; "I'm the prettiest!"

3   Later, it does not surprise me to find myself in Miss Mey's shiny black car, sharing the back seat with the other lucky ones. Does not surprise me that I thoroughly enjoy the fair. At home that night I tell the unlucky ones all I can remember about the merry-go-round, the man who eats live chickens, and the teddy bears, until they say: that's enough, baby Alice. Shut up now, and go to sleep.

4   It is Easter Sunday, 1950. I am dressed in a green, flocked, scalloped-hem dress (handmade by my adoring sister, Ruth) that has its own smooth satin petticoat and tiny hot-pink roses tucked into each scallop. My shoes, new T-strap patent leather, again highly biscuit-polished. I am six years old and have learned one of the longest Easter speeches to be heard that day, totally unlike the speech I said when I was two: "Easter lilies / pure and white / blossom in / the morning light." When I rise to give my speech I do so on a great wave of love and pride and expectation. People in the church stop rustling their new crinolines. They seem to hold their breath. I can tell they

admire my dress, but it is my spirit, bordering on sassiness (womanishness), they secretly applaud:

5   "That girl's a little *mess*," they whisper to each other, pleased.

6   Naturally I say my speech without stammer or pause, unlike those who stutter, stammer, or, worst of all, forget. This is before the world "beautiful" exists in people's vocabulary, but "Oh, isn't she the *cutest* thing!" frequently floats my way. "And got so much sense!" they gratefully add . . . for which thoughtful addition I thank them to this day.

7   *It was great fun being cute. But then, one day, it ended.*

8   I am eight years old and a tomboy. I have a cowboy hat, cowboy boots, checkered shirt and pants, all red. My playmates are my brothers, two and four years older than I. Their colors are black and green, the only difference in the way we are dressed. On Saturday nights we all go to the picture show, even my mother; Westerns are her favorite kind of movie. Back home, "on the ranch," we pretend we are Tom Mix, Hopalong Cassidy, Lash LaRue (we've even named one of our dogs Lash LaRue); we chase each other for hours rustling cattle, being outlaws, delivering damsels from distress. Then my parents decide to buy my brothers guns. These are not "real" guns. They shoot "BBs," copper pellets my brothers say will kill birds. Because I am a girl, I do not get a gun. Instantly I am relegated to the position of Indian. Now there appears a great distance between us. They shoot and shoot at everything with their new guns. I try to keep up with my bow and arrows.

9   One day while I am standing on top of our makeshift "garage"—pieces of tin nailed across some poles—holding my bow and arrow and looking out toward the fields, I feel an incredible blow in my right eye. I look down just in time to see my brother lower his gun.

10   Both brothers rush to my side. My eye stings, and I cover it with my hand. "If you tell," they say, "we will get a whipping. You don't want that to happen, do you?" I do not. "Here is a piece of wire," says the older brother, picking it

up from the roof; "say you stepped on one end of it and the other flew up and hit you." The pain is beginning to start. "Yes," I say. "Yes, I will say that is what happened." If I do not say this is what happened, I know my brothers will find ways to make me wish I had. But now I will say anything that gets me to my mother.

11   Confronted by our parents we stick to the lie agreed upon. They place me on a bench on the porch and I close my left eye while they examine the right. There is a tree growing from underneath the porch that climbs past the railing to the roof. It is the last thing my right eyes sees. I watch as its trunk, its branches, and then its leaves are blotted out by the rising blood.

12   I am in shock. First there is intense fever, which my father tries to break using lily leaves bound around my head. Then there are chills: my mother tries to get me to eat soup. Eventually, I do not know how, my parents learn what has happened. A week after the "accident" they take me to see a doctor. "Why did you wait so long to come?" he asks, looking into my eye and shaking his head. "Eyes are sympathetic," he says. "If one is blind, the other will likely become blind too."

13   This comment of the doctor's terrifies me. But it is really how I look that bothers me most. Where the BB pellet struck there is a glob of whitish scar tissue, a hideous cataract, on my eye. Now when I stare at people—a favorite pastime, up to now—they will stare back. Not at the "cute" little girl, but at her scar. For six years I do not stare at anyone, because I do not raise my head.

14   Years later, in the throes of a mid-life crisis, I ask my mother and sister whether I changed after the "accident." "No," they say, puzzled. "What do you mean?"

15   *What do I mean?*

16   I am eight, and, for the first time, doing poorly in school, where I have been something of a whiz since I was four. We have just moved to the place where the "accident" occurred. We do not know any of the people around us because this is a different county. The only time I see the friends I knew is when we go back to our old church. The

new school is the former state penitentiary. It is a large stone building, cold and drafty, crammed to overflowing with boisterous, ill-disciplined children. On the third floor there is a huge circular imprint of some partition that has been torn out.

17   "What used to be here?" I ask a sullen girl next to me on our way past it to lunch.

18   "The electric chair," says she.

19   At night I have nightmares about the electric chair, and about all the people reputedly "fried" in it. I am afraid of the school, where all the students seem to be budding criminals.

20   "What's the matter with your eye?" they ask, critically.

21   When I don't answer (I cannot decide whether it was an "accident" or not), they shove me, insist on a fight.

22   My brother, the one who created the story about the wire, comes to my rescue. But then brags so much about "protecting" me, I become sick.

23   After months of torture at the school, my parents decide to send me back to our old community, to my old school. I live with my grandparents and the teacher they board. But there is no room for Phoebe, my cat. By the time my grandparents decide there *is* room, and I ask for my cat, she cannot be found. Miss Yarborough, the boarding teacher, takes me under her wing, and begins to teach me to play the piano. But soon she marries an African—a "prince," she says—and is whisked away to his continent.

24   At my old school there is at least one teacher who loves me. She is the teacher who "knew me before I was born" and bought my first baby clothes. It is she who makes life bearable. It is her presence that finally helps me turn on the one child at the school who continually calls me "one-eyed bitch." One day I simply grab him by his coat and beat him until I am satisfied. It is my teacher who tells me my mother is ill.

25   My mother is lying in bed in the middle of the day, something I have never seen. She is in too much pain to speak. She has an abscess in her ear. I stand looking down on her, knowing that if she dies, I cannot live. She is being

treated with warm oils and hot bricks held against her cheek. Finally a doctor comes. But I must go back to my grandparents' house. The weeks pass but I am hardly aware of it. All I know is that my mother might die, my father is not so jolly, my brothers still have their guns, and I am the one sent away from home.

26   "You did not change," they say.

27   *Did I imagine the anguish of never looking up?*

28   I am twelve. When relatives come to visit I hide in my room. My cousin Brenda, just my age, whose father works in the post office and whose mother is a nurse, comes to find me. "Hello," she says. And then she asks, looking at my recent school picture, which I did not want taken, and on which the "glob," as I think of it, is clearly visible, "You still can't see out of that eye?"

29   "No," I say, and flop back on the bed over my book.

30   That night, as I do almost every night, I abuse my eye. I rant and rave at it, in front of the mirror. I plead with it to clear up before morning. I tell it I hate and despise it. I do not pray for sight. I pray for beauty.

31   "You did not change," they say.

32   I am fourteen and baby-sitting for my brother Bill, who lives in Boston. He is my favorite brother and there is a strong bond between us. Understanding my feelings of shame and ugliness he and his wife take me to a local hospital, where the "glob" is removed by a doctor named O. Henry. There is still a small bluish crater where the scar tissue was, but the ugly white stuff is gone. Almost immediately I become a different person from the girl who does not raise her head. Or so I think. Now that I've raised my head I win the boyfriend of my dreams. Now that I've raised my head I have plenty of friends. Now that I've raised my head classwork comes from my lips as faultlessly as Easter speeches did, and I leave high school as valedictorian, most popular student, and *queen*, hardly believing my luck. Ironically, the girl who was voted most beautiful in our class (and was) was later shot twice through the chest

by a male companion, using a "real" gun, while she was pregnant. But that's another story in itself. Or is it?

33   "You did not change," they say.

34   It is now thirty years since the "accident." A beautiful journalist comes to visit and to interview me. She is going to write a cover story for her magazine that focuses on my latest book. "Decide how you want to look on the cover," she says. "Glamorous, or whatever."

35   Never mind "glamorous," it is the "whatever" that I hear. Suddenly all I can think of is whether I will get enough sleep the night before the photography session: if I don't, my eye will be tired and wander, as blind eyes will.

36   At night in bed with my lover I think up reasons why I should not appear on the cover of a magazine. "My meanest critics will say I've sold out," I say. "My family will now realize I write scandalous books."

37   "But what's the real reason you don't want to do this?" he asks.

38   "Because in all probability," I say in a rush, "my eye won't be straight."

39   "It will be straight enough," he says. Then, "Besides, I thought you'd made your peace with that."

40   And I suddenly remember that I have.

41   *I remember*:

42   I am talking to my brother Jimmy, asking if he remembers anything unusual about the day I was shot. He does not know I consider that day the last time my father, with his sweet home remedy of cool lily leaves, chose me, and that I suffered and raged inside because of this. "Well," he says, "all I remember is standing by the side of the highway with Daddy, trying to flag down a car. A white man stopped, but when Daddy said he needed somebody to take his little girl to the doctor, he drove off."

43   *I remember*:

44   I am in the desert for the first time. I fall totally in love with it. I am so overwhelmed by its beauty, I confront for the first time, consciously, the meaning of the doctor's words years ago: "Eyes are sympathetic. If one is blind, the

other will likely become blind too." I realize I have dashed
about the world madly, looking at this, looking at that,
storing up images against the fading of the light. *But I
might have missed seeing the desert!* The shock of that
possibility—and gratitude for over twenty-five years of
sight—sends me literally to my knees. Poem after poem
comes—which is perhaps how poets pray.

ON SIGHT

I am so thankful I have seen
The Desert
And the creatures in the desert
And the desert Itself.

The desert has its own moon
Which I have seen
With my own eye.
There is no flag on it.

Trees of the desert have arms
All of which are always up
That is because the moon is up
The sun is up
Also the sky
The stars
Clouds
None with flags.

If there *were* flags, I doubt
the trees would point.
Would you?

45   *But mostly, I remember this:*
46   I am twenty-seven, and my baby daughter is almost
three. Since her birth I have worried about her discovery
that her mother's eyes are different from other people's.
Will she be embarrassed? I think. What will she say?
Every day she watches a television program called "Big
Blue Marble." It begins with a picture of the earth as it
appears from the moon. It is bluish, a little battered-
looking, but full of light, with whitish clouds swirling

around it. Every time I see it I weep with love, as if it is a picture of Grandma's house. One day when I am putting Rebecca down for her nap, she suddenly focuses on my eye. Something inside me cringes, gets ready to try to protect myself. All children are cruel about physical differences, I know from experience, and that they don't always mean to be is another matter. I assume Rebecca will be the same.

47   But no-o-o-o. She studies my face intently as we stand, her inside and me outside her crib. She even holds my face maternally between her dimpled little hands. Then, looking every bit as serious and lawyerlike as her father, she says, as if it may just possibly have slipped my attention: "Mommy, there's a *world* in your eye." (As in, "Don't be alarmed, or do anything crazy.") And then, gently, but with great interest: "Mommy, where did you *get* that world in your eye?"

48   For the most part, the pain left then. (So what, if my brothers grew up to buy even more powerful pellet guns for their sons and to carry real guns themselves. So what, if a young "Morehouse man" once nearly fell off the steps of Trevor Arnett Library because he thought my eyes were blue.) Crying and laughing I ran to the bathroom, while Rebecca mumbled and sang herself off to sleep. Yes indeed, I realized, looking into the mirror. There *was* a world in my eye. And I saw that it was possible to love it: that in fact, for all it had taught me of shame and anger and inner vision, I *did* love it. Even to see it drifting out of orbit in boredom, or rolling up out of fatigue, not to mention float-ing back at attention in excitement (bearing witness, a friend has called it), deeply suitable to my personality, and even characteristic of me.

49   That night I dream I am dancing to Stevie Wonder's song "Always" (the name of the song is really "As," but I hear it as "Always"). As I dance, whirling and joyous, hap-pier than I've ever been in my life, another bright faced dancer joins me. We dance and kiss each other and hold each other through the night. The other dancer has obvi-ously come through all right, as I have done. She is beauti-ful, whole and free. And she is also me.

Study Guide:

1. This complex essay is deceptively simple in its word choice. For the several rereadings involved in studying it, be sure to know the meanings, in context, of the following words, and add them to your vocabulary list: *subversive, crinoline, to be relegated, cataract, throes, boisterous.*

2. Recognize the allusions to Tom Mix, Hopalong Cassidy, Lash La-Rue, Morehouse College, and Stevie Wonder. And notice in the poem "On Sight" the reference to a "flag" on the moon. This is an allusion to the United States flag planted on the moon in 1969 by the first astronauts to land there. In paragraphs 2 and 4, Alice Walker refers to "biscuit-polished" patent leather shoes. What could she mean by this?

Questions:

1. Look at the structure of this essay.

   a. It is narrated in the present tense, which is unusual and difficult to sustain. Why is the present tense more effective here than the past tense? Where does the tense change? Why?

   b. It is told in a series of **vignettes,** with a space separating each vignette from the others. A vignette is a short literary sketch or scene. What pattern do you see in the beginnings of these vignettes?

   c. These vignettes are organized by theme into four, possibly five, groups. The first group ends after paragraph 6. What is the theme of the first group? The next theme, indeed the major theme of the rest of the essay, is introduced by an isolated, single-line, italicized paragraph. What is that major theme, and why is the first group of vignettes (paragraphs 1–6) important to it?

   d. Within the major theme are stages of development, paragraphs 8–13 providing the basis. The vignettes grouped within paragraphs 14–33 present one stage of development. What is the theme of that stage?

   e. The vignettes following paragraph 33 present at least two more stages of development. What are the themes of those stages?

2. Now take a closer look at the structure.

   a. Paragraphs 13–33 have overlapping themes. One begins with

the final sentence of paragraph 13. Where does that theme
end? The other begins with paragraphs 14 and 15. Where
does it end? Do you see how Alice Walker uses **refrain** to
highlight these themes?

b. Refrain is not the only repetition Walker uses to enrich her
themes. She also repeats bits of dialogue and fragments of
episodes, **motifs,** that play like melodies repeated in different
keys. For instance, the substance of paragraph 12 is repeated
in paragraphs 42 and 44, but this time with the loving understanding of an adult whose emotional wounds are healing.
See also how the substance of paragraph 13 is repeated in
paragraph 44, and of paragraph 14 in paragraph 26. How, on
the other hand, is the substance of paragraph 44 the antithesis of paragraphs 12, 13, and 30? And how does the end of
paragraph 32 tie in with paragraphs 8–13?

c. How does the poem, following paragraph 44, tie in with paragraph 11? How does the "flag" alluded to in the poem tie in
with the eye injury?

3. Look at the images of cruelty and violence in paragraphs 16–22.
Is Alice Walker replacing them with symbols of compassion and peace
in paragraphs 46–48? Or is that reading too much into the essay?
Discuss.

4. Interpret the dream in the final paragraph of the essay.

Composition Topic:

Without getting into a betrayal of family confidences, write an essay in which you make peace with yourself and others after a painful
experience. Attempt it in the present tense.

James Thurber

James Grover Thurber (1894–1961) was born in Columbus, Ohio. At the age of 6, he lost his left eye when one of his brothers accidentally shot an arrow at him. Thirty-five years later a cataract developed in his right eye, and he gradually lost all vision. Despite the handicap, he became a humorist celebrated for his writings and his drawings.

He attended Ohio State University, and though he left before graduating, his talent for writing enabled him to get assignments with several newspapers, first in Columbus, then in Paris, and finally in New York. In 1927 E. B. White introduced Thurber to the staff of *The New Yorker.* He worked there only until 1933, but for the next two decades he continued to contribute essays, stories, and cartoons, and he also wrote extensively for the *Atlantic.*

James Thurber is noted for his creation of frustrated and embattled characters attempting to conduct their lives amid chaos. His most famous story, "The Secret Life of Walter Mitty," is a hilarious illustration that remains timeless. Other works that continue to delight readers and audiences are *The Thirteen Clocks* and *Thurber Country.*

In everything Thurber wrote he exhibits a genius for word play. "Do You Want to Make Something Out of It?" is a wonderful example of his portrayal of character and his fun with words.

DO YOU WANT TO MAKE SOMETHING OUT OF IT?

OR, IF YOU PUT AN "O" ON "UNDERSTO," YOU'LL RUIN MY "THUNDERSTORM"

James Thurber

1951

1   I'm probably not the oldest word-game player in the country, and I know I'm not the ablest, but my friends will all testify that I'm the doggedest. (We'll come back to the word "doggedest" later on.) I sometimes keep on playing the game, all by myself, after it is over and I have gone to bed. On a recent night, tossing and spelling, I spent two hours hunting for another word besides "phlox" that has

"hlo" in it. I finally found seven: "matchlock," "decathlon," "pentathlon," "hydrochloric," "chlorine," "chloroform," and "monthlong." There are more than a dozen others, beginning with "phlo," but I had to look them up in the dictionary the next morning, and that doesn't count.

2   By "the game," I mean Superghosts, as some of us call it, a difficult variation of the familiar parlor game known as Ghosts. In Ghosts, as everybody knows, one of a group of sedentary players starts with a letter, and the spelling proceeds clockwise around the group until a player spells a word of more than three letters, thus becoming "a third of a ghost," or two-thirds, or a whole ghost. The game goes on until everyone but the winner has been eliminated. Superghosts differs from the old game in one small, tricky, and often exacerbating respect: The rules allow a player to *prefix* a letter to the word in progress, thus increasing the flexibility of the indoor sport. If "busines" comes to a player, he does not have to add the final "s"; he can put an "n" in front, and the player who has to add the "e" to "unbusinesslik" becomes part of a ghost. In a recent game in my league, a devious gentleman boldly stuck an "n" in front of "sobsiste," stoutly maintaining the validity of "unsobsisterlike," but he was shouted down. There is a lot of shouting in the game, especially when it is played late at night.

3   Starting words in the middle and spelling them in both directions lifts the pallid pastime of Ghosts out of the realm of children's parties and ladies' sewing circles and makes it a game to test the mettle of the mature adult mind. As long ago as 1930, aficionados began to appear in New York parlors, and then the game waned, to be revived, in my circle, last year. The Superghost aficionado is a moody fellow, given to spelling to himself at table, not listening to his wife, and staring dully at his frightened children, wondering why he didn't detect, in yesterday's game, that "cklu" is the guts of "lacklustre," and priding himself on having stumped everybody with "nehe," the middle of "swineherd." In this last case, "bonehead" would have done, since we allow slang if it is in the dictionary, but "Stonehenge" is out, because we don't allow proper nouns. All

compound and hyphenated words are privileged, even "jack-o'-lantern" and "love-in-a-mist," but the speller must indicate where a hyphen occurs.

4   Many people, who don't like word games and just want to sit around and drink and talk, hate Superghosts and wish it were in hell with Knock, Knock, Who's There? The game is also tough on bad spellers, poor visualizers, mediocre concentrators, ladies and gentlemen of small vocabulary, and those who are, to use a word presently popular with the younger drinking set, clobbered. I remember the night a bad speller, female, put an "m" on "ale," thinking, as she later confessed, that "salamander" is spelled with two "e"s. The next player could have gone to "alemb"—the word "alembic" turns up a lot—but he made it "alema" and was promptly challenged. (You can challenge a player if you think he is bluffing.) What the challenged player had in mind was "stalemate." The man who had challenged him got sore, because he hadn't thought of "stalemate," and went home. More than one game has ended in hard feelings, but I have never seen players come to blows, or friendships actually broken.

5   I said we would get back to "doggedest," and here we are. This word, if it is a word, caused a lot of trouble during one game, when a lady found "ogged" in her lap, refused to be bogged, dogged, fogged, jogged, or logged, and added an "e." She was challenged and lost, since Webster's unabridged dictionary is accepted as the final judge and authority, and while it gives "doggedly" and "doggedness," it doesn't give "doggedest." She could also have got out of "ogged" with an "r" in front, for "frogged" is a good word, and also what might be called a lady's word, but she stuck doggedly to "doggedest." Then there was the evening a dangerous and exasperating player named Bert Mitchell challenged somebody's "dogger." The challenged man had "doggerel" in mind, of course, but Mitchell said, in his irritating voice, "You have spelled a word. 'Dogger' is a word," and he flipped through the unabridged dictionary, which he reads for pleasure and always has on his lap during a game. "Dogger" is indeed a word, and quite a word. Look it up yourself.

6   When I looked up "dogger" the other day, I decided to have a look at "dog," a word practically nobody ever looks up, because everybody is smugly confident that he knows what a dog is. Here, for your amazement, are some dogs other than the carnivorous mammal:

> The hammer in a gunlock. Any of various devices, usually of simple design, for holding, gripping, or fastening something; as: **a** Any of various devices consisting essentially of a spike, rod, or bar of metal, as of iron, with a ring, hook, claw, lug, or the like, at the end, used for gripping, clutching, or holding something, as by driving or embedding it in the object, hooking it to the object, etc. See RAFT DOG, TOE DOG. **b** Specif., either of the hooks or claws of a pair of sling dogs. See CRAMPON. **c** An iron for holding wood in a fireplace; a firedog; an andiron. **d** In a lathe, a clamp for gripping the piece of work and for communicating motion to it from the faceplate. A *clamp dog* consists of two parts drawn together by screws. A *bent-tail dog* has an **L**-shaped projection that enters a slot in the faceplate for communicating motion. A *straight-tail dog* has a projecting part that engages with a stud fastened to or forming part of the faceplate. A *safety dog* is one equipped with setscrews. **e** Any of the jaws in a lathe chuck. **f** A pair of nippers or forceps. **g** A wheeled gripping device for drawing the fillet from which coin blanks are stamped through the opening at the head of the drawbench. **h** Any of a set of adjusting screws for the bed tool of a punching machine. **i** A grapple for clutching and raising a pile-driver monkey or a well-boring tool. **j** A stop or detent; a click or ratchet. **k** A drag for the wheel of a vehicle. **l** A steel block attached to a locking bar or tappet of an interlocking machine, by which locking between bars is accomplished. **m** A short, heavy, sharp-pointed, steel hook with a ring at one end. **n** A steel toothlike projection on a log carriage or on the endless chain that conveys logs into the sawmill.

7   And now, unless you have had enough, we will get back to Superghosts, through the clanging and clatter of all those dogs. The game has a major handicap, or perhaps I should call it blockage. A player rarely gets the chance to

stick the others with a truly tough word, because someone
is pretty sure to simplify the word under construction.
Mitchell tells me that he always hopes he can get around
to "ug-ug" or "ach-ach" on his way to "plug-ugly" and
"stomach-ache." These words are hyphenated in my Webster's, for the old boy was a great hyphenator. (I like his
definition of "plug-ugly": "A kind of city rowdy, ruffian, or
disorderly tough;—a term said to have originated by a
gang of such in Baltimore.") In the case of "ug," the simplifiers usually go to "bug," trying to catch someone with
"buggies," or they add an "l" and the word ends in "ugliness." And "ach" often turns into "machinery," although it
could go in half a dozen directions. Since the simplifiers
dull the game by getting into easy words, the experts are
fond of a variant that goes like this: Mitchell, for example,
will call up a friend and say, "Get out of "ightf" twenty
ways." Well, I tossed in bed one night and got ten: "right-
ful," "frightful," "delightful," "nightfall," "lightfoot,"
"straightforward," "eightfold," "light-fingered," "tight-
fisted," and "tight-fitting." The next day, I thought of
"lightface," "right-footed," and "night-flowering," and came
to a stop. "Right fielder" is neither compounded nor hyphenated by Webster, and I began to wonder about Mitchell's twenty "ightf"s. I finally figured it out. The old devil
was familiar with the ten or more fish and fowl and miscel-
laneous things that begin with "nightf."

8   It must have been about 1932 that an old player I know
figured that nothing could be got out of "dke" except "handkerchief" and then, in a noisy game one night this year, he
passed that combination on to the player at his left. This
rascal immediately made it "dkee." He was challenged by
the lady on *his* left and triumphantly announced that his
word was "groundkeeper." It looked like an ingenious escape from "handkerchief," but old Webster let the fellow
down. Webster accepts only "groundman" and "grounds-
man," thus implying that there is no such word as "groundkeeper."

9   Mitchell threw "abc" at me one night, and I couldn't get
anything out of it and challenged him. "Dabchick," he said

patronizingly, and added blandly, "It is the little grebe." Needless to say, it *is* the little grebe.

10   I went through a hundred permutations in bed that night without getting anything else out of "abc" except a word I made up, which is "grabcheck," one who quickly picks up a tab, a big spender, a generous fellow. I have invented quite a few other words, too, which I modestly bring to the attention of modern lexicographers, if there are any. I think of dictionary-makers as being rigidly conventional gentlemen who are the first to put the new aside. They probably won't even read my list of what I shall call bedwords, but I am going to set it down anyway. A young matron in Bermuda last spring told me to see what I could do with "sgra," and what I did with it occupied a whole weekend. Outside of "disgrace" and its variants, all I could find were "cross-grained" and "misgraff," which means to misgraft (obsolete). I found this last word while looking, in vain, for "misgrade" in the dictionary. Maybe you can think of something else, and I wish you luck. Here, then, in no special order, are my bedwords based on "sgra."

11   **pussgrapple.** A bickering, or minor disturbance; an argument or dispute among effeminate men. Also, less frequently, a physical struggle between, or among, women.

    kissgranny. 1. A man who seeks the company of older women, especially older women with money; a designing fellow, a fortune hunter. 2. An overaffectionate old woman, a hugmoppet, a bunnytalker.

    glassgrabber. 1. A woman who disapproves of, or interferes with, her husband's drinking; a kill-joy, a shushlaugh, a douselight. 2. A man who asks for another drink at a friend's house, or goes out and gets one in the kitchen.

    blessgravy. A minister or cleric; the head of a family; one who says grace. Not to be confused with *praisegravy,* one who extols a woman's cooking, especially the cooking of a friend's wife; a gay fellow, a flirt, a seducer. *Colloq.,* a breakvow, a shrugholy.

    cussgravy. A husband who complains of his wife's cooking, more especially a husband who complains of his wife's cooking in the presence of guests; an ill-tempered fellow, a curmudgeon. Also, sometimes, a peptic-ulcer case.

    messgranter. An untidy housekeeper, a careless housewife. Said of a woman who admits, often proudly, that she has let herself go; a bragdowdy, a frumpess.

hissgrammar. An illiterate fellow, a user of slovenly rhetoric, a father who disapproves of book learning. Also, more rarely, one who lisps, a twisttongue.

chorusgrable. *Orig.* a young actress, overconfident of her ability and future; a snippet, a flappertigibbet. *Deriv.* Betty Grable, an American movie actress.

pressgrape. One who presses grapes, a grape presser. Less commonly, a crunchberry.

pressgrain. 1. A man who tries to make whiskey in his own cellar; hence, a secret drinker, a hidebottle, a sneakslug. 2. One who presses grain in a grain presser. *Arch.*

dressgrader. A woman who stares another woman up and down, a starefrock; hence, a rude female, a hobbledehoyden.

fussgrape. 1. One who diets or toys with his food, a light eater, a person without appetite, a scornmuffin, a shuncabbage. 2. A man, usually American, who boasts of his knowledge of wines, a smugbottle.

bassgrave. 1. Cold-eyed, unemotional, stolid, troutsolemn. 2. The grave of a bass. *Obs.*

lassgraphic. Of, or pertaining to, the vivid description of females; as, the guest was so lassgraphic his host asked him to change the subject or get out. Also said of fathers of daughters, more rarely of mothers.

blissgray. Aged by marriage. Also, sometimes, discouraged by wedlock, or by the institution of marriage.

glassgrail. A large nocturnal moth. Not to be confused with *smackwindow,* the common June bug, or bangsash.

hossgrace. Innate or native dignity, similar to that of the thoroughbred hoss. *Southern U.S.*

bussgranite. Literally, a stonekisser; a man who persists in trying to win the favor or attention of cold, indifferent, or capricious women. Not to be confused with *snatchkiss,* a kitchen lover.

tossgravel. 1. A male human being who tosses gravel, usually at night, at the window of a female human being's bedroom, usually that of a young virgin; hence, a lover, a male sweetheart, and an eloper. 2. One who is suspected by the father of a daughter of planning an elopement with her, a grablass.

12   If you should ever get into a game of Superghosts with Mitchell, by the way, don't pass "bugl" on to him, hoping to

send him into "bugling." He will simply add an "o," making the group "buglo," which is five-sevenths of "bugloss." The word means "hawkweed," and you can see what Mitchell would do if you handed him "awkw," expecting to make him continue the spelling of "awkward." Tough guy, Mitchell. Tough game, Superghosts. You take it from here. I'm tired.

Study Guide:

A master of Superghosts wouldn't want a word missed, so be sure to know the meanings *and spellings* of these words and any others that might be unfamiliar: *phlox, sedentary, exacerbating, devious, validity, pallid, mettle, aficionado, to wane, privileged* (note the context), *mediocre, alembic, unabridged, ingenious, patronizingly, dabchick, blandly, grebe, permutations, tab, lexicographer, conventional, moppet, to extol, curmudgeon, dowdy, frump, slovenly, rhetoric, snippet, flapper, flibbertigibbet, hobbledehoy, hoyden, stolid, graphic, wedlock, innate, indifferent, capricious,* and *dogger* and *doggerel.*

Questions:

1. A **cliché** is a phrase—striking and clever the first time it was used—that has become worn out with overuse. On what cliché does Thurber put a new spin with "tossing and spelling" (paragraph 1)?

2. Why "pallid" Ghosts (paragraph 3), and why "pallid pastime"? Why "clatter and clang of all those dogs" (paragraph 7)?

3. James Thurber is famous for his comic touch. Comedy, however, may come in many forms—slapstick, deadpan, parody, satire, irony, hyperbole, or understatement, to name a few. Analyze Thurber's use of tone and choice of words carefully. What are the precise ingredients in his style that make his humor effective? Do you see incongruity in each of these? Discuss specific examples.

4. One quality essential to a writer of good essays must be a love of words for their own sake. What clues can you find in this essay that reflect Thurber's basic seriousness toward the study of words? Does he think, for instance, that the game "Superghosts" has any practical value for the educated individual? What kind of people does he think would not enjoy "Superghosts," and why?

5. Examine Thurber's list of "sgra" words carefully, and then examine any page of your dictionary with equal care. What similarities in

the style of the definitions can you see? What technique of humor is Thurber employing here (see the list in Question 3)?

6. Discuss the characterization of Bert Mitchell and explain the importance of his role in the essay. How does Thurber feel about him, and why?

7. Discuss the similarities and differences between the tone of Thurber here and that of Benchley in "What Are Little Boys Made Of?"

8. What devices does Thurber use to achieve continuity?

9. What evidence can you amass from this essay that language is constantly changing and developing rather than standing still? In line with this question, imagine the vocabulary problem you might have if you had left the earth in the 1940s and returned to find yourself on Cape Canaveral today.

Classroom Activity:

Devote a classroom period to playing Superghosts, and see what you can learn about words. Be sure to have a first-rate dictionary in the classroom.

Christopher Lehmann-Haupt

Born in Edinburgh, Scotland in 1934, Christopher Lehmann-Haupt received most of his education in the United States. He is a graduate of Swarthmore College and holds a Master of Fine Arts degree from Yale University. At first he had wanted to be an actor and a playwright, but a love of books, which his parents had inspired, soon led to the career that established his renown as an outstanding and fair-minded reviewer of new books.

Hired by the *New York Times Book Review*, he wrote such perceptive criticisms that he was asked to take a more demanding position with the daily paper. He remained and is now senior book reviewer for the *New York Times*. The pressure of reading and deciding whether or not to review any of the dozens of books that come to him each week would seem to be enormous, especially since Lehmann-Haupt considers himself a slow reader, but he also spares time to serve educational communities. He is an instructor for the Orange County secondary school system and community college, and he is a lecturer at colleges and universities here and abroad.

"The Unfunnier Side of Thurber" is an excellent illustration of the sensitivity for which Christopher Lehmann-Haupt is admired by writers and readers. It is book reviewing at its best, beginning with an unusual premise in order to get to the book's treatment of the complex and unhappy man who wrote some of the funniest prose in the English language.

THE UNFUNNIER SIDE OF THURBER

Christopher Lehmann-Haupt

April 3, 1975

Thurber: A Biography. By Burton Bernstein, 532 pages. Illustrated. Dodd, Mead. $15.

1   In a brief foreword to his *Thurber: A Biography, The New Yorker* staff writer Burton Bernstein makes a point that echoes throughout his book and lingers long after one has finished reading it. "When I finished my final draft of the biography," he writes by way of explaining the role that Thurber's widow, Helen, played in the project, "I presented her with a copy for her emendations and comments, in

conformity with our agreement. Her emendations were comparatively few but her comments were numerous. The gist of her complaints was that I had treated her husband's life in too negative a fashion. I am sorry she felt that way. What I did was simply take the facts as they were revealed to me from letters, personal papers, published matter, interviews, and, with a minimum of preconception and using Thurber's own words as much as possible, set them down. In biography—a more profound form of journalism—patent truth can have no surrogate." What this reader wondered was: How could Mrs. Thurber—clearly a woman of integrity, to judge from the portrait of her that emerges from these same pages—possibly have thought otherwise? What could she have had in mind when she complained of Mr. Bernstein's "negativity"? After all, the unhappy aspects of her husband's life seem plain for anyone to see in this the most comprehensive and three-dimensional portrait of Thurber yet to be rendered. How his childhood was disrupted not only by the famous bow-and-arrow accident that cost him one eye (and doomed the other) at the age of six, but also—and more subtly—by family tensions that led to his virtually boarding with a favorite aunt from the age of 10 to 15.

2   How his career at Ohio State University got off to such an unhappy start—what with his failure to make a fraternity, his problems with military drill, and his general loneliness and anonymity—that first he "dropped out" for a year simply by wandering off to the movies or the local library, and then he became such a "regular guy" that his behavior strikes us as embarrassing. (Watching the mature Thurber grow out of the Joe College of the O.S.U. days has always struck me as surreal on the order of a praying mantis being hatched out of a Good and Plenty.)

3   And how he suffered in the years when his health declined: from 1941, when five unsuccessful operations on his remaining eye helped to drive him to nervous collapse, until 1961, when he died after numerous undetected strokes. The irascibility, the self-centeredness, and the paranoia; the drinking, the loss of his comic touch, and the abuse of all who were close to him, especially his wife; and the final

slide into logomania, incontinence, and Lear-like rage: how would it be possible to put all this in a less negative light?

4   And even if one could, how is any biographer to omit or gloss over this extraordinary report from Mark Van Doren: "The afternoon [following the day in 1941 Mr. Van Doren was first introduced to Thurber], we met and I led him to some chairs on the lawn of the house I was staying at. We talked some more about things, and then suddenly he began to cry. To see tears coming from those dead eyes was one of the most touching moments of my life. He was crying, he said, because he had always made fun of people and never praised them as I did. He asked me if I thought that blindness was a punishment for the writing he had done— being trivial and destructive and showing the weaknesses of others, instead of their goodness and strength. That made me uncomfortable, but I knew he was going through an emotional upheaval. Here was a man I admired as a wholly original writer and humorist—a truly unique person—and he was in despair because of his work." Would it have sharpened our perspective of Thurber to have left out this "negative" vignette?

5   Perhaps what Mrs. Thurber had in mind is that all this unhappy news doesn't square with our image of Thurber as a humorist—that he ought to be viewed from the perspective of his writing, which was so far from madness and rage. But the trouble with this approach is that it has already been done—in Charles S. Holmes's *The Clocks of Columbus,* a study that makes the most of the zany side of Thurber's career, but only hints at its darker recesses. And besides, we are always being told that the best humor springs from the most extreme suffering; this is practically a literary cliché. Why not see it illustrated in Thurber's case?

6   So Burton Bernstein has given us the bad news. He has given us some good news too—the news of Thurber's eccentric Ohio forebears, of Harold Ross and the early days at *The New Yorker* and E. B. White and his stylistic influence on Thurber, of the literary companions and the books and the women in Thurber's life. But essentially this is the story of a man who grew up miserable, turned misery into

glorious humor, and then fell back into misery once more. And frankly, I am glad Mr. Bernstein chose to do it that way, and that Mrs. Thurber allowed him to do so despite her complaints. It makes you understand Thurber better, and it makes you appreciate his writing more.

Study Guide:

Add the following words and their meanings in context to your vocabulary list, so that your rereading of the essay will be a richer experience: *emendations, preconception, integrity, comprehensive, to render, virtually, surreal, praying mantis, irascibility, paranoia, logomania, incontinence, to gloss over, unique, eccentric, patent, surrogate.*

Questions:

1. Before getting into the more serious implications of this essay, look at the one striking simile used by Lehmann-Haupt. What does he mean by "Watching the mature Thurber grow out of the Joe College of the O.S.U. days has always struck me as surreal on the order of a praying mantis being hatched out of a Good and Plenty"?

2. A cliché has become a cliché because of its apparent truth as well as its phraseology. Draw upon your own experience (either your own or someone else's whom you know) to write an essay in which you show how suffering was turned by the sufferer into humor.

3. Do you agree or disagree with Christopher Lehmann-Haupt that pulling aside a curtain to reveal a personal tragedy "makes you understand Thurber better, and it makes you appreciate his writing better"? Explain.

4. Discuss the " 'negative' vignette" of Van Doren's visit. How do *you* react to it? Are we better off not knowing such unhappiness about people and life?

5. Reread "Do You Want to Make Something Out of It?" and see what new insights you get from it. Discuss.

6. "Lear-like rage" is an allusion. Investigate and explain its meaning. What dimension does it add to your appreciation of Thurber's character?

7. Organizing a book review effectively is often difficult. Around what central theme does Lehmann-Haupt organize this review? Do you

think it is an effective device for giving the reader an idea of the book and of Lehmann-Haupt's opinion of it? Explain.

Composition Topic:

Think about a book with which you are very familiar and about which you have strong opinions. Then write a review of it, organizing your essay on some central theme that you want to develop.

Joan Didion

Born in the Sacramento Valley of California in 1934, Joan Didion showed her early interest in writing when at age 13 she copied pages of classical literature to see how sentences were put together. In 1956, after earning her B.A degree from the University of California, Berkeley, she entered a writing contest sponsored by *Vogue* and won not only the contest but also a job with *Vogue*.

While working for *Vogue* as associate feature editor, Joan Didion wrote her first novel, *Run River,* which vividly describes the Sacramento Valley. In 1964 she married writer John Gregory Dunne, and both moved to Sacramento as free-lance writers. Essays that Didion wrote for *Vogue,* the *New York Times Magazine,* and the *Saturday Evening Post* during the next 14 years have been published in two collections: *Slouching Towards Bethlehem,* the title taken from William Butler Yeats's poem "The Second Coming," and *The White Album,* after the famous Beatles album.

Two other novels by Didion are *Play It as It Lays* and *A Book of Common Prayer.* She and her husband have also collaborated on screenplays, including *Play It as It Lays.* Her more recent works are *Democracy,* a story written against the backdrop of Vietnam; *Salvador,* a political essay chronicling a trip she took to El Salvador with her husband; and *Miami*, observations on the social and political impact of Cuban exiles on life in Miami.

Joan Didion's writing has been characterized as opinionated yet skeptical, precise yet prophetic. Certainly she has been influenced by Yeats's description of society: "Things fall apart; the centre cannot hold." See if "Rock of Ages" has some of these characteristics.

ROCK OF AGES

Joan Didion

1967

1   Alcatraz Island is covered with flowers now: orange and yellow nasturtiums, geraniums, sweet grass, blue iris, black-eyed Susans. Candytuft springs up through the cracked concrete in the exercise yard. Ice plant carpets the rusting catwalks. "WARNING! KEEP OFF! U.S. PROPERTY," the sign still reads, big and yellow and visible for perhaps a

188

quarter of a mile, but since March 21, 1963, the day they took the last thirty or so men off the island and sent them to prisons less expensive to maintain, the warning has been only *pro forma*, the gun turrets empty, the cell blocks abandoned. It is not an unpleasant place to be, out there on Alcatraz with only the flowers and the wind and a bell buoy moaning and the tide surging through the Golden Gate, but to like a place like that you have to want a moat.

2   I sometimes do, which is what I am talking about here. Three people live on Alcatraz Island now. John and Marie Hart live in the same apartment they had for the sixteen years that he was a prison guard; they raised five children on the island, back when their neighbors were the Birdman and Mickey Cohen, but the Birdman and Mickey Cohen are gone now and so are the Harts' children, moved away, the last married in a ceremony on the island in June 1966. One other person lives on Alcatraz, a retired merchant seaman named Bill Doherty, and, between them, John Hart and Bill Doherty are responsible to the General Services Administration for maintaining a twenty-four-hour watch over the twenty-two-acre island. John Hart has a dog named Duffy, and Bill Doherty has a dog named Duke, and although the dogs are primarily good company they are also the first line of defense on Alcatraz Island. Marie Hart has a corner window which looks out to the San Francisco skyline, across a mile and a half of bay, and she sits there and paints "views" or plays her organ, songs like "Old Black Joe" and "Please Go 'Way and Let Me Sleep." Once a week the Harts take their boat to San Francisco to pick up their mail and shop at the big Safeway in the Marina, and occasionally Marie Hart gets off the island to visit her children. She likes to keep in touch with them by telephone, but for ten months recently, after a Japanese freighter cut the cable, there was no telephone service to or from Alcatraz. Every morning the KGO traffic reporter drops the San Francisco *Chronicle* from his helicopter, and when he has time he stops for coffee. No one else comes out there except a man from the General Services Administration named Thomas Scott, who brings out an occasional congressman or somebody who wants to buy the island or,

once in a while, his wife and small son, for a picnic. Quite a few people would like to buy the island, and Mr. Scott reckons that it would bring about five million dollars in a sealed-bid auction, but the General Services Administration is powerless to sell it until Congress acts on a standing proposal to turn the island into a "peace park." Mr. Scott says that he will be glad to get Alcatraz off his hands, but the charge of a fortress island could not be something a man gives up without ambivalent thoughts.

3   I went out there with him a while ago. Any child could imagine a prison more like a prison than Alcatraz looks, for what bars and wires there are seem perfunctory, beside the point; the island itself was the prison, and the cold tide its wall. It is precisely what they called it: the Rock. Bill Doherty and Duke lowered the dock for us, and in the station wagon on the way up the cliff Bill Doherty told Mr. Scott about small repairs he had made or planned to make. Whatever repairs get made on Alcatraz are made to pass the time, a kind of caretaker's scrimshaw, because the government pays for no upkeep at all on the prison; in 1963 it would have cost five million dollars to repair, which is why it was abandoned, and the $24,000 a year that it costs to maintain Alcatraz now is mostly for surveillance, partly to barge in the 400,000 gallons of water that Bill Doherty and the Harts use every year (there is no water at all on Alcatraz, one impediment to development), and the rest to heat two apartments and keep some lights burning. The buildings seem quite literally abandoned. The key locks have been ripped from the cell doors and the big electrical locking mechanisms disconnected. The tear-gas vents in the cafeteria are empty and the paint is buckling everywhere, corroded by the sea air, peeling off in great scales of pale green and ocher. I stood for a while in Al Capone's cell, five by nine feet, number 200 on the second tier of B Block, not one of the view cells, which were awarded on seniority, and I walked through the solitary block, totally black when the doors were closed. "Snail Mitchel," read a pencil scrawl on the wall of Solitary 14. "The only man that ever got shot for walking too slow." Beside it was a calendar, the months

penciled on the wall with the days scratched off, May, June, July, August of some unnumbered year.

4   Mr. Scott, whose interest in penology dates from the day his office acquired Alcatraz as a potential property, talked about escapes and security routines and pointed out the beach where Ma Barker's son Doc was killed trying to escape. (They told him to come back up, and he said he would rather be shot, and he was.) I saw the shower room with the soap still in the dishes. I picked up a yellowed program from an Easter service *(Why seek ye the living among the dead? He is not here, but is risen)* and I struck a few notes on an upright piano with the ivory all rotted from the keys and I tried to imagine the prison as it had been, with the big lights playing over the windows all night long and the guards patrolling the gun galleries and the silverware clattering into a bag as it was checked in after meals, tried dutifully to summon up some distaste, some night terror of the doors locking and the boat pulling away. But the fact of it was that I liked it out there, a ruin devoid of human vanities, clean of human illusions, an empty place reclaimed by the weather where a woman plays an organ to stop the wind's whining and an old man plays ball with a dog named Duke. I could tell you that I came back because I had promises to keep, but maybe it was because nobody asked me to stay.

Study Guide:

1. Before rereading this essay add these words to your vocabulary list and be sure the meanings fit the context: *pro forma, moat, ambivalent, perfunctory, scrimshaw, penology, devoid, vanities,* and *illusions.*

2. Allusions lend an ironic tone to this essay. What is especially ironic about the title, "Rock of Ages" (are you familiar with the hymn?)? Who were Mickey Cohen, Al Capone, Ma Barker, Doc Barker, and the Birdman of Alcatraz? What is especially ironic about the biblical quotation italicized in the middle of paragraph 4? What might Didion mean by "promises to keep" in the final sentence of the essay? (Think of Robert Frost's poem "Stopping by Woods.")

Questions:

1. What is ironic about the descriptions of flowers blooming on Alcatraz Island? How is this opening paragraph reminiscent of the beginning of A. M. Rosenthal's "No News from Auschwitz"?

2. What is ironic about three human beings and their dogs keeping watch over this abandoned island prison?

3. Is the proposal to make the island a "peace park" appropriate?

4. At the end of paragraph 2, Joan Didion refers to "ambivalent thoughts." How might those two words be the key to the substance and tone of the entire essay and especially the final paragraph?

5. What does Joan Didion mean by the final clause in the last sentence of the essay? How does it reflect antithetically on the first two sentences of paragraph 4?

Composition Topic:

Think of a place where you were when you were younger and which has now changed (been built up or allowed to deteriorate). Write an essay to capture the mood you feel in reflecting on it. Include details of past and present to express your feelings.

Carmen Guerrero Nakpil

Carmen Guerrero Nakpil was born in Manila, in the Philippines. Widowed as a consequence of World War II, she went to work as a journalist, starting out as a proofreader and rising through the ranks until she became an editorial page columnist for the daily *Manila Chronicle*. She remained in that post for 12 years. She also wrote a column for the *Sunday Times Magazine* in Manila. Some of her essays have been reprinted in the *Reader's Digest*.

Fluent in three languages, Filipino, Spanish, and English, Mrs. Guerrero Nakpil has also worked and written in the interest of international peace. For several years she was head of the National Historical Commission for UNESCO (United Nations Educational, Scientific, and Cultural Organization), and she also chaired the Cultural Committee of the Philippine Commission for UNESCO. In 1982 she was elected to the executive board of UNESCO. These appointments and elections have given her important opportunities for travel and for writing.

Interested in writing since childhood, Mrs. Guerrero Nakpil has always been especially fond of the essay as a form. In fact, she once returned to St. Theresa's, the college from which she was graduated in Manila, for a brief stint as a teacher of essay writing. In 1963 she published *Woman Enough and Other Essays*. Ten years later she published *A Question of Identity*, essays intended to give the Western world an idea of what Filipinos are like. Other books are *The Filipinos* (a history) and *The Rice Eaters* (a novel).

"On Time," the first essay in *A Question of Identity*, is a gently humorous introduction to the attitude of Filipinos toward time. Since Montaigne and other early essayists traditionally assigned the preposition *on* to the subject matter in the titles of their essays, Mrs. Guerrero Nakpil has adapted this tradition to the creation of a pun.

ON TIME

Carmen Guerrero Nakpil

13 April 1969

1   Punctuality is the crowning eccentricity in Filipino life. At least, so it seems from where I sit.

2   It is indiscreet to say what one means, and reckless to criticize Americans and certain death to disagree with reli-

193

gious leaders. But those faults have their mitigating circumstances, and are quite likely to be glossed over by kind souls playing part-time psychoanalysts.

3   The one unforgiveable sin is to have a penchant for punctuality. Those who practise it are punished by having to spend a great part of their lives, together with the rest of the unregenerate unbaptized, in a kind of gray limbo of waiting. One waits 45 minutes for a committee meeting to get started, 2 or 3 hours to be served dinner at a party, a week for the delivery of a dress and whole months for a piece of furniture.

4   Except for the few isolated marvels who turn up at the exact time specified on the invitation card or on a notice slip, one finds that there is a general unawareness of time. These members of the smallest cultural minority in the country cast a pall of rectitude over any gathering. People are always venomously shocked when, having asked one to come and have dinner or give a lecture or open a show one makes an appearance at the agreed time. There is a great deal of scurrying about, and grinning and, one suspects, some secret gnashing of teeth. One is immediately put on the defensive. Is it for today? one asks sheepishly. Yes, yes, but we did not expect you to come so early. Just as if punctuality were the greatest affront.

5   One must take refuge in the historical imagination. After all, the social psychology of Filipinos ordains a certain cavalier attitude about time. Traditional Filipinos still reckon time in the vaguest and loosest of terms. At what time will the Chairman be back? *Mamayamaya*—in a little while. At what time did the train leave? *Kanikanina lang*—just a while ago. At what time is the program scheduled to begin? *Sa umaga*—sometime this morning. How much longer will the repairs take? *Sandali na lang*. One often wonders what those enormous timepieces that stare at one everywhere are really for, and why watches and clocks enjoy such brisk sales on the sidewalks. Status symbols? Concessions to the eccentricities of another civilization?

6   The solution is all too obvious. People who issue invitations or summonses anticipate lateness by setting the time

ahead. It's an institution, like the Senate or the jeepney. Everyone—except intransigent little souls like me, apparently—takes it for granted that one is asked to come at seven but is expected at nine.

7   That should not be too difficult to manage. But I insist on being demoralized by not knowing how much of an allowance has been made. A Manila hostess usually allows a thirty minute gap, but provincial undertakings may be a good two or three hours off the mark.

8   I recently received an invitation—which I did not want to accept and did not much enjoy going to—for eight in the morning. After struggling through a premature dawn and careening through unfamiliar highways and byways, I was told, with much amusement at my lack of *savoir faire,* that the proceedings would really begin at eleven. I had a luncheon engagement in Manila at twelve, I objected. You'll never make it, was the disarming reply.

9   I wish it were possible to undertake a radical reshaping of my own habits. Punctuality is bad for the reputation and hardly right for considerations of thrift (if time is really money as the schoolgirl aphorism claims). But I am pinned down more helplessly than a Mangyan or an Ifugao* by the traditions of the exotic and quasi-extinct tribe to which I belong, and who cannot be late if they tried to.

Study Guide:

Before rereading this essay, add these words and their meanings to your list and be sure to understand them in context (some words have very different meanings in different contexts): *punctuality, eccentricity, indiscreet, to mitigate, to gloss over, penchant, unregenerate, limbo, pall, rectitude, venomous, affront, to ordain, cavalier, concession, intransigent, demoralized, provincial, savoir faire, aphorism, exotic,* the prefix *quasi-.*

Questions:

1. The opening sentence immediately transforms our viewpoint to that of the Filipino. How does Carmen Guerrero Nakpil accomplish

*Other peoples of the Philippines, whose customs seem restrictive.

this? How does this sentence set the tone for the humorous incongruity that is basic to this essay?

2. In paragraph 3, Mrs. Guerrero Nakpil uses such religious terms as "unforgivable sin," "unbaptized," and "limbo" as a humorous device to underscore the displeasure with which the average Filipino views a punctual person. How do these terms tie in with paragraph 2? Are they examples of **hyperbole?** Explain.

3. In paragraph 4, how does the majority display "rectitude"? On whom does the word choice "cast a pall of rectitude" put the burden of guilt? Why is it an amusing word choice? Is there an incongruity in the word choice?

4. Explain the pun in the title of the essay.

5. Paragraph 5 shows how language can express a cultural attitude toward time. How would Americans respond to the questions asked in that paragraph? What expressions of time consciousness are embedded in English and European languages?

6. In the second sentence of the final paragraph, what distinction is being made between *punctuality* and *time*? Does the essay suggest that the aphorism about time and money holds true, even among Filipinos?

7. How specific and concrete is this essay? Is it specific enough to make its point about cultural difference?

Composition Topic:

Write an essay in which you show how a difference in attitude toward time can create tension between two people.

Lewis Thomas

Born in New York City in 1913, Lewis Thomas earned his A.B. degree from Princeton University and his M.D. degree from Harvard University. His gifts in research and teaching then led him to an appointment as professor of pediatric research at the University of Minnesota. From there he went on to serve in three capacities at once at the New York University–Bellevue Medical Center: head of the departments of pathology and medicine and dean of the Medical Center. Subsequently he was appointed head of the department of pathology and dean at Yale Medical School. In recent years he has served in New York City as president of the Memorial Sloan-Kettering Cancer Center, where he is now emeritus president.

In addition to this distinguished career in medicine, Lewis Thomas has been a prolific writer, contributing thoughtful and elegantly written essays to *The New Yorker, Scientific American,* the *Atlantic,* and *Harper's.* He is best known, however, for essays that he wrote periodically for the *New England Journal of Medicine.* These have been collected and published in a volume entitled *The Lives of a Cell.* The book was immediately hailed as a treasury of scientific essays, and several years later it was followed by an equally popular collection, *The Medusa and the Snail.*

"The Lives of a Cell," the title essay of Thomas's first volume, requires special care in reading. Go through it once to get the gist of it. You will discover that it is not as difficult as some of the biological terminology would suggest. You will also discover that Thomas is dealing with profound scientific and philosophical ideas and doing so with the skill of a literary artist. Then work at the vocabulary and reread the essay several times. It is worth the effort.

THE LIVES OF A CELL

Lewis Thomas

1973

1   We are told that the trouble with Modern Man is that he has been trying to detach himself from nature. He sits in the topmost tiers of polymer, glass, and steel, dangling his pulsing legs, surveying at a distance the writhing life of the planet. In this scenario, Man comes on as a stupendous lethal force, and the earth is pictured as something deli-

cate, like rising bubbles at the surface of a country pond, or flights of fragile birds.

2   But it is illusion to think that there is anything fragile about the life of the earth; surely this is the toughest membrane imaginable in the universe, opaque to probability, impermeable to death. We are the delicate part, transient and vulnerable as cilia. Nor is it a new thing for man to invent an existence that he imagines to be above the rest of life; this has been his most consistent intellectual exertion down the millennia. As illusion, it has never worked out to his satisfaction in the past, any more than it does today. Man is embedded in nature.

3   The biologic science of recent years has been making this a more urgent fact of life. The new, hard problem will be to cope with the dawning, intensifying realization of just how interlocked we are. The old, clung-to notions most of us have held about our special lordship are being deeply undermined.

4   *Item.* A good case can be made for our nonexistence as entities. We are not made up, as we had always supposed, of successively enriched packets of our own parts. We are shared, rented, occupied. At the interior of our cells, driving them, providing the oxidative energy that sends us out for the improvement of each shining day, are the mitochondria, and in a strict sense they are not ours. They turn out to be little separate creatures, the colonial posterity of migrant prokaryocytes, probably primitive bacteria that swam into ancestral precursors of our eukaryotic cells and stayed there. Ever since, they have maintained themselves and their ways, replicating in their own fashion, privately, with their own DNA and RNA quite different from ours. They are as much symbionts as the rhizobial bacteria in the roots of beans. Without them, we would not move a muscle, drum a finger, think a thought.

5   Mitochondria are stable and responsible lodgers, and I choose to trust them. But what of the other little animals, similarly established in my cells, sorting and balancing me, clustering me together? My centrioles, basal bodies, and probably a good many other more obscure tiny beings at work inside my cells, each with its own special genome, are

as foreign, and as essential, as aphids in anthills. My cells are no longer the pure line entities I was raised with; they are ecosystems more complex than Jamaica Bay.

6   I like to think that they work in my interest, that each breath they draw for me, but perhaps it is they who walk through the local park in the early morning, sensing my senses, listening to my music, thinking my thoughts.

7   I am consoled, somewhat, by the thought that the green plants are in the same fix. They could not be plants, or green, without their chloroplasts, which run the photosynthetic enterprise and generate oxygen for the rest of us. As it turns out, chloroplasts are also separate creatures with their own genomes, speaking their own language.

8   We carry stores of DNA in our nuclei that may have come in, at one time or another, from the fusion of ancestral cells and the linking of ancestral organisms in symbiosis. Our genomes are catalogues of instructions from all kinds of sources in nature, filed for all kinds of contingencies. As for me, I am grateful for differentiation and speciation, but I cannot feel as separate an entity as I did a few years ago, before I was told these things, nor, I should think, can anyone else.

9   *Item.* The uniformity of the earth's life, more astonishing than its diversity, is accountable by the high probability that we derived, originally, from some single cell, fertilized in a bolt of lightning as the earth cooled. It is from the progeny of this parent cell that we take our looks; we still share genes around, and the resemblance of the enzymes of grasses to those of whales is a family resemblance.

10   The viruses, instead of being single-minded agents of disease and death, now begin to look more like mobile genes. Evolution is still an infinitely long and tedious biologic game, with only the winners staying at the table, but the rules are beginning to look more flexible. We live in a dancing matrix of viruses; they dart, rather like bees, from organism to organism, from plant to insect to mammal to me and back again, and into the sea, tugging along pieces of this genome, strings of genes from that, transplanting grafts of DNA, passing around heredity as though at a

great party. They may be a mechanism for keeping new, mutant kinds of DNA in the widest circulation among us. If this is true, the odd virus disease, on which we must focus so much of our attention in medicine, may be looked on as an accident, something dropped.

11   *Item.* I have been trying to think of the earth as a kind of organism, but it is no go. I cannot think of it this way. It is too big, too complex, with too many working parts lacking visible connections. The other night, driving through a hilly, wooded part of southern New England, I wondered about this. If not like an organism, what is it like, what is it *most* like? Then, satisfactorily for that moment, it came to me: it is *most* like a single cell.

Study Guide:

1. Clearly, a student of cellular biology would have an advantage over the average reader in understanding some of the details, but Lewis Thomas wrote this essay for the average reader as well as the cellular biologist, and he expects the average reader to get acquainted with the technical terms. Look up the following words, not all of them technical, and add them to your list so that further study of this essay will be richer in meaning: *tier, polymer, lethal, opaque, impermeable, transient, vulnerable, cilia, millennia, entity, oxidative, mitochondria, posterity, prokaryocyte,* the suffix *-cyte, eukaryote, eukaryotic, precursor, to replicate, DNA, RNA, symbiont, symbiosis, rhizobial, centriole, basal body, genome, aphid, ecosystem, to console, chloroplast, photosynthetic, enterprise, nuclei* (plural of *nucleus,* in this essay the nucleus of a cell), *fusion, contingency, differentiation, speciation, uniformity, progeny, enzyme, matrix, mutant.*

2. Examine photographs of an animal cell and a plant cell, each magnified by an electron microscope, with centrioles, mitochondria, nuclei, and (in the plant cell) chloroplasts labeled. Any standard up-to-date biology text will have such pictures. This will help you to visualize what Thomas is describing.

Questions:

1. In paragraph 4, the phrase *improvement of each shining day* is a slightly inaccurate allusion to Isaac Watts's moralizing poem that begins with the lines "How doth the little busy bee/Improve each shining

hour." How does the allusion give the sentence in which it appears an amusing incongruity?

2. To be sure of an understanding of this essay, look at its organization. The first three paragraphs are the introduction; the following five paragraphs (the first *item*) might be considered the body of the essay; the next two paragraphs (the second *item*) could be the conclusion; and the final paragraph (the last *item*) a footnote.

- a. What illusions is Thomas trying to dispose of in the first two paragraphs?
- b. What sentence in the first two paragraphs gets directly to the point of the essay?
- c. What point is Thomas making in the third paragraph? Does the essay deal with it, or is Thomas asking *us* to deal with it?
- d. What specific details in paragraphs 4–8 illustrate that humankind is embedded in nature?
- e. How do paragraphs 9 and 10 rephrase paragraphs 4–8?
- f. Does paragraph 11 reflect back on paragraph 1?

3. Of all the essays in this book, this comes closest to illustrating that an essay is an "attempt," a window into the writer's thinking process. Thomas is trying to answer questions that have fascinated all thinking human beings: What is this planet? What is life? Who (or what) am I?

- a. In how many ways does he play on the **motif** of what this planet may be?
- b. How does he illustrate the interconnectedness of living substances?
- c. How does he illustrate that we ourselves are not distinct entities?
- d. Which paragraph states a tentativeness in Thomas's philosophical thinking about the earth?

4. Now look at several statements that Thomas makes to shake human beings from illusions about themselves. How do paragraph 6 and the last two sentences of paragraph 10 underscore the middle (the third) sentence of paragraph 2? How does the thinking of paragraph 7 parallel that of paragraph 6?

5. For sheer beauty of style and depth of meaning, paragraph 10 is exceptional. Discuss the metaphors, the parallel constructions, the choice of explicit nouns and verbs, the holistic viewpoint.

6. Compare and contrast this essay with MacLeish's essay "A Reflection: Riders on Earth Together, Brothers in Eternal Cold."

7. Why is it important to be able to understand scientific essays written for laypeople?

A. Zee

Anthony Zee was born in China and reared in Brazil. His advanced education has been in the United States. At Princeton University he received his B.A. degree in 1966, and at Harvard University he received his Ph.D. degree in 1970. He now holds a joint appointment as professor at the University of California and at the Institute for Theoretical Physics at Santa Barbara. He is also an international traveler and lecturer.

In addition to research publications, A. Zee has written a textbook for advanced graduate students of physics, *Unity of Forces in the Universe,* and a book on modern theoretical physics for laypeople, *Fearful Symmetry: The Search for Beauty in Modern Physics.* "Fearful symmetry" is an allusion to "The Tyger," the famous poem by William Blake. In 1990 Zee published *Swallowing Clouds*, a lighthearted book on the language, food, and culture of China.

"Classical versus Quantum" is a vignette from Zee's most recent book on science for the layperson, *An Old Man's Toy: Gravity at Work and Play in Einstein's Universe.* This vignette is a mildly facetious attempt to explain simply a concept that is profoundly complex. In recognition of Anthony Zee's accomplishment in making physics palatable to the lay person, *An Old Man's Toy* was nominated in 1989 for the Pulitzer Prize for nonfiction.

CLASSICAL VERSUS QUANTUM

A. Zee

1989

1   Einstein was wedded to the notion of an unchanging, eternal universe. When he started to study the universe, he first checked to see if his own theory of gravity would allow a static universe. When he saw that it didn't, he was upset and proceeded to muck around with the theory.

2   To understand what Einstein did, let us look at his famous equation of gravity. This theory has a deserved reputation of being difficult to master, but the bottom-line equation of the theory is not hard to understand:

curvature of space and time = distribution of mass and energy

This equation tells us that something is equal to something else. Written out in mathematical form, Einstein's equation says

$$R_{\mu\nu} - \tfrac{1}{2}g_{\mu\nu}R = - T_{\mu\nu}$$

The mess of symbols $R_{\mu\nu} - \tfrac{1}{2}g_{\mu\nu}R$ on the left is just the physicists' way of saying "curvature of space and time," while the symbols $T_{\mu\nu}$ on the right are their way of saying "distribution of mass and energy."

3   Okay, if you want to know what the curvature of the universe is, you have got to tell me how mass and energy are distributed in the universe. Once you tell me that, I just plug it into the equation and obtain the curvature of the universe. In particular, if you give me a uniform distribution of mass and energy, I would obtain a curvature of space and time that describes an expanding universe.

4   But no, Einstein didn't do that! Instead, he wanted an eternal universe so badly that he changed his equation to

$$R_{\mu\nu} - \tfrac{1}{2}g_{\mu\nu}R + \Lambda g_{\mu\nu} = - T_{\mu\nu}$$

He added an extra term, $\Lambda g\mu\nu$, now known to physicists as the cosmological constant term. The Greek letter Λ (lambda) represents the strength of the cosmological constant. Crudely speaking, this term can be thought of as describing the stretching of space and time. The modified equation says

curvature of space and time + stretch of space and time
= distribution of mass and energy

5   By carefully adjusting the strength of the cosmological constant, Einstein was able to obtain a static universe.

6   Quite aside from the fact that the universe is not static, Einstein's move was rather distasteful. The universe stays static only if the effect of the cosmological constant exactly balances the effect of matter in the universe. Were there just a tiny bit less or a tiny bit more matter, the universe would start expanding or contracting. Einstein's solution is analogous to balancing a pencil on its point: Competing effects have to cancel perfectly for the universe to be balanced.

7   Well, as we know, the universe does expand, and Einstein was wrong. Sorry, gang, forget the cosmological constant. I don't need it anymore. Cross it out. The correct equation is the one I wrote down in the first place.

8   So, what's the problem? In classical physics, there is no problem. In writing down an equation, you can include or exclude a term as you please. Of course, then your equation may not agree with experiments. As a classical physicist, you may craft your equation to fit experiments by adding or removing terms as needed.

9   Imagine two classical physicists trying to figure out an equation to describe the motion of the electron. There we are, motion of electron = charge times electric field. Do you think we should also include a term describing how the spinning electron would tumble and shake in a magnetic field? Maybe the equation should be motion of electron = charge times electric field + spin times magnetic field. Beats me, how would I know?

10   To decide, they would have to experiment with an electron in a magnetic field. That's more or less how classical physics proceeds.

11   So Einstein, the consummate classical physicist, felt perfectly free to leave the cosmological constant out. Nobody could stop him. Without the cosmological term, his original equation agrees well with observations, and that's what counts in classical physics.

12   Of course, if you are a classical physicist, you can always include a tiny cosmological constant, tiny enough so it has essentially no effect. Nobody can stop you, either. Astronomical observations can only tell us that the cosmological constant must be smaller than a certain value.

13   The difficulty comes with quantum physics. Because of quantum fluctuations, you are no longer allowed to exclude terms as you please. You must have a reason why a given term should not be there. Roughly, the reason is that quantum physics is probabilistic. Physicists can only determine the probabilities of various processes occurring. Any process not explicitly forbidden by a basic principle will occur, even though the probability of the process actually occurring may be very small.

14   For example, suppose that the two classical physicists did not include a term describing how a spinning electron would tumble in a magnetic field. Since no known principle forbids an electron tumbling in a magnetic field, there is some probability that the electron will do so. Thus the equation has to include a term describing that particular motion.

15   In quantum physics, if you neglect to include a term not specifically forbidden by any principle, quantum fluctuations would force that term on you. Indeed, the equation describing the motion of the electron was first written down without an "anomalous magnetic moment term." Later, physicists realized that quantum fluctuations forced them to include that term. Experimenters then confirmed that the term was indeed necessary to describe the electron's behavior in a magnetic field. Our confidence in the reality of quantum fluctuations has been built up through numerous episodes of this kind.

16   In Theodore White's *The Once and Future King*, the boy Arthur dreams of visiting a kingdom governed on the principle that whatever is not forbidden is required. The story inspired the eminent physicist Murray Gell-Mann to quip that in quantum physics what is not taboo is a commandment.

17   This represents a profound difference between classical physics and quantum physics.

Study Guide:

The following words are essential to understanding this essay, so add them to your list and be sure that the definitions fit the use of the words in context: *quantum* (a dictionary will provide you with barely enough information for this essay), *static, distribution, mass, energy, uniform, cosmological, constant* (in the mathematical sense), *analogous, consummate, fluctuation, probability* and *probabilistic* (in the mathematical sense), *explicitly, anomalous, moment* (in the mechanics sense), *to quip, taboo.*

Questions:

1. In the first four paragraphs, what does Zee do to take the fear out of confronting such an esoteric subject? Some word choices are colloquial, even slangy. What is their effect? How would you describe the **tone** of these first four paragraphs?

2. Paragraphs 5 and 6 are more serious in tone (though the point they make is actually easier). Paragraph 7 is playfully worded but serious in content. Taken together, the first seven paragraphs function as **exposition** for what follows. They fill in the background of information necessary to an understanding of the main substance of the essay. Does this exposition arouse your curiosity?

3. Scientists often use **analogies** to make a point. Is the analogy of the balanced pencil (paragraph 6) instructive?

4. Following the first seven expository paragraphs, which is the first paragraph in which you discover that you are into something deep?

5. Which paragraphs treat the subject most seriously? What do you notice about word choice in those paragraphs as distinguished from word choice in more lighthearted paragraphs?

6. What is the function of paragraph 16? Are you familiar with the allusion? *The Once and Future King* is a modern retelling of the legend of King Arthur. The boy Arthur is taught by the magician Merlin.

7. To test your understanding of this essay, answer these questions:
   a. If in a computerized study of a million frozen snow crystals there is only one chance in 90 octillion that two crystals will be identical, need a classical physicist include in an equation for snow crystal formation a term describing such a remote chance?
   b. If Einstein had been a quantum physicist, would he have left out the cosmological constant?

8. Is the use of the word *profound* in paragraph 17 humorous or serious? Is it ironic in the context of the essay?

9. Is this an effective **didactic** essay?

10. Why is it important to be able to understand such essays?

Maxine Hong Kingston

Maxine Hong Kingston was born in 1940 in Stockton, California, to Chinese parents. She received her college education at the University of California at Berkeley. After her graduation she began a career in education, first as a teacher of English and mathematics at a high school in Hayward, California, and then as a teacher of English in several schools in Hawaii and a teacher of English as a second language at Honolulu Business College. In 1977 she was appointed associate professor of English at the University of Hawaii.

Meanwhile, Maxine Hong Kingston was establishing a reputation as a writer. She was a contributor to *American Girl* and to *American Heritage* as well as to the professional periodical *English Journal*. In 1976 she attracted national attention with the publication of *The Woman Warrior: Memoirs of a Girlhood among Ghosts*. The book won the National Book Critics Circle Award for best work of nonfiction published that year. In 1980 she published *China Men,* a companion piece to *The Woman Warrior.*

"My Mother Talking-Story" is the first essay in a chapter entitled "White Tigers," from *The Woman Warrior.* It is a strangely evocative reflection on the effect storytelling had on a child who was listening to tales from a distant land.

MY MOTHER TALKING-STORY

Maxine Hong Kingston

1976

1   When we Chinese girls listened to the adults talk-story, we learned that we failed if we grew up to be but wives or slaves. We could be heroines, swordswomen. Even if she had to rage across all China, a swordswoman got even with anybody who hurt her family. Perhaps women were once so dangerous that they had to have their feet bound. It was a woman who invented white crane boxing only two hundred years ago. She was already an expert pole fighter, daughter of a teacher trained at the Shao-lin temple, where there lived an order of fighting monks. She was combing her hair one morning when a white crane alighted outside her window. She teased it with her pole, which it pushed aside

with a soft brush of its wing. Amazed, she dashed outside and tried to knock the crane off its perch. It snapped her pole in two. Recognizing the presence of great power, she asked the spirit of the white crane if it would teach her to fight. It answered with a cry that white crane boxers imitate today. Later the bird returned as an old man, and he guided her boxing for many years. Thus she gave the world a new martial art.

2   This was one of the tamer, more modern stories, mere introduction. My mother told others that followed swordswomen through woods and palaces for years. Night after night my mother would talk-story until we fell asleep. I couldn't tell when the stories left off and the dreams began, her voice the voice of the heroines in my sleep. And on Sundays, from noon to midnight, we went to the movies at the Confucius Church. We saw swordswomen jump over houses from a standstill; they didn't even need a running start.

3   At last I saw that I too had been in the presence of great power, my mother talking-story. After I grew up, I heard the chant of Fa Mu Lan, the girl who took her father's place in battle. Instantly I remembered that as a child I had followed my mother about the house, the two of us singing about how Fa Mu Lan fought gloriously and returned alive from war to settle in the village. I had forgotten this chant that was once mine, given me by my mother, who may not have known its power to remind. She said I would grow up a wife and a slave, but she taught me the song of the warrior woman, Fa Mu Lan. I would have to grow up a warrior woman.

4   The call would come from a bird that flew over our roof. In the brush drawings it looks like the ideograph for "human," two black wings. The bird would cross the sun and lift into the mountains (which look like the ideograph "mountain"), there parting the mist briefly that swirled opaque again. I would be a little girl of seven the day I followed the bird away into the mountains. The brambles would tear off my shoes and the rocks cut my feet and fingers, but I would keep climbing, eyes upward to follow the bird. We would go around and around the tallest moun-

tain, climbing ever upward. I would drink from the river, which I would meet again and again. We would go so high the plants would change, and the river that flows past the village would become a waterfall. At the height where the bird used to disappear, the clouds would gray the world like an ink wash.

5   Even when I got used to that gray, I would only see peaks as if shaded in pencil, rocks like charcoal rubbings, everything so murky. There would be just two black strokes—the bird. Inside the clouds—inside the dragon's breath—I would not know how many hours or days passed. Suddenly, without noise, I would break clear into a yellow, warm world. New trees would lean toward me at mountain angles, but when I looked for the village, it would have vanished under the clouds.

6   The bird, now gold so close to the sun, would come to rest on the thatch of a hut, which, until the bird's two feet touched it, was camouflaged as part of the mountainside.

Study Guide:

Add these words to your list and know their meanings before re-reading the essay: *martial, ideograph, opaque, ink wash* (as in art work), *rubbings, murky, thatch.*

Questions:

1. This essay sets a tone in which memory blends into myth and myth blends into dream. Since memories are deceptive and dreams and myths seem insubstantial, their appearance in literature may at first puzzle the reader. There is in this essay, however, a theme, and it is introduced in the first two sentences.

   a. What is the **theme**?

   b. How is that theme given tension and how is it underscored in paragraph 3? Do you see the author's use of **antithesis?**

2. The essay also has at least one **motif,** the motif of the warrior spirit of the white crane.

   a. Where does that motif first appear?

   b. Where is that motif taken up again?

    c. Look at the first sentence of paragraph 3. To whom is Maxine Hong Kingston comparing herself? To what is she comparing her mother talking-story?

    d. What is "the call" that begins paragraph 4?

3. How does the form of this essay illustrate the fourth sentence of paragraph 2: "I couldn't tell where the stories left off and the dreams began . . ."?

4. Look at the art of description in paragraphs 4, 5, and 6. Isn't it like a Chinese painting? Can you see the black wings of the bird against the white mist? Look at the artist's use of contrast: ink-wash gray fading into murky black; then warm yellow and sunlit gold. You might attempt such a painting, drawn from Hong Kingston's words.

5. Paragraph 6 is enigmatic. What could it possibly mean? Is its enigmatic nature appropriate? Explain.

6. Compare and contrast this essay with Jorge Luis Borges's essay "Ragnarök."

Composition Topic:

Write an essay in which you show a dream growing out of a real experience.

Eudora Welty

Born in Jackson, Mississippi, in 1909, and still living in the house that was her father's, Eudora Welty is today a central figure in the renaissance of Southern literature. Her education after high school in Jackson was at Mississippi State College for Women and then at the University of Wisconsin, at Madison, where she received her B.A. degree. After graduation she studied advertising briefly at Columbia University School of Business, but upon the death of her father she returned to Jackson. There she worked for a radio station until she was hired as a society correspondent for a Memphis newspaper. In 1933 she wrote publicity for the WPA (Works Progress Administration, a government-sponsored program to relieve unemployment during the Depression). In 1936 she attracted attention in the arts world through an exhibition of her photographs in New York City and through publication of her first short story, "Death of a Traveling Salesman."

A collection of early short stories published under the title *A Curtain of Green* enhanced her reputation, and the appearance in 1945 of her first novel, *Delta Wedding,* established Eudora Welty as a major writer. The succession of short story collections and novels that have followed has only added to this reputation. Indeed, one of her novels, *The Ponder Heart,* was successfully dramatized on Broadway. Among her many honors is the Gold Medal for the Novel, given by the American Academy and Institute of Arts and Letters for her entire work in fiction.

In the 1980s Eudora Welty appeared on several television interviews and responded to numerous requests to say something about her craft and art. In 1984 Harvard University published *One Writer's Beginnings,* her essays on childhood and her search for a voice as a writer. It is from "Listening," the first chapter in this autobiography, that we have drawn the following vignettes.

FROM *LISTENING*

Eudora Welty

1983

1   In that vanished time in small-town Jackson, most of the ladies I was familiar with, the mothers of my friends in the neighborhood, were busiest when they were sociable. In the afternoons there was regular visiting up and down the

little grid of residential streets. Everybody had calling cards, even certain children; and newborn babies themselves were properly announced by sending out their tiny engraved calling cards attached with a pink or blue bow to those of their parents. Graduation presents to high-school pupils were often "card cases." On the hall table in every house the first thing you saw was a silver tray waiting to receive more calling cards on top of the stack already piled up like jackstraws; they were never thrown away.

2   My mother let none of this idling, as she saw it, pertain to her; she went her own way with or without her calling cards, and though she was fond of her friends and they were fond of her, she had little time for small talk. At first, I hadn't known what I'd missed.

3   When we at length bought our first automobile, one of our neighbors was often invited to go with us on the family Sunday afternoon ride. In Jackson it was counted an affront to the neighbors to start out for anywhere with an empty seat in the car. My mother sat in the back with her friend, and I'm told that as a small child I would ask to sit in the middle, and say as we started off, "Now *talk*."

4   There was dialogue throughout the lady's accounts to my mother. "I said" . . . "He said" . . . "And I'm told she very plainly said" . . . "It was midnight before they finally heard, and what do you think it *was?*"

5   What I loved about her stories was that everything happened in *scenes*. I might not catch on to what the root of the trouble was in all that happened, but my ear told me it was dramatic. Often she said, "The crisis had come!"

6   This same lady was one of Mother's callers on the telephone who always talked a long time. I knew who it was when my mother would only reply, now and then, "Well, I declare," or "You don't say so," or "Surely not." She'd be standing at the wall telephone, listening against her will, and I'd sit on the stairs close by her. Our telephone had a little bar set into the handle which had to be pressed and held down to keep the connection open, and when her friend had said goodbye, my mother needed me to prize her fingers loose from the little bar; her grip had become paralyzed. "What did she say?" I asked.

7   "She wasn't *saying* a thing in this world," sighed my mother. "She was just ready to talk, that's all."

8   My mother was right. Years later, beginning with my story "Why I Live at the P.O.," I wrote reasonably often in the form of a monologue that takes possession of the speaker. How much more gets told besides!

9   This lady told everything in her sweet, marveling voice, and meant every word of it kindly. She enjoyed my company perhaps even more than my mother's. She invited me to catch her doodlebugs; under the trees in her backyard were dozens of their holes. When you stuck a broom straw down one and called, "Doodlebug, doodlebug, your house is on fire and all your children are burning up," she believed this is why the doodlebug came running out of the hole. This was why I loved to call up her doodlebugs instead of ours.

10   My mother could never have told me her stories, and I think I knew why even then: my mother didn't believe them. But I could listen to this murmuring lady all day. She believed everything she heard, like the doodlebug. And so did I.

11   This was a day when ladies' and children's clothes were very often made at home. My mother cut out all the dresses and her little boys' rompers, and a sewing woman would come and spend the day upstairs in the sewing room fitting and stitching them all. This was Fannie. This old black sewing woman, along with her speed and dexterity, brought along a great provision of up-to-the-minute news. She spent her life going from family to family in town and worked right in its bosom, and nothing could stop her. My mother would try, while I stood being pinned up. "Fannie, I'd rather Eudora didn't hear that." "That" would be just what I was longing to hear, whatever it was. "I don't want her exposed to gossip"—as if gossip were measles and I could catch it. I did catch some of it but not enough. "Mrs. O'Neil's oldest daughter she had her wedding dress *tried on*, and all her fine underclothes featherstitched and ribbon run in and then—" "I think that will do, Fannie," said my mother. It was tantalizing never to be exposed long enough to hear the end.

12   Fannie was the worldliest old woman to be imagined. She could do whatever her hands were doing without having to stop talking; and she could speak in a wonderfully derogatory way with any number of pins stuck in her mouth. Her hands steadied me like claws as she stumped on her knees around me, tacking me together. The gist of her tale would be lost on me, but Fannie didn't bother about the ear she was telling it to; she just liked telling. She was like an author. In fact, for a good deal of what she said, I daresay she *was* the author.

13   Long before I wrote stories, I listened for stories. Listening *for* them is something more acute than listening *to* them. I suppose it's an early form of participation in what goes on. Listening children know stories are *there*. When their elders sit and begin, children are just waiting and hoping for one to come out, like a mouse from its hole.

14   It was taken entirely for granted that there wasn't any lying in our family, and I was advanced in adolescence before I realized that in plenty of homes where I played with schoolmates and went to their parties, children lied to their parents and parents lied to their children and to each other. It took me a long time to realize that these very same everyday lies, and the strategems and jokes and tricks and dares that went with them, were in fact the basis of the *scenes* I so well loved to hear about and hoped for and treasured in the conversation of adults.

15   My instinct—the dramatic instinct—was to lead me, eventually, on the right track for a storyteller: the *scene* was full of hints, pointers, suggestions, and promises of things to find out and know about human beings. I had to grow up and learn to listen for the unspoken as well as the spoken—and to know a truth, I also had to recognize a lie.

16   It was when my mother came out onto the sleeping porch to tell me goodnight that her trial came. The sudden silence in the double bed meant my younger brothers had both keeled over in sleep, and I in the single bed at my end of the porch would be lying electrified, waiting for this to be the night when she'd tell me what she'd promised for so

long. Just as she bent to kiss me I grabbed her and asked: "Where do babies come from?"

17   My poor mother! But something saved her every time. Almost any night I put the baby question to her, suddenly, as if the whole outdoors exploded, Professor Holt would start to sing. The Holts lived next door; he taught penmanship (the Palmer Method), typing, bookkeeping and shorthand at the high school. His excitable voice traveled out of their dining-room windows across the two driveways between our houses, and up to our upstairs sleeping porch. His wife, usually so quiet and gentle, was his uncannily spirited accompanist at the piano. "High-ho! Come to the Fair!" he'd sing, unless he sang "Oho ye oho ye, who's bound for the ferry, the briar's in bud and the sun's going down!"

18   "Dear, this isn't a very good time for you to hear Mother, is it?"

19   She couldn't get started. As soon as she'd whisper something, Professor Holt galloped into the chorus, "And 'tis but a penny to Twickenham town!" "Isn't that enough?" she'd ask me. She'd told me that the mother and the father had to both *want* the baby. This couldn't be enough. I knew she was not trying to fib to me, for she never did fib, but also I could not help but know she was not really *telling* me. And more than that, I was afraid of what I was going to hear next. This was partly because she wanted to tell me in the dark. I thought *she* might be afraid. In something like childish hopelessness I thought she probably *couldn't* tell, just as she *couldn't* lie.

20   On the night we came the closest to having it over with, she started to tell me without being asked, and I ruined it by yelling, "Mother, look at the lightning bugs!"

21   In those days, the dark was dark. And all the dark out there was filled with the soft, near lights of lightning bugs. They were everywhere, flashing on the slow, horizontal move, on the upswings, rising and subsiding in the soundless dark. Lightning bugs signaled and answered back without a stop, from down below all the way to the top of our sycamore tree. My mother just gave me a businesslike kiss and went on back to Daddy in their room at the front

of the house. Distracted by lightning bugs, I had missed my chance. The fact is she never did tell me.

22   I doubt that any child I knew ever was told by her mother any more than I was about babies. In fact, I doubt that her own mother ever told her any more than she told me, though there were five brothers who were born after Mother, one after the other, and she was taking care of babies all her childhood.

23   Not being able to bring herself to open that door to reveal its secret, one of those days, she opened another door.

24   In my mother's bottom bureau drawer in her bedroom she kept treasures of hers in boxes, and had given me permission to play with one of them—a switch of her own chestnut-colored hair, kept in a heavy bright braid that coiled around like a snake inside a cardboard box. I hung it from her doorknob and unplaited it; it fell in ripples nearly to the floor, and it satisfied the Rapunzel in me to comb it out. But one day I noticed in the same drawer a small white cardboard box such as her engraved calling cards came in from the printing house. It was tightly closed, but I opened it, to find to my puzzlement and covetousness two polished buffalo nickels, embedded in white cotton. I rushed with this opened box to my mother and asked if I could run out and spend the nickels.

25   "No!" she exclaimed in a most passionate way. She seized the box into her own hands. I begged her; somehow I had started to cry. Then she sat down, drew me to her, and told me that I had had a little brother who had come before I did, and who had died as a baby before I was born. And these two nickels that I'd wanted to claim as my find were his. They had lain on his eyelids, for a purpose untold and unimaginable. "He was a fine little baby, my first baby, and he shouldn't have died. But he did. It was because your mother almost died at the same time," she told me. "In looking after me, they too nearly forgot about the little baby."

26   She'd told me the wrong secret—not how babies could come but how they could die, how they could be forgotten about.

27   I wondered in after years: how could my mother have kept those two coins? Yet how could someone like herself have disposed of them in any way at all? She suffered from a morbid streak which in all the life of the family reached out on occasions—the worst occasions—and touched us, clung around us, making it worse for her; her unbearable moments could find nowhere to go.

28   The future story writer in the child I was must have taken unconscious note and stored it away then: one secret is liable to be revealed in the place of another that is harder to tell, and the substitute secret when nakedly exposed is often the more appalling.

29   Perhaps telling me what she did was made easier for my mother by the two secrets, told and still not told, being connected in her deepest feeling, more intimately than anyone ever knew, perhaps even herself. So far as I remember now, this is the only time this baby was ever mentioned in my presence. So far as I can remember, and I've tried, he was never mentioned in the presence of my father, for whom he had been named. I am only certain that my father, who could never bear pain very well, would not have been able to bear it.

30   It was my father (my mother told me at some later date) who saved her own life, after that baby was born. She had in fact been given up by the doctor, as she had long been unable to take any nourishment. (That was the illness when they'd cut her hair, which formed the switch in the same bureau drawer.) What had struck her was septicemia, in those days nearly always fatal. What my father did was to try champagne.

31   I once wondered where he, who'd come not very long before from an Ohio farm, had ever heard of such a remedy, such a measure. Or perhaps as far as he was concerned he invented it, out of the strength of desperation. It would have been desperation augmented because champagne couldn't be bought in Jackson. But somehow he knew what to do about that too. He telephoned to Canton, forty miles north, to an Italian orchard grower, Mr. Trolio, told him the necessity, and asked, begged, that he put a bottle of his wine on Number 3, which was due in a few minutes to stop in Canton to "take on water" (my father knew everything

about train schedules). My father would be waiting to meet the train in Jackson. Mr. Trolio did—he sent the bottle in a bucket of ice and my father snatched it off the baggage car. He offered my mother a glass of chilled champagne and she drank it and kept it down. She was to live, after all.

32   Now, her hair was long again, it would reach in a braid down her back, and now I was her child. She hadn't died. And when I came, I hadn't died either. Would she ever? Would I ever? I couldn't face *ever*. I must have rushed into her lap, demanding her like a baby. And she had to put her first-born aside again, for me.

33   Of course it's easy to see why they both overprotected me, why my father, before I could wear a new pair of shoes for the first time, made me wait while he took out his thin silver pocket knife and with the point of the blade scored the polished soles all over, carefully, in a diamond pattern, to prevent me from sliding on the polished floor when I ran.

34   As I was to learn over and over again, my mother's mind was a mass of associations. Whatever happened would be forever paired for her with something that had happened before it, to one of us or to her. It became a private anniversary. Every time any possible harm came near me, she thought of how she lost her first child. When a Roman candle at Christmas backfired up my sleeve, she rushed to smother the blaze with the first thing she could grab, which was a dish towel hanging in the kitchen, and the burn on my arm became infected. I was nothing but proud of my sling, for I could wear it to school, and her repeated blaming of herself—for even my sling—puzzled and troubled me.

35   When my mother would tell me that she wanted me to have something because she as a child had never had it, I wanted, or I partly wanted, to give it back. All my life I continued to feel that bliss for me would have to imply my mother's deprivation or sacrifice. I don't think it would have occurred to her what a double emotion I felt, and indeed I know that it was being unfair to her, for what she said was simply the truth.

36   "I'm going to let you go to the Century Theatre with

your father tonight on my ticket. I'd rather you saw *Blossom Time* than go myself."

37   In the Century first-row balcony, where their seats always were, I'd be sitting beside my father at this hour beyond my bedtime carried totally away by the performance, and then suddenly the thought of my mother staying home with my sleeping younger brothers, missing the spectacle at this moment before my eyes, and doing without all the excitement and wonder that filled my being, would arrest me and I could hardly bear my pleasure for my guilt.

38   There is no wonder that a passion for independence sprang up in me at the earliest age. It took me a long time to manage the independence, for I loved those who protected me—and I wanted inevitably to protect them back. I have never managed to handle the guilt. In the act and the course of writing stories, these are two of the springs, one bright, one dark, that feed the stream.

Study Guide:

1. Add the following words to your list so that you will more fully enjoy rereading the essay: *jackstraws, to pertain, affront, crisis, monologue, dexterity, tantalizing, derogatory, gist, strategem, uncannily, covetousness, morbid, appalling, septicemia, augmented, deprivation.*

2. Look up the fairy tale of Rapunzel alluded to in paragraph 24.

Questions:

1. In the first vignette, paragraphs 1–15, what did "listening" teach Eudora Welty about the elements of a good story? In that same vignette, what did she, who did not lie, learn about the crafting of lies and the creation of *scenes?*

2. Show how the **motif** of belief and disbelief, truth and lies runs through this first vignette. Is **antithesis** a part of the fabric of this essay?

3. What is especially good about the simile at the end of paragraph 13?

4. Explain the **paradox** at the end of paragraph 15: "to know a truth, I also had to recognize a lie." Is paragraph 7 also paradoxical?

5. Antithetical elements run through the motifs of the next vignette, paragraphs 16–32. Telling and not telling is one of the motifs. Life and death is another. Show how Eudora Welty plays them together for powerful effect.

6. Do you see how Eudora Welty uses *scenes* to lead into the powerfully effective abstract statement in paragraph 26 and the equally effective final sentence of paragraph 32? Explain.

7. Explain the humorous incongruities in paragraphs 17–19.

8. Paragraph 10 is notable for its evocative and accurate description of fireflies. Try in as few sentences as possible to evoke just such vivid images of some other natural phenomenon.

9. The third vignette, paragraphs 33–38, develops the pattern of antithetical elements into a statement in which Eudora Welty interprets her art as a writer. What do the scenes reveal about Eudora Welty's development as a person? What are the antithetical elements? How does she think her emotional being affects her writing?

10. Discuss how in these three vignettes Eudora Welty has fed the stream of her writing with the two springs, "one bright, one dark."

Composition Topic:

Sometimes you may be required to write essays that reveal something about yourself. Eudora Welty sets a standard for style and honesty in these vignettes. Think of a scene in your life that reveals something of who and what you are, and work it into an essay.

PART FOUR

For the Interested Reader

The following essays are given as further examples of the works of five authors represented earlier in the book.

As you read these essays, notice particularly the gracefulness of style, so characteristic of the authors' writing. We will ask no questions at the ends of these essays, but we hope that your reading will raise many. We hope, also, that you will accept the essays in the spirit in which we present them to you, as a special gift to a reader who has been stimulated to go this far into an understanding of the essay.

UNTYING THE KNOT

Annie Dillard

1974

1   Yesterday I set out to catch the new season, and instead I found an old snakeskin. I was in the sunny February woods by the quarry; the snakeskin was lying in a heap of leaves right next to an aquarium someone had thrown away. I don't know why that someone hauled the aquarium deep into the woods to get rid of it; it had only one broken glass side. The snake found it handy, I imagine; snakes like to rub against something rigid to help them out of their skins, and the broken aquarium looked like the nearest likely object. Together the snakeskin and the aquarium made an interesting scene on the forest floor. It looked like an exhibit at a trial—circumstantial evidence—of a wild scene, as though a snake had burst through the broken side of the aquarium, burst through his ugly old skin, and disappeared, perhaps straight up in the air, in a rush of freedom and beauty.

2   The snakeskin had unkeeled scales, so it belonged to a nonpoisonous snake. It was roughly five feet long by the yardstick, but I'm not sure because it was very wrinkled and dry, and every time I tried to stretch it flat it broke. I ended up with seven or eight pieces of it all over the kitchen table in a fine film of forest dust.

3   The point I want to make about the snakeskin is that, when I found it, it was whole and tied in a knot. Now there have been stories told, even by reputable scientists, of snakes that have deliberately tied themselves in a knot to prevent larger snakes from trying to swallow them—but I couldn't imagine any way that throwing itself into a half hitch would help a snake trying to escape its skin. Still, ever cautious, I figured that one of the neighborhood boys could possibly have tied it in a knot in the fall, for some whimsical boyish reason, and left it there, where it dried and gathered dust. So I carried the skin along thoughtlessly as I walked, snagging it sure enough on a low

branch and ripping it in two for the first of many times. I saw that thick ice still lay on the quarry pond and that the skunk cabbage was already out in the clearings, and then I came home and looked at the skin and its knot.

4   The knot had no beginning. Idly I turned it around in my hand, searching for a place to untie; I came to with a start when I realized I must have turned the thing around fully ten times. Intently, then, I traced the knot's lump around with a finger: it was continuous. I couldn't untie it any more than I could untie a doughnut; it was a loop without beginning or end. These snakes *are* magic, I thought for a second, and then of course I reasoned what must have happened. The skin had been pulled inside-out like a peeled sock for several inches; then an inch or so of the inside-out part—a piece whose length was coincidentally equal to the diameter of the skin—had somehow been turned right-side out again, making a thick lump whose edges were lost in wrinkles, looking exactly like a knot.

5   So I have been thinking about the change of seasons. I don't want to miss spring this year. I want to distinguish the last winter frost from the out-of-season one, the frost of spring. I want to be there on the spot the moment the grass turns green. I always miss this radical revolution; I see it the next day from a window, the yard so suddenly green and lush I could envy Nebuchadnezzar down on all fours eating grass. This year I want to stick a net into time and say "now," as men plant flags on the ice and snow and say, "here." But it occurred to me that I could no more catch spring by the tip of the tail than I could untie the apparent knot in the snakeskin; there are no edges to grasp. Both are continuous loops.

6   I wonder how long it would take you to notice the regular recurrence of the seasons if you were the first man on earth. What would it be like to live in open-ended time broken only by days and nights? You could say, "it's cold again; it was cold before," but you couldn't make the key connection and say, "it was cold this time last year," because the notion of "year" is precisely the one you lack. Assuming that you hadn't yet noticed any orderly progres-

sion of heavenly bodies, how long would you have to live on earth before you could feel with any assurance that any one particular long period of cold would, in fact, end? "While the earth remaineth, seedtime and harvest, and cold and heat, and summer and winter, and day and night shall not cease": God makes this guarantee very early in Genesis to a people whose fears on this point had perhaps not been completely allayed.

7   It must have been fantastically important, at the real beginnings of human culture, to conserve and relay this vital seasonal information, so that the people could anticipate dry or cold seasons, and not huddle on some November rock hoping pathetically that spring was just around the corner. We still very much stress the simple fact of four seasons to schoolchildren; even the most modern of modern new teachers, who don't seem to care if their charges can read or write or name two products of Peru, will still muster some seasonal chitchat and set the kids to making paper pumpkins, or tulips, for the walls. "The people," wrote Van Gogh in a letter, "are very sensitive to the changing seasons." That we are "very sensitive to the changing seasons" is, incidentally, one of the few good reasons to shun travel. If I stay at home I preserve the illusion that what is happening on Tinker Creek is the very newest thing, that I'm at the very vanguard and cutting edge of each new season. I don't want the same season twice in a row; I don't want to know I'm getting last week's weather, used weather, weather broadcast up and down the coast, old-hat weather.

8   But there's always unseasonable weather. What we think of the weather and behavior of life on the planet at any given season is really all a matter of statistical probabilities; at any given point, anything might happen. There is a bit of every season in each season. Green plants—deciduous green leaves—grow everywhere, all winter long, and small shoots come up pale and new in every season. Leaves die on the tree in May, turn brown, and fall into the creek. The calendar, the weather, and the behavior of wild creatures have the slimmest of connections. Everything overlaps smoothly for only a few weeks each season,

and then it all tangles up again. The temperature, of course, lags far behind the calendar seasons, since the earth absorbs and releases heat slowly, like a leviathan breathing. Migrating birds head south in what appears to be dire panic, leaving mild weather and fields full of insects and seeds; they reappear as if in all eagerness in January, and poke about morosely in the snow. Several years ago our October woods would have made a dismal colored photograph for a sadist's calendar: a killing frost came before the leaves had even begun to brown; they drooped from every tree like crepe, blackened and limp. It's all a chancy, jumbled affair at best, as things seem to be below the stars.

9   Time is the continuous loop, the snakeskin with scales endlessly overlapping without beginning or end, or time is an ascending spiral if you will, like a child's toy Slinky. Of course we have no idea which arc on the loop is our time, let alone where the loop itself is, so to speak, or down whose lofty flight of stairs the Slinky so uncannily walks.

10   The power we seek, too, seems to be a continuous loop. I have always been sympathetic with the early notion of a divine power that exists in a particular place, or that travels about over the face of the earth as a man might wander—and when he is "there" he is surely not here. You can shake the hand of a man you meet in the woods; but the spirit seems to roll along like the mythical hoop snake with its tail in its mouth. There are no hands to shake or edges to untie. It rolls along the mountain ridges like a fireball, shooting off a spray of sparks at random, and will not be trapped, slowed, grasped, fetched, peeled, or aimed. "As for the wheels, it was cried unto them in my hearing, O wheel." This is the hoop of flame that shoots the rapids in the creek or spins across the dizzy meadows; this is the arsonist of the sunny woods: catch it if you can.

A HANGING

George Orwell

1931

1 It was in Burma, a sodden morning of the rains. A sickly light, like yellow tinfoil, was slanting over the high walls into the jail yard. We were waiting outside the condemned cells, a row of sheds fronted with double bars, like small animal cages. Each cell measured about ten feet by ten and was quite bare within except for a plank bed and a pot for drinking water. In some of them brown silent men were squatting at the inner bars, with their blankets draped round them. These were the condemned men, due to be hanged within the next week or two.

2 One prisoner had been brought out of his cell. He was a Hindu, a puny wisp of a man, with a shaven head and vague liquid eyes. He had a thick, sprouting moustache, absurdly too big for his body, rather like the moustache of a comic man on the films. Six tall Indian warders were guarding him and getting him ready for the gallows. Two of them stood by with rifles and fixed bayonets, while the others handcuffed him, passed a chain through his handcuffs and fixed it to their belts, and lashed his arms tight to his sides. They crowded very close about him, with their hands always on him in a careful, caressing grip, as though all the while feeling him to make sure he was there. It was like men handling a fish which is still alive and may jump back into the water. But he stood quite unresisting, yielding his arms limply to the ropes, as though he hardly noticed what was happening.

3 Eight o'clock struck and a bugle call, desolately thin in the wet air, floated from the distant barracks. The superintendent of the jail, who was standing apart from the rest of us, moodily prodding the gravel with his stick, raised his head at the sound. He was an army doctor, with a grey toothbrush moustache and a gruff voice. "For God's sake hurry up, Francis," he said irritably. "The man ought to have been dead by this time. Aren't you ready yet?"

4   Francis, the head jailer, a fat Dravidian in a white drill suit and gold spectacles, waved his black hand. "Yes sir, yes sir," he bubbled, "All is satisfactorily prepared. The hangman is waiting. We shall proceed."

5   "Well, quick march, then. The prisoners can't get their breakfast until this job's over."

6   We set out for the gallows. Two warders marched on either side of the prisoner, with their rifles at the slope; two others marched close against him, gripping him by arm and shoulder, as though at once pushing and supporting him. The rest of us, magistrates and the like, followed behind. Suddenly, when we had gone ten yards, the procession stopped short without any order or warning. A dreadful thing had happened — a dog, come goodness knows whence, had appeared in the yard. It came bounding among us with a loud volley of barks, and leapt round us wagging its whole body, wild with glee at finding so many human beings together. It was a large woolly dog, half Airedale, half pariah. For a moment it pranced round us, and then, before anyone could stop it, it had made a dash for the prisoner and, jumping up, tried to lick his face. Everyone stood aghast, too taken aback even to grab at the dog.

7   "Who let that bloody brute in here?" said the superintendent angrily. "Catch it, someone!"

8   A warder, detached from the escort, charged clumsily after the dog, but it danced and gambolled just out of his reach, taking everything as part of the game. A young Eurasian jailer picked up a handful of gravel and tried to stone the dog away, but it dodged the stones and came after us again. Its yaps echoed from the jail walls. The prisoner, in the grasp of the two warders, looked on incuriously, as though this was another formality of the hanging. It was several minutes before someone managed to catch the dog. Then we put my handkerchief through its collar and moved off once more, with the dog still straining and whimpering.

9   It was about forty yards to the gallows. I watched the bare brown back of the prisoner marching in front of me. He walked clumsily with his bound arms, but quite stead-

ily, with that bobbing gait of the Indian who never straightens his knees. At each step his muscles slid neatly into place, the lock of hair on his scalp danced up and down, his feet printed themselves on the wet gravel. And once, in spite of the men who gripped him by each shoulder, he stepped slightly aside to avoid a puddle on the path.

10   It is curious, but till that moment I had never realized what it means to destroy a healthy, conscious man. When I saw the prisoner step aside to avoid the puddle I saw the mystery, the unspeakable wrongness, of cutting a life short when it is in full tide. This man was not dying, he was alive just as we are alive. All the organs of his body were working—bowels digesting food, skin renewing itself, nails growing, tissues forming—all toiling away in solemn foolery. His nails would still be growing when he stood on the drop, when he was falling through the air with a tenth-of-a-second to live. His eyes saw the yellow gravel and the grey walls, and his brain still remembered, foresaw, reasoned—reasoned even about puddles. He and we were a party of men walking together, seeing, hearing, feeling, understanding the same world; and in two minutes, with a sudden snap, one of us would be gone—one mind less, one world less.

11   The gallows stood in a small yard, separate from the main grounds of the prison, and overgrown with tall prickly weeds. It was a brick erection like three sides of a shed, with planking on top, and above that two beams and a crossbar with the rope dangling. The hangman, a grey-haired convict in the white uniform of the prison, was waiting beside his machine. He greeted us with a servile crouch as we entered. At a word from Francis the two warders, gripping the prisoner more closely than ever, half led half pushed him to the gallows and helped him clumsily up the ladder. Then the hangman climbed up and fixed the rope round the prisoner's neck.

12   We stood waiting, five yards away. The warders had formed in a rough circle round the gallows. And then, when the noose was fixed, the prisoner began crying out to his god. It was a high, reiterated cry of "Ram! Ram! Ram! Ram!" not urgent and fearful like a prayer or cry for help,

but steady, rhythmical, almost like the tolling of a bell. The dog answered the sound with a whine. The hangman, still standing on the gallows, produced a small cotton bag like a flour bag and drew it down over the prisoner's face. But the sound, muffled by the cloth, still persisted, over and over again: "Ram! Ram! Ram! Ram! Ram!"

13   The hangman climbed down and stood ready, holding the lever. Minutes seemed to pass. The steady, muffled crying from the prisoner went on and on, "Ram! Ram! Ram!" never faltering for an instant. The superintendent, his head on his chest, was slowly poking the ground with his stick; perhaps he was counting the cries, allowing the prisoner a fixed number—fifty, perhaps, or a hundred. Everyone had changed color. The Indians had gone grey like bad coffee, and one or two of the bayonets were wavering. We looked at the lashed, hooded man on the drop, and listened to his cries—each cry another second of life; the same thought was in all our minds: oh, kill him quickly, get it over, stop that abominable noise!

14   Suddenly the superintendent made up his mind. Throwing up his head he made a swift motion with his stick. "Chalo!" he shouted almost fiercely.

15   There was a clanking noise, and then dead silence. The prisoner had vanished, and the rope was twisting on itself. I let go of the dog, and it galloped immediately to the back of the gallows; but when it got there it stopped short, barked, and then retreated into a corner of the yard, where it stood among the weeds, looking timorously out at us. We went round the gallows to inspect the prisoner's body. He was dangling with his toes pointed straight downwards, very slowly revolving, as dead as a stone.

16   The superintendent reached out with his stick and poked the bare brown body; it oscillated slightly. *"He's* all right," said the superintendent. He backed out from under the gallows, and blew out a deep breath. The moody look had gone out of his face quite suddenly. He glanced at his wrist-watch. "Eight minutes past eight. Well, that's all for this morning, thank God."

17   The warders unfixed bayonets and marched away. The dog, sobered and conscious of having misbehaved itself,

slipped after them. We walked out of the gallows yard, past the condemned cells with their waiting prisoners, into the big central yard of the prison. The convicts, under the command of warders armed with lathis, were already receiving their breakfast. They squatted in long rows, each man holding a tin panikin, while two warders with buckets marched round ladling out rice; it seemed quite a homely, jolly scene, after the hanging. An enormous relief had come upon us now that the job was done. One felt an impulse to sing, to break into a run, to snigger. All at once everyone began chattering gaily.

18   The Eurasian boy walking beside me nodded towards the way we had come, with a knowing smile: "Do you know, sir, our friend [he meant the dead man] when he heard his appeal had been dismissed, he pissed on the floor of his cell. From fright. Kindly take one of my cigarettes, sir. Do you not admire my new silver case, sir? From the boxwalah, two rupees eight annas. Classy European style."

19   Several people laughed—at what, nobody seemed certain.

20   Francis was walking by the superintendent, talking garrulously: "Well, sir, all hass passed off with the utmost satisfactoriness. It was all finished—flick! like that. It iss not always so—oah, no! I have known cases where the doctor wass obliged to go beneath the gallows and pull the prisoner's legs to ensure decease. Most disagreeable!"

21   "Wriggling about, eh? That's bad," said the superintendent.

22   "Ach, sir, it iss worse when they become refractory! One man, I recall, clung to the bars of his cage when we went to take him out. You will scarcely credit, sir, that it took six warders to dislodge him, three pulling at each leg. We reasoned with him, 'My dear fellow,' we said, 'think of all the pain and trouble you are causing to us!' But no, he would not listen! Ach, he wass very troublesome!"

23   I found that I was laughing quite loudly. Everyone was laughing. Even the superintendent grinned in a tolerant way. "You'd better all come out and have a drink," he said quite genially. "I've got a bottle of whisky in the car. We could do with it."

24   We went through the big double gates of the prison into the road. "Pulling at his legs!" exclaimed a Burmese magistrate suddenly, and burst into a loud chuckling. We all began laughing again. At that moment Francis' anecdote seemed extraordinarily funny. We all had a drink together, native and European alike, quite amicably. The dead man was a hundred yards away.

THE RING OF TIME

E. B. White

Fiddler Bayou, March 22, 1956

1   After the lions had returned to their cages, creeping angrily through the chutes, a little bunch of us drifted away and into an open doorway nearby, where we stood for a while in semidarkness, watching a big brown circus horse go harumphing around the practice ring. His trainer was a woman of about forty, and the two of them, horse and woman, seemed caught up in one of those desultory treadmills of afternoon from which there is no apparent escape. The day was hot, and we kibitzers were grateful to be briefly out of the sun's glare. The long rein, or tape, by which the woman guided her charge counterclockwise in his dull career formed the radius of their private circle, of which she was the revolving center; and she, too, stepped a tiny circumference of her own in order to accommodate the horse and allow him his maximum scope. She had on a short-skirted costume and a conical straw hat. Her legs were bare and she wore high heels, which probed deep into the loose tanbark and kept her ankles in a state of constant turmoil. The great size and meekness of the horse, the repetitious exercise, the heat of the afternoon, all exerted a hypnotic charm that invited boredom; we spectators were experiencing a languor—we neither expected relief nor felt entitled to any. We had paid a dollar to get into the grounds, to be sure, but we had got our dollar's worth a few minutes before, when the lion trainer's whiplash had got caught around a toe of one of the lions. What more did we want for a dollar?

2   Behind me I heard someone say, "Excuse me, please," in a low voice. She was halfway into the building when I turned and saw her—a girl of sixteen or seventeen, politely threading her way through us onlookers who blocked the entrance. As she emerged in front of us, I saw that she was barefoot, her dirty little feet fighting the uneven ground. In most respects she was like any of two or three dozen

showgirls you encounter if you wander about the winter quarters of Mr. John Ringling North's circus, in Sarasota—cleverly proportioned, deeply browned by the sun, dusty, eager, and almost naked. But her grave face and the naturalness of her manner gave her a sort of quick distinction and brought a new note into the gloomy octagonal building where we had all cast our lot for a few moments. As soon as she had squeezed through the crowd, she spoke a word or two to the older woman, whom I took to be her mother, stepped to the ring, and waited while the horse coasted to a stop in front of her. She gave the animal a couple of affectionate swipes on his enormous neck and then swung herself aboard. The horse immediately resumed his rocking canter, the woman goading him on, chanting something that sounded like "Hop! Hop!"

3   In attempting to recapture this mild spectacle, I am merely acting as recording secretary for one of the oldest of societies—the society of those who, at one time or another, have surrendered, without even a show of resistance, to the bedazzlement of a circus rider. As a writing man, or secretary, I have always felt charged with the safekeeping of all unexpected items of worldly or unworldly enchantment, as though I might be held personally responsible if even a small one were to be lost. But it is not easy to communicate anything of this nature. The circus comes as close to being the world in microcosm as anything I know; in a way, it puts all the rest of show business in the shade. Its magic is universal and complex. Out of its wild disorder comes order; from its rank smell rises the good aroma of courage and daring; out of its preliminary shabbiness comes the final splendor. And buried in the familiar boasts of its advance agents lies the modesty of most of its people. For me the circus is at its best before it has been put together. It is at its best at certain moments when it comes to a point, as through a burning glass, in the activity and destiny of a single performer out of so many. One ring is always bigger than three. One rider, one aerialist, is always greater than six. In short, a man has to catch the circus unawares to experience its full impact and share its gaudy dream.

4   The ten-minute ride the girl took achieved—as far as I
was concerned, who wasn't looking for it, and quite unbe-
knownst to her, who wasn't even striving for it—the thing
that is sought by performers everywhere, on whatever
stage, whether struggling in the tidal currents of Shakespeare or bucking the difficult motion of a horse. I somehow
got the idea she was just cadging a ride, improving a shining ten minutes in the diligent way all serious artists seize
free moments to hone the blade of their talent and keep
themselves in trim. Her brief tour included only elemen-
tary postures and tricks, perhaps because they were all she
was capable of, perhaps because her warmup at this hour
was unscheduled and the ring was not rigged for a real
practice session. She swung herself off and on the horse
several times, gripping his mane. She did a few knee-
stands—or whatever they are called—dropping to her
knees and quickly bouncing back up on her feet again.
Most of the time she simply rode in a standing position,
well aft on the beast, her hands hanging easily at her
sides, her head erect, her straw-colored ponytail lightly
brushing her shoulders, the blood of exertion showing
faintly through the tan of her skin. Twice she managed a
one-foot stance—a sort of ballet pose, with arms outstretched. At one point the neck strap of her bathing suit
broke and she went twice around the ring in the classic
attitude of a woman making minor repairs to a garment.
The fact that she was standing on the back of a moving
horse while doing this invested the matter with a clownish
significance that perfectly fitted the spirit of the circus—
jocund, yet charming. She just rolled the strap into a neat
ball and stowed it inside her bodice while the horse rocked
and rolled beneath her in dutiful innocence. The bathing
suit proved as self-reliant as its owner and stood up well
enough without the benefit of strap.

5   The richness of the scene was in its plainness, its natural condition—of horse, of ring, of girl, even to the girl's
bare feet that gripped the bare back of her proud and ridiculous mount. The enchantment grew not out of anything
that happened or was performed but out of something that
seemed to go round and around and around with the girl,

attending her, a steady gleam in the shape of a circle—a ring of ambition, of happiness, of youth. (And the positive pleasures of equilibrium under difficulties.) In a week or two, all would be changed, all (or almost all) lost: the girl would wear makeup, the horse would wear gold, the ring would be painted, the bark would be clean for the feet of the horse, the girl's feet would be clean for the slippers that she'd wear. All, all would be lost.

6   As I watched with the others, our jaws adroop, our eyes alight, I became painfully conscious of the element of time. Everything in the hideous old building seemed to take the shape of a circle, conforming to the course of the horse. The rider's gaze, as she peered straight ahead, seemed to be circular, as though bent by force of circumstance; then time itself began running in circles, and so the beginning was where the end was, and the two were the same, and one thing ran into the next and time went round and around and got nowhere. The girl wasn't so young that she did not know the delicious satisfaction of having a perfectly be-haved body and the fun of using it to do a trick most people can't do, but she was too young to know that time does not really move in a circle at all. I thought: "She will never be as beautiful as this again"—a thought that made me acutely unhappy—and in a flash my mind (which is too much of a busybody to suit me) had projected her twenty-five years ahead, and she was now in the center of the ring, on foot, wearing a conical hat and high-heeled shoes, the image of the older woman, holding the long rein, caught in the treadmill of an afternoon long in the future. "She is at that enviable moment in life [I thought] when she believes she can go once around the ring, make one complete circuit, and at the end be exactly the same age as at the start." Everything in her movements, her expression, told you that for her the ring of time was perfectly formed, changeless, predictable, without beginning or end, like the ring in which she was travelling at this moment with the horse that wallowed under her. And then I slipped back into my trance, and time was circular again—time, pausing quietly with the rest of us, so as not to disturb the balance of a performer.

7   Her ride ended as casually as it had begun. The older woman stopped the horse, and the girl slid to the ground. As she walked toward us to leave, there was a quick, small burst of applause. She smiled broadly, in surprise and pleasure; then her face suddenly regained its gravity and she disappeared through the door.

8   It has been ambitious and plucky of me to attempt to describe what is indescribable, and I have failed, as I knew I would. But I have discharged my duty to my society; and besides, a writer, like an acrobat, must occasionally try a stunt that is too much for him. At any rate, it is worth reporting that long before the circus comes to town, its most notable performances have already been given. Under the bright lights of the finished show, a performer need only reflect the electric candle power that is directed upon him; but in the dark and dirty old training rings and in the makeshift cages, whatever light is generated, whatever excitement, whatever beauty, must come from original sources—from internal fires of professional hunger and delight, from the exuberance and gravity of youth. It is the difference between planetary light and the combustion of stars.

9   The South is the land of the sustained sibilant. Everywhere, for the appreciative visitor, the letter "s" insinuates itself in the scene: in the sound of sea and sand, in the singing shell, in the heat of sun and sky, in the sultriness of the gentle hours, in the siesta, in the stir of birds and insects. In contrast to the softness of its music, the South is also cruel and hard and prickly. A little striped lizard, flattened along the sharp green bayonet of a yucca, wears in its tiny face and watchful eye the pure look of death and violence. And all over the place, hidden at the bottom of their small sandy craters, the ant lions lie in wait for the ant that will stumble into their trap. (There are three kinds of lions in this region: the lions of the circus, the ant lions, and the Lions of the Tampa Lions Club, who roared their approval of segregation at a meeting the other day— all except one, a Lion named Monty Gurwit, who declined to roar and thereby got his picture in the paper.)

10   The day starts on a note of despair: the sorrowing dove, alone on its telephone wire, mourns the loss of night, weeps at the bright perils of the unfolding day. But soon the mockingbird wakes and begins an early rehearsal, setting the dove down by force of character, running through a few slick imitations, and trying a couple of original numbers into the bargain. The redbird takes it from there. Despair gives way to good humor. The Southern dawn is a pale affair, usually, quite different from our northern daybreak. It is a triumph of gradualism; night turns to day imperceptibly, softly, with no theatrics. It is subtle and undisturbing. As the first light seeps in through the blinds I lie in bed half awake, despairing with the dove, sounding the A for the brothers Alsop.* All seems lost, all seems sorrowful. Then a mullet jumps in the bayou outside the bedroom window. It falls back into the water with a smart smack. I have asked several people why the mullet incessantly jump and I have received a variety of answers. Some say the mullet jump to shake off a parasite that annoys them. Some say they jump for the love of jumping—as the girl on the horse seemed to ride for the love of riding (although she, too, like all artists, may have been shaking off some parasite that fastens itself to the creative spirit and can be got rid of only by fifty turns around a ring while standing on a horse).

11   In Florida at this time of year, the sun does not take command of the day until a couple of hours after it has appeared in the east. It seems to carry no authority at first. The sun and the lizard keep the same schedule; they bide their time until the morning has advanced a good long way before they come fully forth and strike. The cold lizard waits astride his warming leaf for the perfect moment; the cold sun waits in his nest of clouds for the crucial time.

12   On many days, the dampness of the air pervades all life, all living. Matches refuse to strike. The towel, hung to dry, grows wetter by the hour. The newspaper, with its headlines about integration, wilts in your hand and falls limply

---

*Joseph and Stewart Alsop, columnists whose articles had a tone of gloom rather than of cheery optimism.

into the coffee and the' egg. Envelopes seal themselves. Postage stamps mate with one another as shamelessly as grasshoppers. But most of the time the days are models of beauty and wonder and comfort, with the kind sea stroking the back of the warm sand. At evening there are great flights of birds over the sea, where the light lingers; the gulls, the pelicans, the terns, the herons stay aloft for half an hour after land birds have gone to roost. They hold their ancient formations, wheel and fish over the Pass, enjoying the last of day like children playing outdoors after supper-time.

13   To a beachcomber from the North, which is my present status, the race problem has no pertinence, no immediacy. Here in Florida I am a guest in two houses—the house of the sun, the house of the State of Florida. As a guest, I mind the manners and do not criticize the customs of my hosts. It gives me a queer feeling, though, to be at the center of the greatest social crisis of my time and see hardly a sign of it. Yet the very absence of signs seems to increase one's awareness. Colored people do not come to the public beach to bathe, because they would not be made welcome there; and they don't fritter away their time visiting the circus, because they have other things to do. A few of them turn up at the ballpark, where they occupy a separate but equal section of the left-field bleachers and watch Negro players on the visiting Braves team using the same bases as the white players, instead of separate (but equal) bases. I have had only two small encounters with "color." A colored woman named Viola, who had been a friend of my wife's sister years ago, showed up one day with some laundry of ours that she had consented to do for us, and with the bundle she brought a bunch of nasturtiums, as a sort of natural accompaniment to the delivery of clean clothes. The flowers seemed a very acceptable thing and I was touched by them. We asked Viola about her daughter, and she said she was at Kentucky State College, studying voice.

14   The other encounter was when I was explaining to our cook, who is from Finland, the mysteries of bus travel in the American Southland. I showed her the bus stop, armed her with a timetable, and then, as a matter of duty, men-

tioned the customs of the Romans. "When you get on the bus," I said, "I think you'd better sit in one of the front seats—the seats in back are for colored people." A look of great weariness came into her face, as it does when we use too many dishes, and she replied, "Oh, I know—isn't it silly!"

15   Her remark, coming as it did all the way from Finland and landing on this sandbar with a plunk, impressed me. The Supreme Court said nothing about silliness, but I suspect it may play more of a role than one might suppose. People are, if anything, more touchy about being thought silly than they are about being thought unjust. I note that one of the arguments in the recent manifesto of Southern Congressmen in support of the doctrine of "separate but equal" was that it had been founded on "common sense." The sense that is common to one generation is uncommon to the next. probably the first slave ship, with Negroes lying in chains on its decks, seemed commonsensical to the owners who operated it and to the planters who patronized it. But such a vessel would not be in the realm of common sense today. The only sense that is common, in the long run, is the sense of change—and we all instinctively avoid it, and object to the passage of time, and would rather have none of it.

16   The Supreme Court decision is like the Southern sun, laggard in its early stages, biding its time. It has been the law in Florida for two years now, and the years have been like the hours of the morning before the sun has gathered its strength. I think the decision is as incontrovertible and warming as the sun, and, like the sun, will eventually take charge.

17   But there is certainly a great temptation in Florida to duck the passage of time. Lying in warm comfort by the sea, you receive gratefully the gift of the sun, the gift of the South. This is true seduction. The day is a circle—morning, afternoon, and night. After a few days I was clearly enjoying the same delusion as the girl on the horse—that I could ride clear around the ring of day, guarded by wind and sun and sea and sand, and be not a moment older.

18   P.S. (April 1962). When I first laid eyes on Fiddler Bayou, it was wild land, populated chiefly by the little crabs that gave it its name, visited by wading birds and by an occasional fisherman. Today, houses ring the bayou, and part of the mangrove shore has been bulkheaded with a concrete wall. Green lawns stretch from patio to water's edge, and sprinklers make rainbows in the light. But despite man's encroachment, Nature manages to hold her own and assert her authority: high tides and high winds in the Gulf sometimes send the sea crashing across the sand barrier, depositing its wrack on lawns and ringing everyone's front door bell. The birds and the crabs accommodate themselves quite readily to the changes that have taken place; every day brings herons to hunt around among the roots of the mangroves, and I have discovered that I can approach to within about eight feet of a Little Blue Heron simply by entering the water and swimming slowly toward him. Apparently he has decided that when I'm in the water, I am without guile—possibly even desirable, like a fish.

19   The Ringling circus has quit Sarasota and gone elsewhere for its hibernation. A few circus families still own homes in the town, and every spring the students at the high school put on a circus, to let off steam, work off physical requirements, and provide a promotional spectacle for Sarasota. At the drugstore you can buy a postcard showing the bed John Ringling slept in. Time has not stood still for anybody but the dead, and even the dead must be able to hear the acceleration of little sports cars and know that things have changed.

20   From the all-wise *New York Times*, which has the animal kingdom ever in mind, I have learned that one of the creatures most acutely aware of the passing time is the fiddler crab himself. Tiny spots on his body enlarge during daytime hours, giving him the same color as the mudbank he explores and thus protecting him from his enemies. At night the spots shrink, his color fades, and he is almost invisible in the light of the moon. These changes are synchronized with the tides, so that each day they occur at a different hour. A scientist who experimented with the crabs to learn more about the phenomenon discovered that even

when they are removed from their natural environment and held in confinement, the rhythm of their bodily change continues uninterrupted, and they mark the passage of time in their laboratory prison, faithful to the tides in their fashion.

A BOOK THAT INFLUENCED ME

E. M. Forster

1944

1   It was rather a little book, and that introduces my first point. One's impulse, on tackling the question of influence, is to search for a great book, and to assume that here is the force which has moulded one's outlook and character. Looking back upon my own half-century of reading, I have no doubt which my three great books have been: Dante's *Divine Comedy*, Gibbon's *Decline and Fall*, and Tolstoy's *War and Peace*. All three are great both in quality and in bulk. Bulk is not to be despised. Combined with quality, it gives a long book a pull over a short one, and permits us to call it monumental. Here are three monuments. But they have not influenced me in the least, though I came across them all at an impressionable age. They impressed me by their massiveness and design, and made me feel small in the right way, and to make us feel small in the right way is a function of art; men can only make us feel small in the wrong way. But to realise the vastness of the universe, the limits of human knowledge, the even narrower limits of human power, to catch a passing glimpse of the medieval universe, or of the Roman Empire on its millennial way, or of Napoleon collapsing against the panorama of Russian daily life—that is not to be influenced. It is to be extended. Perhaps those three books were too monumental, and human beings are not much influenced by monuments. They gaze, say "Oh!" and pass on unchanged. They are more likely to be influenced by objects nearer their own size. Anyhow, that has been my own case.

2   The book in question is Samuel Butler's *Erewhon*, a work of genius, but with Dante, Gibbon and Tolstoy setting our standards not to be called great. It has been better described as "a serious book not written too seriously."

3   Published as far back as 1872, it is difficult to classify— partly a yarn, partly an account of Utopia, partly a satire on Victorian civilisation. It opens with some superb descrip-

tions of mountain scenery: this part is taken from Butler's New Zealand experiences. The hero is a bit of a scamp, and not so much a living character as a vehicle for the author's likes and dislikes, and for his mischievousness. He has left England under a cloud for a distant colony, with the intention of converting some lost tribe to Christianity at a handsome profit. He hears that beyond the mountain range there are terrible figures, and still more terrible sounds. He sets out, and presently discovers enormous and frightful statues, through whose hollow heads the wind moans. They are the guardians of Erewhon. Struggling past them, he enters the unknown country, and the fantasy proper begins. The descent on the further side beyond the statues is exquisitely related, and the scenery now suggests the Italian slopes of the Alps. He is politely imprisoned by the mountaineers until instructions as to his disposal can come up from the capital. But there are two hitches. One of them occurs when his watch is discovered on him. The other is with his jailer's daughter, Yram (Erewhonian for Mary). He and she get on well, and when he catches a cold he makes the most of it, in the hope of being cosseted by her. She flies into a fury.

4   By now he has learnt the language, and is summoned to the capital. He is to be the guest of a Mr. Nosnibor and the account of Mr. Nosnibor puzzles him. "He is," says his informant, "a most delightful man, who has but lately recovered from embezzling a large sum of money under singularly distressing circumstances; you are sure to like him." What can this all mean? It's wrong to have a watch, wrong to catch a cold, but embezzlement is only a subject for sympathy. The reader is equally puzzled, and skilfully does Butler lead us into the heart of this topsy-turvy country, without explaining its fantasies too soon. Take the Musical Banks. Erewhon, it seems, has two banking systems, one of them like ours, the other is Musical Banking. Mr. Nosnibor, as befits a dubious financier, goes constantly to the first sort of bank, but never attends the offices of the second, though he is ostensibly its ardent supporter. Mrs. Nosnibor and her daughters go once a week. Each bank has its own coinage, the coins of the musical banks being

highly esteemed, but of no commercial value, as the hero
soon discovers when he tries to tip one of its officials with
them. Just as in Swift we read for a bit about the Yahoos
without realising that he intends them for ourselves, so we
read about the Musical Banks, and only gradually realise
that they caricature the Church of England and its connections with Capitalism. There was a great row over this
chapter as soon as it was understood; the "enfant terrible,"
as he called himself, had indeed heaved a brick. He also
shocked people by reversing the positions of crime and illness. In Erewhon it is wicked to be ill—that is why Yram
was angry when the hero had a cold. Embezzlement, on the
other hand, is a disease. Mr. Nosnibor is treated for it
professionally and very severely. "Poor papa," says his
charming daughter, "I really do not think he will steal any
more." And as for possessing a watch—all machinery invented after a certain date has been destroyed by the Ere-
whonians, lest it breeds new machines, who may enslave
men. And there are further brilliant inventions—for instance, the College of Unreason, who teach a Hypothetical
Language, never used outside their walls, and in whom we
must reluctantly recognise the ancient universities of Oxford and Cambridge, and their schools of Latin and Greek.
And there is the worship of the Goddess Ydgrun (Mrs.
Grundy); for worship is mostly bad, yet it produces a few
fine people, the High Ydgrunites. These people were conventional in the right way: they hadn't too many ideas, and
they were always willing to drop a couple to oblige a
friend. In the High Ydgrunites we come to what Butler
thought desirable. Although a rebel, he was not a reformer.
He believed in the conventions, provided they are observed
humanely. Grace and graciousness, good temper, good
looks, good health and good sense; tolerance, intelligence,
and willingness to abandon any moral standard at a pinch.
That is what he admired.

5   The book ends, as it began, in the atmosphere of adventure. The hero elopes with Miss Nosnibor in a balloon. The
splendid descriptions of natural scenery are resumed, they
fall into the sea and are rescued, and we leave him as
secretary of the Erewhon Evangelisation Company in Lon-

don, asking for subscriptions for the purpose of converting the country to Christianity with the aid of a small expeditionary force. "An uncalled-for joke?" If you think so, you have fallen into one of Butler's little traps. He wanted to make uncalled-for jokes. He wanted to write a serious book not too seriously.

6   Why did this book influence me? For one thing, I have the sort of mind which likes to be taken unawares. The frontal full-dress presentation of an opinion often repels me, but if it be insidiously slipped in sidewise I may receive it, and Butler is a master of the oblique: Then, what he had to say was congenial, and I lapped it up. It was the food for which I was waiting. And this brings me to my next point. I suggest that the only books that influence us are those for which we are ready, and which have gone a little farther down our particular path than we have yet got ourselves. I suggest, furthermore, that when you feel that you could almost have written the book yourself— that's the moment when it's influencing you. You are not influenced when you say, "How marvellous! What a revelation! How monumental. Oh!" You are being extended. You are being influenced when you say "I might have written that myself if I hadn't been so busy." I don't suppose that I could have written the *Divine Comedy* or the *Decline and Fall*. I don't even think I could have written the *Antigone* of Sophocles, though of all the great tragic utterances that comes closest to my heart, that is my central faith. But I do think (quite erroneously) that I could have turned out this little skit of Erewhon if the idea of it had occurred to me. Which is strong evidence that it has influenced me.

7   *Erewhon* also influenced me in its technique. I like that idea of fantasy, of muddling up the actual and the impossible until the reader isn't sure which is which, and I have sometimes tried to do it when writing myself. However, I mustn't start on technique. Let me rather get in an observation which was put to me the other day by a friend. What about the books which influence us negatively, which give us the food we don't want, or, maybe, are unfit for, and so help us to realise what we do want? I have amused myself by putting down four books which have influenced

me negatively. They are books by great writers, and I have appreciated them. But they are not my sort of book. They are: *The Confessions* of St. Augustine, Macchiavelli's *Prince,* Swift's *Gulliver,* and Carlyle on *Heroes and Hero Worship.* All these books have influenced me negatively, and impelled me away from them towards my natural food. I know that St. Augustine's *Confessions* is a "good" book, and I want to be good. But not in St. Augustine's way. I don't want the goodness which entails an asceticism close to cruelty. I prefer the goodness of William Blake. And Macchiavelli—he is clever—and unlike some of my compatriots I want to be clever. But not with Macchiavelli's cold, inhuman cleverness. I prefer the cleverness of Voltaire. And indignation—Swift's indignation in *Gulliver* is too savage for me; I prefer Butler's in *Erewhon.* And strength—yes, I want to be strong, but not with the strength of Carlyle's dictator heroes, who foreshadow Hitler. I prefer the strength of Antigone.

A REPLY TO JENNY SIMPER*

Richard Steele

January 24, 1712

Mr. Spectator,

1   I am clerk of the parish from whence Mrs. Simper†
sends her complaint in your yesterday's *Spectator*. I must
beg of you to publish this as a public admonition to the
aforesaid Mrs. Simper; otherwise all my honest care in the
disposition of the greens in the church will have no effect. I
shall therefore with your leave lay before you the whole
matter.

2   I was formerly, as she charges me, for several years a
gardener in the County of Kent. But I must absolutely
deny that 'tis out of any affection I retain for my old em-
ployment that I have placed my greens so liberally about
the church, but out of a particular spleen I conceived
against Mrs. Simper (and others of the same sisterhood)
some time ago. As to herself, I had one day set the hun-
dredth psalm, and was singing the first line in order to put
the congregation into the tune. She was all the while curt-
sying to Sir Anthony in so affected a manner that the
indignation I conceived at it made me forget myself so far
as from the tune of that psalm to wander into Southwell
tune, and from thence into Windsor tune, still unable to
recover myself till I had with the utmost confusion set a
new one. Nay, I have often seen her rise up and smile and
curtsy to one at the lower end of the church in the midst of
a Gloria Patri; and when I have spoken the assent to a
prayer with a long "Amen" uttered with decent gravity, she
has been rolling her eyes around about in such a manner
as plainly showed, however she was moved, it was not towards an Heavenly object. In fine, she extended her conquests so far over the males, and raised such envy in the

---

*See "Christmas Greens," pages 24–25.

†*Mistress* Simper. In the eighteenth century, *mistress* was a term of address
for a woman, whether she is married or not.

females, that what between love of those and the jealousy of these, I was almost the only person that looked in the prayer book all the church-time.

3   I had several projects in my head to put a stop to this growing mischief; but as I have long lived in Kent, and there often heard how the Kentish men evaded the conqueror by carrying green boughs over their heads, it put me in mind of practicing this device against Mrs. Simper. I find I have preserved many a young man from her eyeshot by this means; therefore humbly pray the boughs may be fixed till she shall give security for her peaceable intentions.

Your humble servant,
FRANCIS STERNHOLD

A Glossary of Literary Terms

Abstraction: (a) A general idea, principle, or pattern derived from definite sensory observations of specific objects or experiences. Abstractions of this sort can exist at various levels. For instance, the idea of an evergreen is derived from observations of specific hemlocks, pines, spruces, and so on. The idea or conception of a tree is derived from observations of evergreens and deciduous trees. See also *Generalization*. (b) A term applied to ideas that are philosophical or emotional, not concrete or tangible, yet that are derived from experience—for example, truth, liberty, freedom. See also *Concrete terms*. (See pages 13, 15–16, 26–28.)

Alliteration: Repetition of *beginning consonant* sounds in words in succession or in close association. Example: " . . . first, fawn tiptoed toward . . ." (See page 38.)

Allusion: A reference to a person, saying, object, or incident from literature, history, mythology, or religion. (See pages 26, 55–59.)

Analogy: A comparison, often figurative, between two objects or experiences that attempts to explain one in terms of the other. "A sail is to a ship as a motor is to a car" is a simple analogy. A more complex analogy is given in physics courses when sound waves are compared to the concentric ripples created by a stone's being dropped into a still pond. (See pages 93, 122, 207.)

Antithesis: Strong contrast shown through the juxtaposition of opposing words, phrases, clauses, sentences, or ideas. For instance, Emerson's statement: "Every sweet has its sour; every evil its good." (See pages 95, 173, 220–221.)

Assonance: Repetition, from word to word, of stressed *vowel* sounds *within* words. The words may be in succession or in less close association, usually within one or two lines of prose or poetry. Example: "hooting," "woodland," and "hooraar," pages 38.

Cliché: A strikingly worded expression that is worn out from too much use. Examples are: "hard as a rock," "sadder but wiser." More broadly, the term can also be applied to an idea, point of view, or situation, as in Christopher Lehmann-Haupt's "Unfunnier Side of Thurber." (See pages 181, 186.)

Coherence: Literally, a sticking together. Coherence refers to the successions and connections of phrases, clauses, sentences, and transitional devices that provide clear overall meaning and fluent continuity of thought. See also *Transition*.

Comparison: An examination designed to expose similarities between two objects or ideas. See also *Contrast*.

Concrete terms: Terms that represent, and often attempt to evoke, images or experiences of specific, tangible objects or entities. Concrete terms are usually thought of as opposed to abstract or general terms. It should be remembered, however, that many abstractions are derived from and made vital by specific, concrete material. For instance, our abstract idea of Nathan Hale's patriotism is derived from his concrete statement, "I only regret that I have but one life to lose for my country," made moments before he was executed. (See pages 13, 15.) See also *Abstraction.*

Connotation: A definition or implication that goes beyond the narrowest, most literal meaning (or denotation) of a word. For instance, *to discriminate* means, by denotation, to compare and to note differences. Broader senses of the word involve emotional and judgmental implications or connotations. *To discriminate* has favorable connotations when it refers to the ability to distinguish between graceful and clumsy writing. It has unfavorable connotations when it refers to distinctions and attitudes based on prejudice. (See pages 36, 106.) See also *Denotation.*

Context: The situation or the specific literary background within which a word or idea is expressed. A statement depends on the surrounding words and tone for its full meaning. Thus it may be misleading to take a statement out of its context. For instance, it is common in theater advertising for just the favorable words of an unfavorable review to be lifted out of context and quoted to create the impression that the play or movie was well received by the critics.

Contrast: A device by which two objects or ideas are put in opposition to one another to show and emphasize the differences between them. See also *Comparison.*

Denotation: The dictionary definition of a word that comes closest to the actuality for which the word stands. (See pages 28 41, 106.) The *denotation* of *sphere* is any round body or figure having the surface equally distant from the center at all points. The denotation of a word is isolated from the emotional and judgmental implications that are typical of *connotations.* For instance, a *connotation* of *sphere* could be one's area of experience or influence. (See also *Connotation.*)

Didactic essay: An essay written specifically to teach or instruct the reader. (See pages 132, 207.)

Explicit: Clear, precise, definite, plain to see. A good writer who uses explicit nouns and verbs will not have to rely too heavily on adjectives and adverbs. (See pages 36, 116, 201.)

Exposition: A kind of writing designed to explain. Expository material explains the nature of an object, idea, or theme. The term may also refer to introductory material that supplies background information necessary to an understanding of the whole, especially in drama or the short story.

Figurative language: Language that uses figures of speech.

Figure of speech: A form of imagery. An expression or literary construction (as in a simile, a metaphor, or a hyperbole) that conveys its meaning through an imaginative, nonliteral use of words, often by comparison or analogy. For instance, the eyes of an angry person might be said to "flash with rage." (See pages 20, 41–42, 115.) See also *Hyperbole, Metaphor, Simile, Understatement.* See especially *Imagery.*

Generalization: The abstraction of a general idea, principle, or pattern from the observation of particular objects, events, or experiences. A statement that is broad enough to cover or describe characteristics that are common to a variety of particular objects, events, or experiences. For instance, we generalize that a person is honest if, under a variety of specific circumstances and specific temptations, he or she behaves in an honorable manner. (See pages 27, 28.) See also *Abstraction (a).*

Humor: A conjunction of incongruous situations or images in a surprising manner that evokes amusement. Humor may range from the lighthearted and harmless to the critical and derisive. Pure humor is devoid of criticism and is derived solely from the amusing surprises of its incongruities. (See pages 48–50, 54.) See also *Incongruity.*

Hyperbole: Deliberate exaggeration used to produce heightened dramatic effects or humorous or ironic effects. (See pages 60–61.) See also *Satire.*

Imagery: The use of words to produce mental images of specific sensory experiences. Not all mental images are visual in conception. They may also be related to sound, touch, taste, or smell. They may even be emotional.

Literal, or factual, imagery attempts *directly* to evoke *accurate* images of *actual* objects or experiences. The words used in literal imagery are as close as possible in denotation and connotation (cf.) to the objects or experiences they represent. For instance, "the salivant sourness of a slice of lemon" are words that evoke directly an unmistakably accurate image of the actual taste of lemon.

Imaginative imagery attempts by a use of *figurative* language to create vivid *imaginary* images, in order by *indirection* to evoke and enhance images of *actual* objects or experiences. For instance, in his poem "The Highwayman," Alfred Noyes evokes a factual image of clouds scudding across the moon by creating an imaginary image: "The moon was a ghostly galleon tossed upon cloudy seas." Here the imaginary image of the "ghostly galleon" enhances our factual image of the moon and gives it an eerie quality. Such imaginative imagery is called figurative language. (See pages 41–42.) See also *Figure of speech.*

Implicit: Suggested or understood without being directly stated. To imply is to suggest rather than to state. An incident can imply an idea that would otherwise have to be stated. (See pages 15, 36.)

Incongruity: A disharmony or incompatibility between two or more objects, ideas, or experiences that are examined together. Humor and irony depend, in part, upon the element of unexpected incongruity. (See pages 21–23, 49–50.) See also *Humor* and *Irony.*

Inference: An arrived at understanding or conclusion through deduction from evidence. Inferring from that which is *implied* or *implicit.* (See pages 15, 36.)

Irony: A term for situations and for written and spoken observations and inventions in which there is a discrepancy (often opposite in nature) between what is apparent and what is expected. This quality of discrepancy is called *incongruity* (cf.).

Literary irony is an appreciation of the absurdities of life. It is an excellent antidote for sentimentality. In tone it can be bitter, funny, satiric, tragic. It can be loosely categorized into verbal irony, dramatic irony, and irony of situation.

Verbal irony is irony consciously spoken or written ironically. When a student who is humiliated in front of a class responds by saying, "Thanks!" the student's facial expression and tone of voice show that the opposite is meant. Verbal irony has been expressed.

Irony of situation is the unexpected twist in any situation that has developed from events that had appeared to lead in an expected direction. The emotional response to such irony may be amusement, surprise, dismay, shock, or disappointment. An example of irony of situation is in Aesop's fable of the widow and the hen. A poor widow, hoping to double the number of eggs laid by her hen, started to feed the bird a double measure of grain. Ironically, the increased diet made the hen so fat and lazy that she laid no eggs at all.

Dramatic irony appears in two related forms: (1) In which a character or narrator unconsciously reveals to other characters and to the audience (or reader) some knowledge of himself or herself contrary to the impression he or she wishes to make. (2) In which the character or narrator acts and reacts in ignorance of some vital external knowledge held by one or more of the other characters and by the audience (or reader). When it leads to tragic consequences, this latter form of dramatic irony is sometimes known as *tragic irony.* (See pages 21–23, 26, 61.)

Jargon: Words and phrases that are the special conversational vocabulary of a profession or some other interest. Jargon is often unintelligible to people unfamiliar with the special interest. (See page 137.)

Juxtaposition: Side-by-side placement of sentences or ideas for the effect that can be implied by such immediate placement. (See pages 22–23, 102.)

Literal meaning: The direct, accurate, unembellished meaning of a statement or word; a meaning as nearly devoid as possible of connotative meanings. (See page 28.) See *Denotation* and *Connotation.*

Metaphor: An implied, imaginative direct equation or analogy between two objects, ideas, or experiences. For instance, a poet who describes the fading stars at dawn by saying, "Night's candles are burnt out," is equating, by implication, stars with burning candles; the poet is calling stars "candles." (See pages 42, 43.)

Motif: A recurring idea that is woven like a design in the fabric of a literary work. (See pages 173, 220–221.) The term is also used for melodic phrases that recur in music, as in Wagner's use of the *leitmotif* in the *Ring* operas.

Objective: Impersonal; free from the author's feelings, attitudes, and prejudices. (See pages 28, 158.) See also *Subjective*.

Parable: A short, simple, often symbolic story designed to illustrate a moral or religious truth. (See pages 77, 100.) See also *Symbol*.

Paradox: A self-contradictory statement that may state a truth. An example is the following statement by Thomas Fuller: "The way to be safe is never to be secure." (See pages 00, 000.)

Parallel construction: The expression of sequential and related thoughts in similar syntactical form. The principle of parallelism can be applied to words, phrases, clauses, sentences, paragraphs, and still larger units. Parallelism gives the reader a sense of a balanced and rational ordering of thought. (See pages 44–45.)

Parody: An imitation of the style and content of a specific literary work, often humorous and intended to ridicule or criticize. Informal parody is called a takeoff. (See page 92.)

Refrain: The repetition, at intervals, of a word or group of words for effect. For example, the word "nevermore" in Poe's "Raven" becomes a refrain. (See the opening and closing paragraphs of "No News from Auschwitz.")

Restraint: Less a literary device than an example of good taste. There are some things in literature that are more effective left unsaid. Just as a good joke can be ruined by the teller who feels the need to explain the point, so a literary description or narration can be ruined by the addition of some unnecessary explanation. Much of the trashy literature found in magazine stalls is characterized by lack of restraint—a morbid lingering over sordid or gruesome incidents, or an overindulgence in sentimentality. (See page 40.)

Sarcasm: A cutting remark, written or spoken, designed to make fun of, and hurt, its object. Sarcasm often employs irony.

Satire: A humorous or witty method of criticizing characteristics and institutions of human society. Its purpose is to correct as well as to expose and ridicule; thus it is not purely destructive. The satire found in the essays of Addison and Steele is a gentle form of ridicule. Other satire, such as that found in Swift's "Modest Proposal," is savage.

Much satire is ironic. *Ironic satire* expresses one thought while implying its opposite. Its value as criticism and ridicule is apparent only to the reader who is sensitive to the implied incongruity of the irony. (See page 23.)

Another popular device of satire is hyperbole (cf.). When used in satire, hyperbole seems to insinuate itself into a popular idea, and then, like a balloon, inflates the idea so that the details become exaggerated and enormously vulnerable to the pin pricks of ridicule. (See page 137.)

Sentimentality: An expression of emotion in excess of that warranted by the subject. (See page 40.)

Simile: A nonliteral comparison between two objects, ideas, or experiences. The comparison is *stated* as such, using the word *like, as,* or *than.* Generally the comparison is between two things essentially unlike, and the author's perception of their resemblance in one or more aspects is the basis of the comparison. For instance, when Rossetti wrote "the dragon-fly hangs like a blue thread loosened from the sky," he was comparing two objects in a simile based on their common quality of blue thinness. (See page 42.) See *Imagery.*

Solecism: An error in, or violation of, a rule of grammar or usage. For instance, "She graduated college" is a common solecism. Properly, one would say, "She was graduated from college." Solecisms are often heard in jargon. (See pages 134–138.)

Style: An author's selection and arrangement of words and details to express thoughts in literary form. (See pages 27–28.)

Subjective: Personal; closely allied to an author's feelings, attitudes, prejudices, and personal reactions. (See page 28.) See also *objective.*

Symbol: A specific object, incident, or person intended to represent some abstract idea. For example, the American flag is a symbol not only of the United States but also of such abstract qualities as patriotism, pride, and democracy. (See page 77.)

Theme: The major underlying idea in a specific literary work.

Tone: The tone of a literary work is said to express the author's apparent *attitudes* toward subject matter and reader. It is created by word choice, rhythm, sentence structure (and length), and setting. It is also achieved through the author's selection of symbols and imagery. Tone may be described in terms like "stuffy," "light-hearted," "gloomy," "teasing," and so on. Our perception of tone is not always reliable, however, because of the biases we may have and because the author may be disguising his or her real attitudes. (See pages 48–50.)

Transition: A device usually a word or phrase, sometimes a sentence or even a paragraph) for guiding the reader from thought to thought within a literary work. (See pages 46–47.) See *Coherence.*

Understatement: The representation of something as less than it really is, for ironic effect. Understatement (also called *meiosis*) is the opposite of hyperbole (cf.). (See page 61.)

Vignette: A short literary sketch designed to create a single effect or express a single theme. (See page 172.) Vignette is also a motion picture term describing a brief scene that has a single effect.

INDEX

Abstract ideas. *See also* Generalizations
  concrete details in, 28
    development of, 115
  in Darwin, 33
  defined, 13, 27
  developed, as analogy, 122
    through concrete and specific details,
      13, 15–16. *See also* Concrete
      details *and* Specific details.
  generalization in, 27
  selection of details for, 26
  subjective, 35
Abstraction, defined, 253
Addison, Joseph, 8, 21, 24
Adjectives, in word choice, 36
Adverbs, in word choice, 36
Alliteration, 253
Allusion, 26, 55–59, 203, 253
  cultural literacy and, 55–59
  in specific essays, 26, 55–59, 61, 72,
    92, 93, 95, 102, 106, 132, 149, 150,
    172, 173, 186, 191, 200, 201, 207,
    220
Analogy
  defined, 253
  in specific essays, 92–93, 122, 207
Antithesis, 95, 253
  in specific essays, 95, 99, 102,173, 192,
    210, 220–221
"Assassination, The," *104–105*
  "Ragnarök" and, 103
Assonance, defined, 253

Bacon, Sir Francis, 8
Baker, Russell, 55
Baldwin, James, 139
"Beauty: When the Other Dancer Is the
  Self," *163–171*
Benchley, Robert, 89
"Benign Intentions," *68–71*
Biographical sketches. *See specific
  authors*
"Black Prisoners, White Law," *151–155*
"Book That Influenced Me, A," *246–250*

Borges, Jorge Luis, 100

Chrisman, Robert, 151
"Christmas Greens," *24–25*, 27
  referred to in "A Reply to Jenny
  Simper," 251–252
"Classical versus Quantum," *203–206*
  tone of, 207
Clemens, Samuel Langhorne, 48
Cliché, 181, 186, 253
Close Encounters of the Third Kind,
  review of, *68–71*
Coherence, defined, 253–254. *See also*
  Continuity and transition
Comparison
  defined, 253
  in figures of speech, 41–42
Concrete details, 13. *See also* Abstract
  ideas, Details, *and* Specific details
  in analogy, 122
  in Darwin's style, 27
  in developing abstract ideas, 13, 15,
    28, 115
  terms, defined, 253
Connotation, 36, 254
  and denotation, in "The Assassination,"
    106
Context, defined, 254
Continuity, devices used by Thurber, 182
  and transitions, 46–47
Contrast
  defined, 254
  selection of details for, 35–36
Contrasting details, in "Twins," 39
Cultural literacy, 8
  acquiring, 16
  allusion and, 55–59
  in "What Are Little Boys Made Of?"
    92

Darwin, Charles, 27–28
  tone of style, 48
Deadpan humor, 48–50
  in specific essays, 52–53, 93, 158